THE MAKING OF THE ENGLISH
LANDSCAPE

THE SHROPSHIRE LANDSCAPE

THE MAKING OF THE ENGLISH LANDSCAPE

The Shropshire Landscape

by

TREVOR ROWLEY

HODDER AND STOUGHTON

LONDON SYDNEY AUCKLAND TORONTO

Copyright © 1972 by Trevor Rowley. First Printed 1972. ISBN 0 340 02373 2
All rights reserved. No part of this publication may be reproduced or transmitted in
any form or by any means, electronic or mechanical, including photocopy, recording,
or any information storage and retrieval system, without permission in writing from the
publisher. Printed in Great Britain for Hodder and Stoughton Limited St Paul's
House Warwick Lane London EC4P 4AH by The Camelot Press Limited London
and Southampton.

To my parents

Preface

SHROPSHIRE HAS BEEN, until recently, comparatively neglected by topographical and historical geographers. This reflects the county's rather isolated position in the middle of the Welsh Marches, a situation that has often daunted scholars outside the county from pursuing their enquiries in the necessary detail.

In recent years, however, there has been an increasing amount of historical work on the county, particularly its industrial history. This book is intended to draw together some of this work and expand a number of the ideas expressed in my unpublished Oxford thesis, 'The History of the South Shropshire Landscape, 1086–1800'. I hope that it will act as a stimulus to students to investigate those many aspects of the beautiful Shropshire countryside which I have merely touched upon. There is room for work in every sphere, above all perhaps in vernacular architecture and settlement history.

The county possesses no definitive historical survey. Only Volume 1 (1908) and the excellent Volume 8 (1968) of the *Victoria County History* have been published; Volumes 2 and 3 are in preparation. The county is fortunate, however, in possessing the Rev. E. W. Eyton's *Antiquities of Shropshire* (1854–60), twelve volumes of antiquarian local history probably unsurpassed in England. The *Transactions of the Shropshire Archaeological Society* contain a number of useful papers, as does the *Shropshire Newsletter*, and there is some excellent topographical material in the volumes of the *Transactions of the Caradoc and Severn Valley Society*.

The County Record Office possesses several important

documentary collections, including a great deal of topographical material and a fine set of estate maps. Shrewsbury Public Library houses an excellent local history collection, which I have found of the greatest value. I would like to express my thanks to members of both these institutions for their help and patience over the past years.

The writing of this book has only been made possible by the assistance and inspiration of a number of individuals. My deepest debt is to Mr Alec Gaydon, Editor of the *Victoria County History of Shropshire*, for his advice and for allowing me access to much unpublished material. I should like to thank Mr Philip Barker, whose enthusiasm first aroused my interest in the Shropshire landscape, and who has been a constant source of help; also Mr Barrie Trinder for his help with the industrial history. I am grateful to Miss L. MacLean for typing, indexing and helping with the proof-reading of the book.

Finally I must thank Professor Hoskins, for his help as general editor of the series and for his book *The Making of the English Landscape*, which for me, as for many, was the beginning of my ventures into landscape history.

R. T. ROWLEY

Wheatley,
  Oxfordshire

Contents

List of Plates

Between pages 40 *and* 41
1 Old Oswestry hill fort
2 Wroxeter—'Old Work'
3 *Viroconium* defences with ploughed-out ridge-and-furrow
4 The Berth, Baschurch
5 Offa's Dyke in the Clun Forest

Between pages 56 *and* 57
6 Stoke St Milborough Church
7 Minton village green
8 Haughmond Abbey
9 Heath Chapel
10 Bold Chapel, 1791
11 More, castle and deserted village earthworks

Between pages 88 *and* 89
12 Stokesay Castle
13 Acton Burnell, castle and church
14 Pickthorn deserted village
15 Moreton Corbet Castle

Between pages 120 *and* 121
16 Attingham Hall
17 Blake Mere and Oteley Hall
18 Broadstone field system, 1770
19 Lubberland, medieval coal-pits and squatter encroachments

Between pages 168 *and* 169
20 Hopton Wafers, parliamentary enclosure road

11

ACKNOWLEDGMENTS

The author wishes to thank the following for permission to use their photographs and plans:
Aerofilms Limited: Plates 1, 8, 16, 17, 25, 42
National Monuments Record: Plates 3 (photograph by W. A. Baker), 15, 24, 27, 28, 34 (Crown Copyright Reserved)

The Committee for Aerial Photography, Cambridge: Plates 4, 11, 13, 14, 19, 21, 23, 32 (photographs by J. K. St Joseph, Cambridge University Collection: copyright reserved)

West Midland Photo Services: Plate 29

C. Crosthwaite: Plates 30, 31

A. F. Kersting: Plate 33

A. P. Wallace: Plate 40

All other photographs copyright of the author.

Fig. 2 is based on a plan by G. Webster; Fig. 7 is reproduced by permission of E. M. Yates; Fig. 8 was drawn by Miss J. M. Talou; Fig. 9 was drawn by J. Bond; Figs. 18, 19 and 20 were compiled by M. Aston; Fig. 24 was compiled by D. Pannett and R. Machin

List of maps and plans

NOTE ON ABBREVIATIONS

A.H.R.	*Agricultural History Review*
Arch. Camb.	*Archaeologia Cambrensis*
Arch. J.	*Archaeological Journal*
B.M.	British Museum
J.B.A.A.	*Journal of the British Archaeological Association*
P.R.O.	Public Record Office
S.N.L.	*Shropshire Newsletter*
S.P.L.	Shrewsbury Public Library
S.R.O.	Shropshire Record Office
T.C.S.V.S.	*Transactions of the Caradoc and Severn Valley Society*
T.R.H.S.	*Transactions of the Royal Historical Society*
T.S.A.S.	*Transactions of the Shropshire Archaeological Society*
V.C.H.	*Victoria County History*

Editor's Introduction

SOME SIXTEEN YEARS ago I wrote: "Despite the multitude of books about English landscape and scenery, and the flood of topographical books in general, there is not one book which deals with the historical evolution of the landscape as we know it. At the most we may be told that the English landscape is the man-made creation of the seventeenth and eighteenth centuries, which is not even a quarter-truth, for it refers only to country houses and their parks and to the parliamentary enclosures that gave us a good deal of our modern pattern of fields, hedges, and by-roads. It ignores the fact that more than a half of England never underwent this kind of enclosure, but evolved in an entirely different way, and that in some regions the landscape had been virtually completed by the eve of the Black Death. No book exists to describe the manner in which the various landscapes of this country came to assume the shape and appearance they now have, why the hedgebanks and lanes of Devon should be so totally different from those of the Midlands, why there are so many ruined churches in Norfolk or so many lost villages in Lincolnshire, or what history lies behind the winding ditches of the Somerset marshlands, the remote granite farmsteads of Cornwall, and the lonely pastures of upland Northamptonshire.

"There are indeed some good books on the geology that lies behind the English landscape, and these represent perhaps the best kind of writing on the subject we have yet had, for they deal with facts and are not given to the sentimental and formless slush which afflicts so many books concerned only with superficial appearances. But the geologist, good though he may be, is concerned with only one aspect of the subject, and beyond a certain point he is obliged to leave the historian and geographer to continue and complete it. He explains to us the bones of the landscape, the fundamental structure that gives form and colour to the scene and produces a certain kind of topography and natural vegetation. But the flesh that covers the bones, and the details of the features, are the concern of the historical geographer, whose task it is to show how man has clothed the geological skeleton during the comparatively recent past—mostly within the last fifteen centuries, though in some regions much longer than this."

In 1955 I published *The Making of the English Landscape*. There I claimed that it was a pioneer study, and if only for that reason it could not supply the answer to every question. Four books, in a series published between 1954 and 1957, filled in more detail for the counties of Cornwall, Lancashire, Gloucestershire, and Leicestershire.

Much has been achieved since I wrote the words I have quoted. Landscape-history is now taught in some universities, and has been studied for many parts of England and Wales in university theses. Numerous articles have been written and a few books published, such as Alan Harris's *The Rural Landscape of the East Riding 1700–1850* (1961) and more recently Dorothy Sylvester's *The Rural Landscape of the Welsh Borderland* (1969).

Special mention should perhaps be made of a number of landscape-studies in the series of Occasional Papers published by the Department of English Local History at the University of Leicester. Above all in this series one might draw attention to *Laughton: a study in the Evolution of the Wealden Landscape* (1965) as a good example of a microscopic scrutiny of a single parish, and Margaret Spufford's *A Cambridgeshire Community* (*Chippenham*) published in the same year. Another masterly study of a single parish which should be cited particularly is Harry Thorpe's monograph entitled *The Lord and the Landscape,* dealing with the War-wickshire Parish of Wormleighton, which also appeared in 1965.[1] Geographers were quicker off the mark than his-torians in this new field, for it lies on the frontiers of both disciplines. And now botany has been recruited into the field, with the recent development of theories about the dating of hedges from an analysis of their vegetation.

But a vast amount still remains to be discovered about the man-made landscape. Some questions are answered, but new questions continually arise which can only be answered by a microscopic examination of small areas even within a county. My own perspective has enlarged greatly since I published my first book on the subject. I now believe that some features in our landscape today owe their origin to a much more distant past than I had formerly thought pos-sible. I think it highly likely that in some favoured parts of England farming has gone on in an unbroken continuity since the Iron Age, perhaps even since the Bronze Age; and that many of our villages were first settled at the same time. In other words, that underneath our old villages, and underneath the older parts of these villages, there may well be evidence of habitation going back for some two or three thousand years. Conquests only meant in most places a change of landlord for better or for worse, but the farming life went on unbroken, for even conquerors would have starved without its continuous activity. We have so far failed to find this continuity of habitation because sites have been built upon over and over again and have never been wholly cleared and examined by trained archaeologists.

At the other end of the time-scale the field of industrial archaeology has come into being in the last few years, though I touched upon it years ago under the heading of Industrial Landscapes. Still, a vast amount more could now be said about this kind of landscape.

[1] *Transactions of the Birmingham Archaeological Society,* Vol. 80, 1965.

Purists might say that the county is not the proper unit for the study of landscape-history. They would say perhaps that we ought to choose individual and unified regions for such an exercise; but since all counties, however small, contain a wonderful diversity of landscape, each with its own special history, we get, I am sure, a far more appealing book than if we adopted the geographical region as our basis.

The authors of these books are concerned with the ways in which men have cleared the natural woodlands, reclaimed marshland, fen, and moor, created fields out of a wilderness, made lanes, roads, and footpaths, laid out towns, built villages, hamlets, farmhouses and cottages, created country houses and their parks, dug mines and made canals and railways, in short with everything that has altered the natural landscape. One cannot understand the English landscape and enjoy it to the full, apprehend all its wonderful variety from region to region (often within the space of a few miles), without going back to the history that lies behind it. A commonplace ditch may be the thousand-year-old boundary of a royal manor; a certain hedge-bank may be even more ancient, the boundary of a Celtic estate; a certain deep and winding lane may be the work of twelfth-century peasants, some of whose names may be made known to us if we search diligently enough. To discover these things, we have to go to the documents that are the historians' raw material, and find out what happened to produce these results and when, and precisely how they came about.

But it is not only the documents that are the historian's guide. One cannot write books like these by reading someone else's books, or even by studying records in a muniment room. The English landscape itself, to those who know how to read it aright, is the richest historical record we possess. There are discoveries to be made in it for which no

written documents exist, or have ever existed. To write the
history of the English landscape requires a combination of
documentary research and of fieldwork, of laborious
scrambling on foot wherever the trail may lead. The result
is a new kind of history which it is hoped will appeal to all
those who like to travel intelligently, to get away from the
guide-book show-pieces now and then, and to know the
reasons behind what they are looking at. There is no part
of England, however unpromising it may appear at first
sight, that is not full of questions for those who have a
sense of the past. So much of England is still unknown and
unexplored. Fuller enjoined us nearly three centuries ago

"Know most of the rooms of thy native country
before thou goest over the threshold thereof.
Especially seeing England presents thee with
so many observables."

These books on The Making of the English Landscape
are concerned with the observables of England, and the
secret history that lies behind them.

Exeter, 1970   W. G. HOSKINS

1. Shropshire Landscapes

Natural landscapes. *The pattern of settlement.*

Natural landscapes

SHROPSHIRE IS THE largest inland county in Great Britain with a total area of 1346 square miles. It is a county of contrast with a wide variety of scenery within its borders. Much of this variety derives from Shropshire's position as a border county, both geographically between the Midland plain and the Welsh mountains, and culturally between England and Wales. The main division in the county is between the northern plains and the southern hills and dales (Fig. 1). The river Severn forms both a link and a barrier between the two, and Shrewsbury, 'Islanded in Severn Stream', lies at the heart of Shropshire and acts as the nucleus on which communications from both regions naturally converge.

Within this basic division a variety of landscapes reflect underlying geology and soils as well as different cultural responses. To the north of the Severn the Shropshire plain is made up of undulating trias, blanketed by glacial drift, with meres and peat mosses in the hollows. The surface of the plain is broken only by upstanding sandstone ridges such as Nesscliffe, Pim Hill, Grinshill and Hawkstone. Towards Cheshire the plain is occupied by scattered red-brick farms and cottages connected by a maze of roads. The landscape here is largely a product of post-seventeenth-century drainage and accordingly there are few villages. Much of the area is now agriculturally prosperous, although

21

in places such as Whixall Moss true wild fenland vegetation is returning.

In the extreme north-west of the county there is a small area, west of Oswestry, where the Denbighshire hills overspill into Shropshire. The landscape here is largely Welsh in character, with small stone cottages, pastoral farming and limestone-quarrying as well as a predominance of Welsh place-names. Woodland clearance in this area was not completed until the seventeenth century, and small scattered farms are far more common than nucleated villages.

To the east, beyond the Wrekin, lie Wellington and the Shropshire coalfield where the only extensive industrial landscape in the county is to be seen. Compared with many other British coalfields there has been little twentieth-century development and consequently this area is full of relics of early industry. The coalfield extends from Lilleshall in the north-east to Coalbrookdale and Broseley in the south-west and from Wrockwardine in the west to Oakengates in the east, forming a well-defined triangle. This is a comparatively small area, made up of valleys and escarpments, where settlement and landscape patterns found elsewhere in the county have been distorted by a frenzy of coal-mining, iron and pottery manufacturing, and all the other physical remains of unplanned industrial activity.

It is sadly fitting that the massive cooling towers of the new electric power-station at Buildwas, symbols of our technological society, which now dominate the central Shropshire skyline, should be sited so close to Abraham Darby's Coalbrookdale works. For it is from here that the Industrial Revolution was triggered off. The new town of Telford, named after one of our greatest civil engineers, is to be built over much of the coalfield as an overspill city for the industrial Midlands.

In the south-east beyond the Severn there is a rich sandstone countryside, originally part of Worcestershire, based

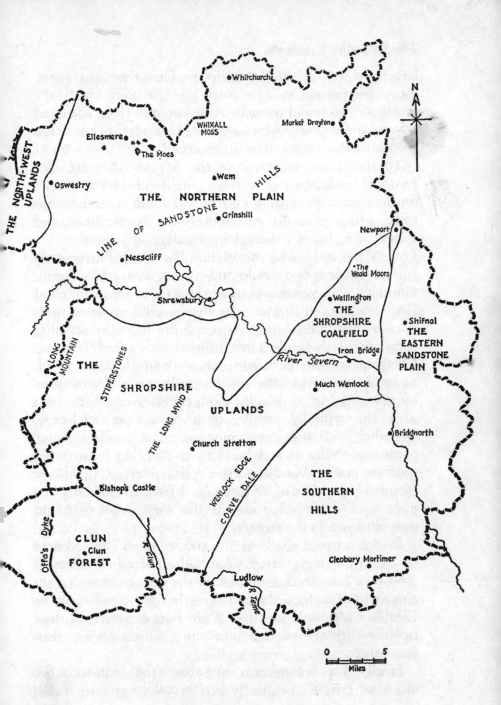

Fig. 1. Shropshire: natural regions

largely on the ancient Morfe Forest. Here there are larger, more prosperous villages such as Claverley, with the remains of scattered moated farms and numerous scattered coverts and coppices which serve as reminders of the dense woodland that once covered this area.

To the south and west of the Severn there are two principal landscape types: firstly, the highland areas based on the ancient pre-Cambrian rocks of south central Shropshire, which generally run south-west to north-east and include the Long Mountain, Stapeley, Stiperstones, the Long Mynd and the Stretton Hills. The Shropshire uplands are very varied; open, wild and barren, with rocks, heath, moorland and mountain pasture, but with many rich and fertile valleys folded away among the hills. In some parts open moorland used only for rough grazing is found lying comfortably alongside areas of enclosed mixed farming. Villages, except in the valleys, tend to be small and scattered. Secondly, there are the subtle sandstone and limestone escarpments such as Wenlock Edge and Hoar Edge which form the typically gentle south Shropshire landscape. Together with the intervening vales and its numerous picturesque villages and hamlets, this region is probably the most beautiful and evocative within the county. It is the essential Shropshire of Housman's *A Shropshire Lad*, centred upon Ludlow, which today is the most impressive and unspoilt town in the county.

In the extreme south of the county is an isolated area based on the 'high-reared' Clee Hills. These basalt-capped sandstone hills are the highest in the county, reaching up almost to 1800 feet. Beyond them lies the small town of Cleobury Mortimer and the Wyre Forest, which in their isolation belong more naturally to Worcestershire than Shropshire.

Finally, there is another remote area in the south-west, the old Clun Forest, still partly Welsh and completely rural.

Here the slopes become much steeper and trees and hedges less frequent except in the valleys; here too the isolated stone farmhouse is the most common form of settlement.

As for the buildings of the county, the survival of Norman architecture in many Shropshire churches is particularly striking. But there are few grand secular buildings in the county, and there is no definite regional style. Building materials vary considerably throughout the county, reflecting the availability of wood, stone or brick. Thus in the north, half-timbered houses and red brick predominate, while in the south, local sandstone and limestone has been extensively used. Recent research into vernacular architecture in the county suggests that a considerable number of medieval timber buildings have survived, unrecognised, encased in a later brick shell. For example, there are no fewer than six houses of encased medieval cruck construction to be found in the village of Condover alone.

Shropshire, unlike much of England, is still largely unspoilt. To the west of the River Severn, it (like Herefordshire and parts of Worcestershire) remains unbruised. Suburban sprawl, motorways and highly mechanised agriculture have not seriously affected the county. These essential, but often brutal, features of late twentieth-century industrial society cannot be comfortably absorbed into a rural landscape that has been so long in the making.

The pattern of settlement

Although Shropshire does not form a distinct geographical unit, there is a recognisable Shropshire landscape. This landscape is characterised poignantly through the fields, hedges and buildings and that essential feature of Shropshire rural life, the hamlet. Hamlets, or townships as they are sometimes called, are more common in Shropshire than proper villages. Such settlements often consist of no more than half a dozen dwellings; and frequently they have no school, shop, chapel or even inn.

The Shropshire settlement pattern has in the past received little serious attention and recent attempts, largely by geographers, to classify Shropshire's villages and hamlets have been only partly successful. However, Mr Alec Gaydon in Volume 8 of the *Victoria County History of Shropshire*, clearly demonstrates that in central and western Shropshire the basic unit of settlement from the early Middle Ages at least, was the nucleated village and hamlet and that the isolated farmhouse did not appear as a common feature of the Shropshire landscape until towards the end of the thirteenth century.

Over much of the county a clearly defined system of mother-villages and daughter-settlements has been identified. Mother-villages, which were often at the head of large Saxon estates or parishes, may represent the earlier phases of the English settlement or possibly occupy sites settled before the Saxons arrived. Daughter, or dependent hamlets, of which some large manors had several dozen, were secondary creations, often planted during a colonising phase in wood, moor or heath. Some medieval daughter-settlements later achieved complete parochial and manorial independence, while others maintained their links with the mother-village and the remainder simply faded away.

Superficially, the modern settlement pattern reflects that of the Middle Ages. However, in reality over much of the county we see a decayed settlement pattern. Many village-names have survived in the form of parish, hamlet or farm names, frequently giving an impression of continuity when in fact the basic pattern of settlement has radically changed. In Condover Hundred, for instance, of the sixty-one hamlets which appear to have existed at the time of the Domesday Survey in 1086, eight have been deserted and thirty-one have shrunk to one or two farms. Elsewhere in

Shropshire dozens of 'lost' villages have been found and many more undoubtedly remain to be identified. Indeed, rural depopulation is still taking place over much of Shropshire and the shrinkage of many remote hamlets continues.

The fossilisation of parishes has meant that their boundaries remained virtually static from the Middle Ages to the end of the nineteenth century, and even today reflect administrative units that in some cases have long since disappeared. For instance, Deuxhill, a few miles south of Bridgnorth, appears as a parish on modern Ordnance Survey maps, but the village has long since disappeared and the ruins of the church are to be found behind the only surviving dwelling, Hall Farm. Such fossilisation can be very useful to the landscape historian and can often help with the interpretation of medieval settlement patterns. However, settlement studies, based only on the modern map or even tithe maps of the nineteenth century, taken at their face value can be extremely misleading.

Many hamlets and towns later contracted or were abandoned completely as a result of changing economic conditions. From the thirteenth century there was a movement away from the sands and gravels that had attracted early settlers to the heavier clays and marls. Whereas on the lighter soils the traditional form of settlement had been the nucleated hamlet with its open fields, on the clays the isolated farm with enclosed fields was much more common. This slow but inexorable process was fundamental to the making of the modern landscape. The enclosure of open fields, too, was responsible for the gradual decline of many nucleated villages. The centralised village lying in the middle of its open fields was particularly suitable for strip-farming; each farm lying more or less at an equal distance from its scattered strips. Following enclosure and the creation of compact farms, villages often disintegrated; as the farmhouses in the villages fell into decay they were replaced by new houses lying in the middle of their fields, often far away from the old village. This process, which continued over several centuries, was responsible for extensive settlement shrinkage throughout Shropshire. Indeed, enclosure may be regarded as the main force in the weakening of the village fabric.

Another important factor in the changing fortune of some villages was the decline of strategic sites. Many settlements which were deliberately planted or extended to meet the demands of Welsh border conflict in the twelfth and thirteenth centuries later lost their military function and decayed gradually.

The element of deliberate creation or destruction in the settlement pattern is very strong in Shropshire—much stronger, I believe, than has previously been imagined. All the market towns with the possible exception of Shrewsbury were planted or at least stimulated in the Middle Ages. A process of planned expansion, often associated with the building of small medieval castles, also appears to have been responsible for the shape of many smaller villages in the county. On the other hand, the movement or even destruction of villages brought about by the creation or extension of parkland is a recurring theme in the Shropshire countryside right up to the middle of the nineteenth century.

The impact of industry on traditional settlement patterns has also been significant. In the coalfield the original villages and hamlets have been absorbed or transformed by a wide variety of industrial activities and associated piecemeal settlement over the past three centuries. Changes have been brought about, too, by the establishment of transport links, often serving industry. The building of a canal, turnpike road or railway line has frequently initiated a shift from the original village and encouraged subsequent development along the new route.

Finally, a word about squatters. From the early sixteenth century onwards, groups of landless peasants encroached and built cottages on the edge of common land. In some parts, particularly the heathlands of north Shropshire, the squatter-cottage is a much more important element in the landscape than the village.

SELECT BIBLIOGRAPHY

The Land of Britain—Shropshire, Ed. E. J. Howell (1941).
Pevsner, N., *The Buildings of England—Shropshire* (1958).
Trueman, A. E., *The Scenery of England and Wales* (1938).
Victoria County History, *Shropshire*, Vol. 1 (1908), pp. 1-50.
Watts, W. W., *Shropshire: The Geography of the County* (Shrewsbury, 1939).

2. Shropshire before the Norman Conquest

Prehistoric Shropshire. The Romans in Shropshire. The British and the English settlement. Offa's Dyke. Saxon burhs.

Prehistoric Shropshire

As SHROPSHIRE DID not exist as an administrative unit until the early eleventh century, it is a little unrealistic to think in terms of county boundaries when talking about the impact of early man on the landscape. Counties, however, have provided convenient units for archaeological research in the past, so, bearing in mind that the administrative boundaries of the twentieth century would have had no conceivable meaning to early settlers, we can examine the imprint of prehistoric man on this assumption.

As a landlocked and heavily forested region on the edge of the Welsh mountains, much of Shropshire was not particularly attractive to early settlers. No trace has been found in the county of Palaeolithic man and there have been few finds of Mesolithic character. Apart from the axe-factory just over the Montgomeryshire border at Hyssington under Corndon Hill only a thin scattering of Neolithic material has been recovered, indicating that during this period traffic was largely confined to river valleys and open hills. The Portway, which runs along the crest of the Long Mynd, was used by Neolithic axe-traders onwards and was still recognised as a king's highway in the Middle Ages.

During the Bronze Age, communication was principally along ridgeways; the best known of these, the Clun–Clee ridgeway, ran across the southern part of the county and has been traced by Miss Chitty from thousands of flints found in the area. The ridgeway remained important until at least the eighth century A.D., and parts of it in the south-west of the county are still in use today. It is possible that the villages of Clunbury and Onibury, whose churches lie directly along the line of the ridgeway, are settlements of great antiquity. Other Bronze Age trackways have been identified in Shropshire; along Stapeley Hill, for instance, runs *Yr Hen Ffordd* (the Old Road), which probably gave its name to the hamlet Hemford (*Hen-Ford*). In the north of the county a trackway, known as *Ffordd Saeson*, which, starting near Oswestry, connected Anglesey with the Severn Valley and was used by Bronze Age Irish axe-traders, whose wares have been found in Shropshire; forging a link between the Welsh Borderland and Ireland that was to last at least until the early Saxon period.[1] However, apart from some *tumuli* following the line of the Portway and a few stone circles—the best known of which is Mitchell's Fold—little visible imprint of Bronze Age man survives in the landscape.

The most obvious legacies of the prehistoric period, and indeed the most outstanding ancient monuments in the county, are the hill forts, the majority of which appear to date from the Iron Age, probably reflecting a period of rapid expansion and colonisation in the county. Most of the hills in the western part of the county are topped by some form of prehistoric fortification. Among the most formidable of these in the south are Bury Ditches, Hopesay, Burrow Camp and Caer Caradoc. In the north, the hill fort at Old Oswestry is the most spectacular (Plate 1). Sir Cyril Fox described it

[1] Miss L. F. Chitty, 'The Clun–Clee Ridgeway: A Prehistoric Trackway across South Shropshire', *Culture and Environment: Essays in Honour of Sir Cyril Fox* (1963); C. A. Gresham and H. C. Irvine, 'Prehistoric Routes across North Wales', *Antiquity*, No. 145 (1963).

as "the outstanding work of the early Iron Age type on the Marches of Wales". It covers forty acres, and underwent many vicissitudes between its beginnings about 250 B.C. and its initial abandonment after the Claudian conquest. Originally it consisted of two huge earthen banks, but at a later stage a third bank was added, and finally the whole structure was enclosed by an enormous double compound. Old Oswestry is particularly interesting as it is one of the Shropshire hill forts that were probably reoccupied in the fifth century after the Romans left.

Many other Shropshire forts are made up of multiple earth ramparts with fine inturned entrances. At Caynham Camp and Titterstone Clee hill fort, evidence of rock cut ditches and stone ramparts has been found. On many sites there was probably earlier occupation, but little excavation has taken place to prove this. At Abdon Burf on Brown Clee, a massive fort destroyed by quarrying, evidence of occupation from Neolithic to Romano-British times has been found. [2]

It has been suggested that some hill forts in the county were interdependent; recent work on a group of forts around Pontesbury, for instance, indicates that they share the same cultural background, and that some of the small forts in the area acted as satellites. [3] Evidence of trackways linking these sites may remain to be found in the footpaths, bridleways and parish boundaries of western Shropshire. Such a trackway may be postulated running north-west from Earl's Hill, Pontesford, to the Breidden hill fort, still partly preserved in minor roads and footpaths. The hill forts make impressive landmarks, in some places dominating the skyline, but their influence on subsequent landscape

[2] B. H. St J. O'Neil, 'Excavations at Titterstone Clee Camp', *Arch. Camb.*, Vol. 89 (1934); G. Harding Webster, 'The Riddle of Abdon Burf', *T.S.A.S.*, Vol. 45 (1929).

[3] J. Forde-Johnston, 'Earl's Hill, Pontesbury and related hillforts in England and Wales', *Arch. J.*, Vol. 119 (1962).

development has, on the whole, been small. Such fortifications, however, often helped to shape the countryside in a minor, but fascinating way. Norton Camp, lying at about 1000 feet on the southernmost tip of Wenlock Edge near Craven Arms, encloses about ten acres and is one of the least accessible sites in the county. Commanding the Onny Valley and the western approaches to Corvedale, its prominence and deeply engraved defences have meant that in historic times it has acted as a natural feature and helped shape the immediate topography. The outer rampart on the northern and western sides forms Culmington parish boundary, and fields have evolved in a circular pattern around the camp; the defences, too steep for cultivation, have remained wooded.

Recent archaeological research along the gravel terraces of the Severn and in south Shropshire clearly shows that lowland settlement during the Bronze and Iron Ages was far more important than had previously been thought. Many settlement sites have been identified from crop-marks visible only from the air.[4] Although no surface evidence has survived, this erased landscape reflects intensive prehistoric settlement and farming on the river gravels and lighter soils. Some clusters of crop-marks may possibly mark the beginnings of later Shropshire villages. Significantly, one of the greatest concentrations of crop-marks is along the Severn Valley, near Shrewsbury. This area was later intensively occupied by the Romans and emerged by the time of Domesday Book (1086) as a region of prosperous arable farming. Although one must be cautious, the historian seeking evidence of continuity in settlement and farming would do well to study the Severn Valley between Montford Bridge and Buildwas, using the results of aerial photography and archaeological research.

[4] S. Stanford, 'Excavations at Bromfield', *S.N.L.*, No. 31 (Nov. 1966), and information from Mr A. Baker.

Finally, there are the traces of Celtic fields on the Long Mynd. These small enclosures are almost certainly related to hilltop occupation and may be associated with prehistoric 'cattle-ranching'. Few of the numerous hill forts and their associated earthworks in the county have been even partly excavated, and accurate plans for the vast majority of sites simply do not exist. Our understanding of prehistoric settlement in the region will remain fragmentary until such detailed archaeological research is carried out; the need for this work is emphasised by the threat to upland sites posed by the spread of forestry plantations and deep ploughing.

The Romans in Shropshire

Traditionally an account of the Romans in this area begins with Caratacus, the legendary Belgic Prince, who having fled from the Romans in England, carried on a desperate rearguard action in the foothills of Wales. The site of his last stand is described by Tacitus in his *Annals* thus: "He then threw up on the more accessible parts of the highest hills a kind of rampart of stone; below and in front of which was a river difficult to ford . . ." Generations of antiquaries have tried, but failed, to supply a satisfactory identity to this site, the topography of which can be matched by a dozen or so forts in the Marchlands. Detailed archaeological excavation may one day provide the answer, probably outside the modern county of Shropshire, but until then attempts at identification must fall into the realm of speculation.

During the early phase of the Roman occupation, Shropshire lay on the edge of the Civil Zone, where the Romans established a series of military forts. The best preserved of these is at Wall near Cleobury Mortimer, where the siting of the fort suggests a Roman crossing of the Severn near

Bewdley. Today a farm lies within this small square earth-work and the road cuts across the outer ramparts and ditches. Similar forts are known to have existed at Red Hill (Oakengates), Wroxeter and Whitchurch. Recent aerial reconnaissance, by Mr Arnold Baker in particular, has produced evidence in the form of crop-marks, of a consider-able number of previously unidentified forts and marching camps in Shropshire.

The largest Roman monument in the county is at Wroxeter, *Viroconium Cornoviorum*, a city built on a flat glacial plateau overlooking the Severn. Originally estab-lished as a military base on the Severn prior to the Roman Conquest of Wales, Wroxeter was developed as a civil town after the western command was transferred to Chester about A.D. 78. At Wroxeter, Watling Street first makes contact with the Severn and the foothills of the Welsh mountains can be seen rising in the distance; it would have been a convenient place for a base from which to conduct the conquest of Wales. At least three other military sites are known in the immediate area as well as several marching camps.

Towards the end of the first century the army moved from *Viroconium* and the site was handed over to the civil authorities. The town became the cantonal capital of the British tribe of the *Cornovii*, whose original headquarters had been in the hill fort on top of the Wrekin.[5] A remarkable inscription, from over the entrance to the Forum, was erected about A.D. 130 in honour of the Emperor Hadrian by the *Civitas Cornovii*. This inscription was smashed into many fragments when the Forum gateway collapsed into the street. It has been restored and is now housed in Rowley's House Museum in Shrewsbury.

Capitals such as Wroxeter were distinguished from lesser

[5] Miss K. M. Kenyon, 'Excavations on the Wrekin, Shropshire, 1939', *Arch. J.*, Vol. 99 (1942–3).

towns by the regular street-grid, the public law court and market, the large public bath-house and the provision of a water supply and drainage system.[6] What is surprising about Wroxeter is that the size and apparent wealth of the town is hardly commensurate with the known state of the tribe in pre-Roman times, and we can only assume that our picture is at present far from complete.

The visible buildings at *Viroconium* represent part of a large bath-house complex with the famous 'Old Work' forming the bath entrance. It is one of the very few extensive lengths of civilian Roman walling to have survived in Britain (Plate 2). Outside the baths, the main lines of the grid-pattern street-plan with associated buildings have been identified from air photographs and earthworks (Fig 2). The total area of the town was about 180 acres, the fourth largest in Britain. The defences of the town have been identified largely from aerial photographs and Plate 3 shows the relationship between the town ditches and the ploughed-out medieval ridge-and-furrow. Although the original site of the fort at *Viroconium* was chosen for strategic reasons, it is almost certain that there already existed native British estates capable of producing food for the city. Furthermore, a considerable number of cropmarks within a few miles of *Viroconium* along the Severn, probably representing a system of Romano-British farms, have been identified.[7] On these grounds a fairly well-developed Iron Age farming system in the area can be assumed.

Little light has yet been thrown on the physical collapse

---

[6] *The Civitas Capitals of Roman Britain*, Ed. J. S. Wacher (Leicester, 1966).

[7] Information from Mr J. Pickering. Current work on the military situation in the first century A.D. suggests that there are considerably more forts and marching camps in the county than had been previously realised. By inference there may well be many Romano-British civil sites awaiting discovery. See G. Webster, 'The Military situation in Britain between A.D. 43 and 71', *Britannia*, Vol. 1 (1970).

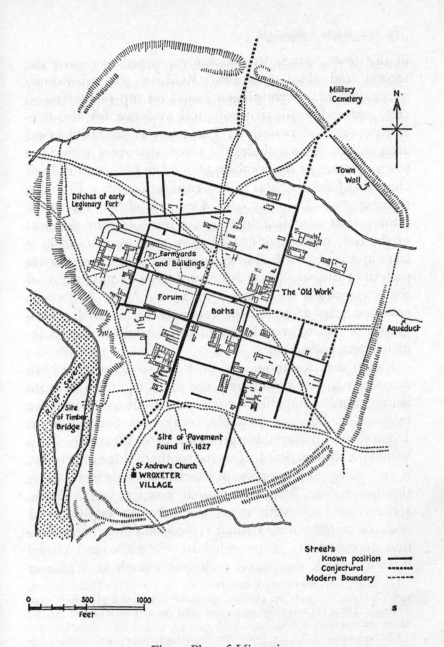

Fig. 2. Plan of *Viroconium*

Viroconium was the fourth largest town in Roman Britain. This plan shows the relationship of the village of Wroxeter to the town defences.

of this town, which was certainly prosperous during the second and third centuries. Evidence of sub-Roman occupation has recently been found on top of the ruined city, and additional archaeological evidence for the late- and post-Roman periods at *Viroconium* is gradually being accumulated. This includes the recent discovery within the town defences of the tombstone of a late fifth-century Irish chieftain, Cunorix, and the identification of a Frankish throwing-axe of similar date. One can add to this aerial photographs of a field within the north-eastern defences of the city, where crop-marks show what appears to be a large area of timber buildings contained within a rectilinear pattern of ditches. There are also dozens of pits, many of them rectangular and aligned with the ditches. The whole complex bears a remarkable resemblance to aerial photographs of the excavated sites of early Anglo-Saxon settlements with *grübenhauser*.[8]

Earlier theories about a violent end to *Viroconium* have now been largely discounted, the idea of gradual collapse being more compatible with recent discoveries. The relationship between possible continuous occupation at *Viroconium* and the shrunken village of Wroxeter, lying within the Roman defences on the southern side of the town, is intriguing and worthy of further investigation. It is significant that Wroxeter church contains early Saxon architecture built with stone from Roman buildings, as does the neighbouring church at Atcham.[9] Another indication of continuity is provided by the glebe and chapel interests which the Saxon collegiate church at Wroxeter

[8] P. A. Barker, 'Wroxeter: Excavations on the site of the Baths Basilica, 1970', *S.N.L.*, No. 39 (Dec. 1970). *Grübenhauser* is a term applied to sunken dwellings; these are normally associated with the earliest stages of Anglo-Saxon settlement in Britain.

[9] J. Taylor and H. Taylor, *Saxon Architecture in England* (Cambridge, 1965). The fabric of the north wall of Wroxeter church consists of re-used Roman stones and two Roman columns serve rather incongruously as gateposts at the entrance to the churchyard.

possessed in the neighbouring townships of Uckington, Beslow, Donnington, Drayton, Rushton, *Severalsdon* (lost), Norton, Uppington, Eyton and Little Buildwas; thus forming the basis of a considerable ecclesiastical estate between the Severn and the Wrekin, which in turn may well represent an earlier Roman estate. The ancient link between Wroxeter and Upton Magna, a considerable manor in 1086, may also be pre-Saxon, and the ancient parish boundaries between the rivers Severn and Tern and the Wrekin have a regularity that suggests at one stage they may have formed one large unit. It is too early yet to make any firm statement, but there is a growing body of evidence to imply at least the partial continuity of a large Romano-British estate into the Saxon period in this part of the Severn–Tern valley.

There is a long history of excavation at Wroxeter. The earliest recorded digging here was in 1292 when four men were brought to court for having "dug by night at *Wroccestre* in search of treasure".[10] The Roman city has provided a ready source of worked stone over the centuries for non-archaeological excavators. Telford noted that the site of the city was distinguished "by a blacker and richer soil or mould than the adjacent fields, and the stone foundations of ancient buildings, at no great depth under the surface of the ground, are manifest in long continued drought, so that when the occupiers of the land need any stones for building, they mark the scorched parts and after the harvest dig out what serves their purpose". This is possibly the first description of 'parch-marks', features which have been widely used by archaeologists to identify sites from the air in recent years. Telford, who made a remarkable impact on Shropshire in many spheres, undertook archaeological excavations at Wroxeter, and claims to have first identified

[10] Rev. E. W. Eyton, *Antiquities of Shropshire*, Vol. 7, p. 311, fn. It was reported that they had found nothing.

baths here. After some small pillars and a paved floor had been found, Telford "caused the place to be cleared to a considerable extent and thus brought to light a set of Roman Baths".[11]

Apart from Wroxeter, little obvious evidence of Roman occupation survives in Shropshire. The site of the small town of *Mediolanum* has been identified as Whitchurch, in the north of the county. A military fort was built here in the first century A.D. on the road running from *Viroconium* to the legionary base at Chester; later a small civil settlement grew up here. The modern High Street follows the line of the original Roman road and the basic street-plan reflects the Roman town-plan.[12]

A number of Romano-British villa sites have been identified and a few have been excavated, principally Yarchester in Harley parish and Lea Cross near Hanwood. There is little evidence as yet to suggest, however, that Roman Shropshire was particularly prosperous or intensively occupied. There is even less trace of the native British settlements that must have existed in the countryside.

Some evidence of Roman involvement in the mineral deposits of western Shropshire has survived. Lead was mined at Shelve and Linley, where Roman workings have been identified. Lead, copper and zinc were mined at Llanymynech hill which is honeycombed with old shafts and workings, some of which are Roman.

Part of the Roman road system has been preserved in the pattern of modern communications. The eventual movement of the trade centre from *Viroconium* to Shrewsbury, however, brought about a subtle adaptation of the original network. Watling Street, which linked Wroxeter with

[11] *Life of Thomas Telford*, Ed. J. Rickman (1838), p. 23. Telford was also involved in excavations at Lea Cross Roman Villa and his drawing of a tesselated pavement there appears in the *Telford Atlas*.

[12] G. D. B. Jones and P. V. Webster, 'Mediolanum: Excavations at Whitchurch, 1965–6', *Arch. J.*, Vol. 125 (1968).

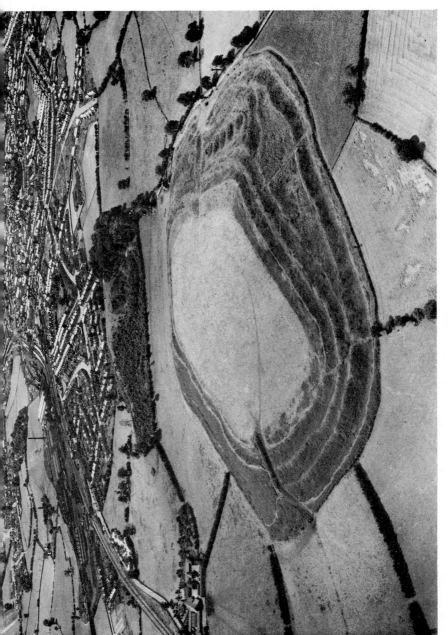

Plate 1 Old Oswestry Iron Age hill fort. The fort was reoccupied in the fifth century, and was the site of the Battle of *Maserfelth* (A.D. 641). The line of the eighth-century linear earthwork, Watt's Dyke, used the western boundary of the fort, but is not visible on this photograph. Oswestry's suburban and railway development can be seen in the background.

Plate 2   The baths entrance at Wroxeter (*Viroconium*), traditionally known as the 'Old Work'. (The remains of the excavated baths can be seen in the foreground.) This is one of the largest stretches of surviving civil Roman masonry in Britain. *Viroconium* was the capital of the British *Cornovii* tribe; previously their headquarters were in the hill fort on top of the Wrekin, here seen in the background.

Plate 3   Crop-marks showing the ploughed-out defences of *Viroconium*. Traces of medieval ridge-and-furrow belonging to the open-fields of Wroxeter are superimposed on top of the defences. The Severn and the village of Wroxeter can be seen in the background.

Plate 4 The Berth, near Baschurch; possibly the site of Pengwern. The defences of the central earthwork are wooded. The pattern of regular parliamentary enclosure fields surrounds the earthworks.

Plate 5 Offa's Dyke winding across open country in the Clun Forest. The line of the earthwork is mirrored by a ditch and road on the Welsh side.

Red Hill (*Uxacona*), Penkridge (*Pennocrucium*), and eventually London, has been preserved in the line of the A5. A minor detour from the Roman road at Overley hill formed part of Telford's improvements to the London–Holyhead road, early in the nineteenth century; the ancient road alignment is, however, preserved in parish boundaries. West of Shrewsbury, the Roman road joining *Viroconium* to the massive fort at Forden Gaer (*Lavrobrinta*) is preserved as a secondary road only as far as Westbury. The Roman road then proceeded westwards over the top of the Long Mountain, the line being demarcated for two miles by Westbury parish boundary. The modern road, however, follows the river Rea southwards, implying that during the Roman period the marshy Rea Valley did not provide convenient access into central Wales. The modern trunk road from Shrewsbury to central Wales lies a few miles to the north, reflecting the northwards movement of the trading centre in late Saxon times. The road from *Viroconium* to *Mediolanum* is preserved in short stretches as a modern road, but can be identified in field boundaries and from crop-marks. The road running southwards from *Viroconium* to Leintwardine (*Bravonium*) is easily identifiable on the ground running south-westwards through the Church Stretton gap. There is a remarkable stretch of Roman road between Craven Arms and Leintwardine which stands out very clearly in aerial photographs. Wistanstow church, a pre-Conquest foundation, lies on this stretch of road and the village appears to have developed along it.[13]

In the east of the county the line of the road running from *Pennocrucium* to *Mediolanum* can be traced in the modern road pattern. A stretch of this road, which crosses the flood plain of the river Tern to the south of Market Drayton, has been known as the 'Longford' since at least the thirteenth century. The name Pave or Pavement Lane, found in

[13] See p. 77.

41

Woodcote parish near Newport and elsewhere in the county, may also refer back to a former Roman road. Shrewsbury did not emerge as the new trading centre until well after the initial English settlement and the Roman road system must have served the incoming peoples. There are six villages in the county with the name Stretton indicating settlement by, or along, an existing Roman road; the preservation of Roman roads as parish boundaries strongly suggests that these roads too were still functioning in the early Saxon period.

With the establishment of new market centres in the Saxon and medieval periods the county road pattern changed to link Shrewsbury with the other towns. Even so, the Roman system was largely preserved until the era of turnpiking in the eighteenth century, when some roads were nominally improved at the expense of others. Very frequently it was the old Roman routes which were then finally abandoned.

The British and the English settlement

The Dark Ages are nowhere darker than in Shropshire. There are few tangible remains of the centuries following the collapse of the Roman administration. We have to be content with the tantalising evidence provided by early historians, charters and place-names. There can be little doubt, however, that the six centuries between the end of the Roman occupation and the coming of the Normans were of immense importance in the shaping of the Shropshire countryside. We need not be too concerned with the details of folk-settlement during this period, but there are three questions which are worthy of consideration here. What happened after the Romans left, what was the extent and nature of the English settlement and what was the degree of native British survival in the area?

In the fifth century A.D. a British kingdom of Powys was created, possibly by a chieftain with the Roman-sounding name of Vortigern; it has been suggested that this kingdom was co-extensive with the old territory of the *Cornovii* tribe.[14] Some of the western prehistoric hill forts were almost certainly reoccupied after the Romans left, notably Old Oswestry camp and Breidden fort (in Montgomeryshire). It has been suggested that there are even closer links between the Border hill forts and the English settlement. Attention has been drawn to the fact that of some twenty major forts in Shropshire no less than thirteen adjoined important lowland centres in the eleventh century, implying that there was a direct movement from the hill forts to the new lowland settlements in the early Saxon period.[15] Although this theory may prove a useful starting point for further research, there is as yet no archaeological evidence to support it, and indeed, numerous major hill forts were not adjoined by important Saxon manors.

Miss Chitty has convincingly argued that the Berth, near Baschurch, was a site of considerable importance during the Dark Ages, a theory which has been reinforced by the discovery here of a sixth-century bronze cauldron. The Berth is a fortified glacial hillock ringed by a rampart with an inturned entrance and linked by causeways across the encircling marsh to dry land and to a second mount (Plate 4). This is possibly Pengwern, the site of the Hall of the Welsh Prince Cynddylan, for long identified as Shrewsbury. Cynddylan was a chieftain of Powys, slain in the seventh

[14] N. K. Chadwick, 'Celtic Background and Early Anglo-Saxon England', *Studies in Early British History* (1954). Indeed, Professor Thomas, *Britain and Ireland in Early Christian Times* (1971), points out that the Roman *civitas* was probably composed of constituent *pagi* or subdistricts, and these must have been previously native divisions. *Pagus* survived to become Welsh *pen*: Powys comes from *pagenses*, 'the people who dwell in the *pagus*'.

[15] G. R. J. Jones, 'The settlement pattern of the Welsh Border', *A.H.R.*, Vol. 8 (1960).

century and buried in the Churches of Bassa, *Eglwyseu Bassa*, now Baschurch. It is possible that the Berth took over from *Viroconium* as the administrative and trade centre for the Welsh border, later to be replaced by Shrewsbury. Pengwern, the capital of Powys, was sacked in the mid-seventh century; its collapse was probably matched by the development of Shrewsbury (making its first appearance under its English name in a Wenlock charter dated A.D. 901), which had clearly emerged as the regional centre by the late ninth century.

There is some evidence to suggest Irish contact with the region during the Dark Ages; the fifth-century tombstone of an Irish chieftain has already been referred to. Early Mercian literature contains a marked Irish influence and recent work in central Wales has indicated Irish settlement and fields. Such traces may well be found in Shropshire.[16]

The early history of Mercia, of which the later county of Shropshire formed a part, is hazy. The initial conquest and occupation of the area was probably undertaken by the Kings of Wessex in the late sixth century. The Mercians were an obscure people, politically dependent upon the northern kingdom of Deira. In A.D. 628 the Mercians, led by Penda, broke into the region of the lower Severn. Later, in alliance with Cadwallon of Gwynned, the most powerful Welsh King of the day, Penda ravaged Deira and in A.D. 641 defeated Oswald at the battle of *Maserfelt*, a place better known as Oswestry. Oswald, a Christian, was later canonised and the later Norman town was named after St Oswald's Tree. The resulting kingdom of the *Magonsaete* embraced both Shropshire south of the Severn, and the plain of Herefordshire. The boundaries of this territory are still preserved in the diocese of Hereford. Bishops of

---

[16] C. Crampton, 'Ancient Settlement Patterns in Mid-Wales', *Arch. Camb.*, Vol. 116 (1967).

Worcester were frequently styled bishops of the Hwicce, and analogy suggests that the bishops of Hereford were originally regarded as bishops of the *Magonsaetan*. In the early eleventh century the eastern boundary of Hereford diocese followed the Dowles brook (still part of Shropshire's southern boundary); thence it ran up the Severn to Quatford.[17] The northern part of what is now Shropshire, formed part of the kingdom of the *Wroecensaetan*.

In the south of the county there are a small group of *'ham'* place-name endings,[18] representing perhaps the earliest phase of English settlement—Corfham (River Corve), Caynham (River Key), Lydham (River Lyde), Attingham (lying on the River Severn near to *Viroconium*). Dinham is a street-name in Ludlow near to the castle, possibly derived from a Saxon village on the site of the later town. The history of the Saxon occupation and colonisation, however, poses many problems. Apart from the extensive linear earthworks known as Offa's Dyke and a few Saxon churches, obvious relics of the settlement are rare. Nevertheless, by the time the first major topographical document appeared, the Domesday Survey of 1086, the framework for the modern landscape had been fashioned. The majority of Shropshire villages had been founded and named; large areas of virgin forest and heath had been cleared and cultivated; a new farming system which was to last a thousand years had been

[17] H. P. R. Finberg, 'Bishop Athelstan's Boundary', *The Early Charters of the West Midlands*. This boundary (dated between A.D. 1012 and 1056) was described as following the River Severn to Eardington. It obviously left the Severn at its confluence with the Mor brook and followed the straight road to Eardington. Afterwards it "ran up the Severn to Quatford"; as Quatford lies due east of Eardington across the Severn the terminology is obviously wrong or Quatford lay further upstream at this date, thus adding further confusion to the vexed question of the late Saxon history of the Bridgnorth region; see p. 187.

[18] *Ham* place-name endings are normally associated with early settlement when attached to British river-names. Attingham which has become abbreviated to Atcham over the centuries, had the early -*ingham* ending as well as having a church dedicated to a seventh-century saint.

introduced, and the basic road system and administrative boundaries had all been established. Why then are there so few tangible remains of their presence here? The answer is that the Saxon settlers who came to Shropshire were village-dwellers who built in wood. It is a mistake to think of the Saxons in this area as warlike invaders; they were initially colonisers and later farmers with no tradition of town life. They also had no tradition of pottery, and Saxon pottery has yet to be found in any quantity in Shropshire.[19] Also, Saxon settlements in many instances must lie underneath our modern villages. The recovery of information about such settlements, where decayed wooden buildings are evident only from subtle changes in soil colour and texture, requires meticulous excavation techniques. Eventually, however, traces of Saxon timber dwellings with their associated occupation will undoubtedly be found in Shropshire.

Soon after the establishment of the *Magonsaete* kingdom, a convent of monks and nuns was founded at Much Wenlock about A.D. 680. The site was purchased from Merewalh, Penda's son and the first recorded king of *Magonsaete*;[20] and in due course Merewalh's daughter Mildburge, who was later canonized, became its abbess. Wenlock, which was endowed with a scattered estate of over 200 hides in south Shropshire, must at the time of St Mildburge's death in the early eighth century have ranked as the leading monastic foundation in western Mercia.

A late seventh-century charter states that Merchelm (whose name survives in Marchamley, a village five miles east of Wem) and Milfred granted to their sister Mildburge,

[19] Late Saxon pottery has recently been found in the centre of Shrewsbury. *S.N.L.*, No 35 (1968).

[20] Merewalh was converted to Christianity in A.D. 660 by the Northumbrian missionary Eadfrith. The rarity of known pagan burial grounds in the Welsh Marches suggests there was, in fact, no great interval between the Saxon settlement of West Mercia and its conversion to Christianity.

with the consent of King Ethelred, sixty-three 'manentes' (hides) in various places, some around the hill called Clie (Clee), some by the River Corf (Corve), some in the place called Kenbecleag (possibly Kenley), and some in Chilmers (Chelmarsh). The land in the vicinity of Clee Hill almost certainly included Stoke St Milborough, the scene of a legendary incident in the saint's life. In 1066 the church of Wenlock held twenty hides there and two hides at Clee Stanton. The evidence from an early tenth-century charter suggests that the property by the River Corve included Easthope and Patton; to which the Domesday holdings in Bourton, Shipton and Sutton may be added.[21] There are fewer than a dozen surviving land charters for the county, so that those dealing with the Wenlock estate assume particular importance. The framework of this estate survived for almost a thousand years until the dissolution of the monasteries, and therefore deserves close attention.

The scattered nature of the property even in the seventh century implies the existence of widespread early or possibly pre-English settlement in this area. Wenlock's original endowment contained some Welsh estates, including land in the Monnow Valley and at Llanfillo, a village five miles north-east of Brecon. Professor Finberg has used this as part of his argument that at this time the Mercians and the native Welsh were living peaceably side by side.

The foundation at Wenlock, initially a daughter of the famous East Anglian house founded by St Botolf, was a double monastery. It was common in such establishments to have two churches, and it has now been shown that there were three, possibly four, churches within the Saxon monastery. This partly explains the siting of the parish church of Holy Trinity so close to the Priory ruins. The traditional assumption that Wenlock was ravaged by the

---

[21] H. P. R. Finberg, *The Early Charters of the West Midlands* (Leicester, 1961), p. 147. Wenlock also held Beckbury and Eardington before 1066.

Danes has recently been questioned, but whatever the truth the monastery was out of use by the late ninth century, although it was later refounded by Leofric *c.* 1050 as a minster church, endowed with much of its original estate.[22]

During the eighth and ninth centuries enormous parishes were created; some of them in the west were co-extensive with hundreds, and churches such as that at Stottesdon acted as small monasteries (*monasterium*) with a small group of resident clergy ministering to large numbers of surrounding villages and hamlets. The process of chapel-foundation, which was to assume such importance during the early medieval period, had already begun. It is thought that the small church at Barrow which contains eighth-century architecture was originally founded as an oratory or chapel from Wenlock.

Early Christianity in relationship to the Saxon occupation of the county needs to be closely examined. Reference has already been made to St Andrew's church at Wroxeter, which was possibly built at about the same time as the first buildings at Wenlock in the late seventh century. The neighbouring church at Atcham has a unique dedication to St Eata (d. A.D. 685), a companion to St Aidan, and it has been suggested that the earliest parts of the church were contemporary with those at Wroxeter. Nearby at Cressage the ancient church was dedicated to the Welsh St Samson (d. ?A.D. 565).[23] A group of Saxon churches in Corvedale possibly reflect the influence of Wenlock. Some remarkable Saxon carving and masonry is to be found in the parish churches of Culmington, Stanton Lacy, Diddlebury and the church at Tugford. Outside the Corvedale Stottesdon and Rushbury churches also contain interesting Saxon material.

[22] E. D. C. Jackson and Sir E. Fletcher, 'The Pre-Conquest churches at Much Wenlock', *J.B.A.A.*, Vol. 28, 3rd ser. (1965).

[23] Cressage—O.E. 'Christ's Oak'. Possibly a reference to a prominent tree at which the gospel was preached, cf. Oswestry—St Oswald's Tree.

The very survival of these churches in Shropshire is significant. In the southern Midlands the prosperity of the later Middle Ages, usually resulting from the wool trade, led to the wholesale rebuilding of churches. Shropshire, on the other hand, remained a comparatively poor county down to at least the sixteenth century. Accordingly many more early churches (particularly Norman) escaped rebuilding. Fortunately for us an attempt to rebuild the cruciform Saxon church at Stanton Lacy in the thirteenth century was abandoned because of lack of funds before much work was carried out.

In our present state of knowledge, Saxon place-name evidence points to a slow but reasonably intensive occupation of the county associated with woodland clearance. '*Wood*' names indicative of woodland clearance are common in Shropshire particularly in the west. The *ley* (*leah* = O.E. 'woodland clearing') ending is more common, however, in the south and east. The colonisation of woodland which appears to have been particularly important during the ninth and tenth centuries was carried out by satellite or daughter-hamlets, which by 1086 had often established themselves as villages in their own right. Stoke St Milborough, lying at 700 feet to the south of Brown Clee hill, appears to have been one of Wenlock's most important colonising centres (*Stoc* = O.E. 'daughter-settlement') (Plate 6); from this centre small dependent townships and their fields were won from the waste and woodland. Heath, where there is a striking isolated Norman chapel, provides a good example of this process (Plate 9). The hamlet which lay on the margin of farming at about 850 feet, remained parochially tied to Stoke St Milborough until 1871. By 1086 Stoke St Milborough had established six other dependent hamlets including two with the self-explanatory names of Newton and More.

Throughout Shropshire the Saxon unit of settlement

D

appears to have been the nucleated hamlet, in some cases probably consisting of no more than half a dozen dwellings. There is little evidence, except perhaps for hunting lodges and granges, to indicate the existence of isolated farmsteads before the thirteenth century. On the western fringes it is probable that Welsh pastoral farmers living in scattered communities existed alongside the nucleated Saxon villages, but little research on this aspect of Shropshire settlement history has yet been carried out.

During the Saxon period many township and parish boundaries were created. Such boundaries often remained unaltered until the late nineteenth century. A boundary in the countryside once created often persists long after the meaning for its creation has been forgotten. Thus these Saxon boundaries formed a framework on which later landscape changes hung. The old parish boundary patterns around the Brown Clee suggest that the Clee parishes may have originally formed one large estate (Fig. 3).

We must now look at the difficult problem of native British or Welsh survival in Shropshire. The western boundary of the Anglo-Saxon settlement, which is now crystallised in the boundary between England and Wales, has never been clearly defined. Both Offa's Dyke and the present boundary, drawn in 1536, were rationalisations and inevitably cut off some Welsh communities from their motherland. Recent work has indicated that not only did British communities survive the coming of the Saxons but also that during the early Middle Ages parts of the Marchlands were reoccupied by Welsh-speaking settlers.

Place-names provide the most convincing evidence for the survival of pre-Saxon communities; Hodnet (*Hoddnant*—peaceful valley), Lizard Hill (*Llysgarth*—hall by the hill), Prees (*Prys*—brushwood) and Wenlock (*Gwen loc*—white church) are all British place-names. While Celtic names of hills and rivers such as Clee, Caer Caradoc, Severn and

Lawley, might have been picked up by the incoming Saxons from a few survivors, the adoption of British settlement-names implies the continued existence of British rural communities. Such survivals may only hint at the degree of continuity; many villages which are thought of as Saxon foundations because of their place-names could have been founded much earlier, changing their names only as English became the dominant language. In western Shropshire there are nine Waltons and four Walcots; the place-name element *walh* was a derogatory term used by the Saxons for the Celts, and in these cases almost certainly refers to the survival of British settlements. Extremely valuable evidence of Celtic survival is provided by a study of dialect peculiar to border shires. This shows that up to the eighteenth century the linguistic frontier between English and Welsh ran from a point between Ellesmere and Oswestry to Upton Magna, about two miles east of Shrewsbury, thence along the Severn to Bewdley. West of this line it is suggested the inhabitants were the descendants of Welsh-speakers. And the English of the region was traditionally a 'Welsh English'. Many places in the county had alternate Welsh names throughout the Middle Ages, for instance, Wenlock was *Llan Meilen*, 'sacred enclosure', and Shrewsbury was *Amwithig*, 'defensive stronghold'.

The survival of the Welsh language, however, together with Welsh inheritance customs, may have been partly due to a later eastward movement of the Welsh. By the time of the Domesday Survey at the end of the eleventh century, the Hundred of *Mersete* had a considerable proportion of Welshmen (fifty-three out of a total of sixty-seven in Shropshire). *Mersete*, which is an Old English name meaning 'the settlers by the boundary', lies in the extreme north-west of the county. All the major manors in the hundred had English names, but most of the township and field-names were Welsh by the thirteenth century, the date of the first detailed

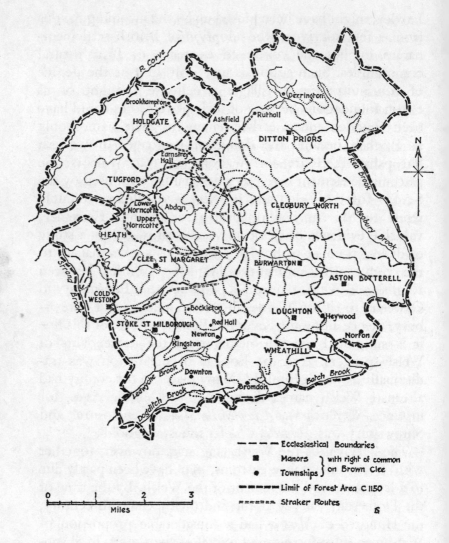

Fig. 3. Parish boundaries on Brown Clee
The parishes surrounding Brown Clee share the upland common
between them. Together they have a unity suggesting that once they
formed one estate. The straker routes were the tracks taken by drovers
on their way to Brown Clee common land; grazing rights on Brown
Clee were enjoyed by all the townships that had lain within the Forest
of Clee, demarcated on the plan.

surveys. Common Welsh place-name elements found in western Shropshire are *tre, bettws, llan, cefn, nant, pen, pant* and *pentre*. Some English place-names were made Welsh-sounding by changing the last syllable, for instance exchanging *tyn* for *ton* in Sellatyn and Sychtyn. This suggests that while there may have been initial English settlement here, later occupation and colonisation was Welsh. A similar situation appears to have occurred in the manor of Tempsitur (O.E. 'the Teme settlers'), in the Honour of Clun. Tempsitur was a long strip of land along the north bank of the River Teme containing twenty-three townships in the late Middle Ages. Offa's Dyke passes through it, leaving half of the manor on the Welsh side of the Dyke. However, by the thirteenth century the population of Tempsitur was almost exclusively Welsh.[24]

In the north-west and in parts of Ford Hundred the system of *gwaeli bond*, a form of Welsh communal ownership, may have contributed to the fragmented nature of the fields and holdings, as the tenurial system was based on partible inheritance, i.e. the equal division of lands amongst all the sons as distinct from the more usual custom of primogeniture. The western manors of Caus, Oswestry, Knockin and Clun all had their *Walcheria* throughout the Middle Ages. Additionally, Welsh dues continued to be paid in parts of the county; *Trethnedion*, a tribute of oxen, was observed in the Honour of Clun, and indeed a special Welsh court was held at Clun throughout the Middle Ages. Similarly Welsh dues survived in Oswestry until the seventeenth century. Oswestry was for all practical purposes a Welsh town until comparatively recently; there were always Welsh burgesses in the town and place-names within the

[24] T. Salt, 'Ancient Documents Relating to the Honour, Forest and Borough of Clun', *T.S.A.S.*, Vol. 11 (1887). The terms British, Welsh and Celtic are here used synonymously to distinguish the native inhabitants from the incoming English.

liberties were Welsh. There were well-known links between the Welsh bards and Oswestry: in the fifteenth century Guto'r Glyn was made a freeman of the borough for his poem (*cywydd*) in praise of Oswestry.

During the seventeenth and eighteenth centuries, however, a process of anglicisation went on, and English traditions and language gradually replaced their Welsh counterparts. Today little Welsh is spoken in Shropshire except perhaps on market days.[25]

Offa's Dyke

The first major attempt to settle the frontier between the English and the Welsh was made by the Mercian King, Offa (A.D. 757–96). The great linear earthwork known as Offa's Dyke is the most tangible legacy of the Old English occupation of Shropshire. The Dyke runs in and out of England, still forming part of Shropshire's border with Wales to the west of Chirk. The most complete section of the whole Dyke is in the south-west of the county where it runs through some of Shropshire's wildest countryside (Plate 5). Recent research appears to suggest that the Dyke represents a negotiated boundary between the Mercians and the Welsh, possibly associated with cattle-breeding. The Dyke certainly left to the Welsh some portions of lands which in earlier days the Mercians had made their own. The Welsh historian Asser claimed that Offa "ordered the great Dyke between Wales and Mercia to be made from sea to sea". It runs from the estuary of the Dee near Prestatyn in the north to the Severn estuary near Chepstow in the south. Sir Cyril Fox considered the Dyke to be "the product of one mind and of one generation of men". Earthworks of this size almost

[25] B. G. Charles, 'The Welsh, their Language and Place-names in Archenfield and Oswestry', *Angles and Britons* (1963). The process of anglicisation is demonstrated in minor place-names, Hayford farm in Westbury was Hafod when the tithe map was drawn up.

always attract legend and superstition often associated with supernatural forces. A long-held belief in the Welsh Borderland was that Offa's Dyke was ploughed by the Devil in a single night.

The Dyke which runs mostly across the grain of the countryside, that is north to south, is rarely able to follow a straight line and tends to follow a switch-back course, constantly changing direction (see Fig. 1). Generally it follows contour lines and not hilltops or ridges. Only occasionally, as at Llyncys Hill, south of Oswestry, it is replaced by natural topographical features, in this instance a cliff face. The engineers who constructed the Dyke made use of west-facing slopes wherever possible, even if this meant taking the boundary eastwards in the case of the Teme valley. There is also a remarkable eastern detour between Whitehaven and Llanymynech in order to exploit west-facing slopes.

In the north the Dyke is almost always accompanied by a western ditch, frequently with a counterscarp, but in the south the ditch is less common and over short stretches an eastern ditch is found. The average height of the bank above the accompanying ditch is about eighteen feet in the north and ten feet or less in the south. The Dyke has acted as a natural feature and influenced subsequent topographical history, very much as a natural ridge would have done. Parish and field boundaries often use it and only in a few places has it been effectively ploughed out. The Dyke frequently forms a woodland boundary and carries a tree cover in otherwise open areas. Despite the mammoth pioneer work by Sir Cyril Fox, a great deal remains to be done both on the interpretation of the overall scheme and in the critical examination of individual stretches.[26]

Traditionally the Dyke has been known as Offa's Ditch, and 'Ditches' farm, lying on the line of the Dyke near

[26] Sir C. Fox, *Offa's Dyke* (Oxford, 1955).

Chirbury, is a reminder of the ancient name *Offediche*. The importance of Offa's Dyke has been emphasised by its political and ethnic implications; even when not serving as the boundary between England and Wales it still kept its demarcation function. In the Middle Ages the Dyke acted as the boundary between Chirbury Hundred and the Marcher lordship of Montgomery. Thus in 1223 the King bade "the men of *Cherberi* Hundred on this side of *Offediche*, to give heed to the Sheriff of Shropshire in all matters which relate to the Hundred". Largely through the efforts of Mr Frank Noble, the line of Offa's Dyke has now been opened as a National Footpath (July 1971), an imaginative development for this ancient and much-neglected earthwork. In the Clun Forest two other short linear earthworks known as the Upper and Lower short ditches, run parallel to, and are possibly contemporary with, Offa's Dyke. On the English side Watt's Dyke, probably the work of an earlier Mercian ruler, Aethelbold (A.D. 716–57), extends from the Dee estuary, terminating at the Morda Brook south of Oswestry. At Whittington the modern road and parish boundary follow Watt's Dyke for a few hundred yards to Old Oswestry.

Saxon burhs

Towns played very little part in Saxon Shropshire, though during the ninth and tenth centuries a number of market centres were fortified. In the early tenth century Queen Aethelflaed began a systematic programme of fortress building to combat the Danes. In all some ten fortresses were constructed in the Midlands. One of the *burhs*, as these fortified enclosures were called, was built at Bridgnorth (*Brycge*) in A.D. 912 blocking a Severn crossing that had already been used by the Danes. The site of a second of Aethelflaed's *burhs, aet Cyricbyrig* (A.D. 915), is thought to

Plate 6 The ancient church of Stoke St Milborough in the foothills of the Clee hills. St Milborough's well, the scene of a legendary incident in the seventh-century saint's life, can still be found nearby.

Plate 7 The village of Minton surrounding an ancient green, now partly enclosed. The earthworks of a medieval motte-and-bailey castle lie in the coppice immediately behind the green. Minton originally lay within the Long Forest. It still lies on the margin of cultivation.

Plate 8 The ruins of Haughmond Abbey near Shrewsbury. Although the abbey was founded *c.* 1135, most of the surviving architecture is late twelfth century. Originally founded in a forest area, the escarpment to the east of the abbey is wooded. Note the outlying earthworks, including fishponds, and the precinct boundary which has a hedge growing on it.

Plate 9 Heath Chapel, an almost perfect twelfth-century building. The earthworks of the deserted village lie behind the chapel.

Plate 10 Remains of Bold Chapel, incorporated into farm buildings, drawn by the Rev. E. Williams in 1791. Extensive earthworks of the deserted village are still to be seen in the field to the south of the chapel ruins.

Plate 11 The ring-work and deserted medieval village at More. The horseshoe shape of the surrounding fields demarcates the ancient precinct, which is almost certainly indicative of early medieval village plantation. Note also the road on the left of the picture, which used to serve the castle and village, but was later diverted.

lie at Chirbury. Excavation of the rectangular earthwork, known as the 'castle' at Chirbury, was undertaken by the late Professor Wainwright in 1958, but failed to provide archaeological confirmation that this was the site of Aethelflaed's fortress. Taking other factors into account, however, its defensive position, its relation to an ancient gap in nearby Offa's Dyke, its control of a main route into (and from) central Wales, and its place in the national system of defence against the Danes, it is possible to conclude the so-called 'castle' at Chirbury is the site of a Saxon *burh*.[27] The siting of the *burh* at Shrewsbury is discussed later.[28]

A considerable number of Shropshire place-names carry the *-bury* ending, including Shrewsbury itself, and it seems probable that many of these places were fortified during this period, although no documentary record has survived.[29] A great deal of research remains to be carried out on the identification and plotting of late village defence works. At Pontesbury, which stands on the north-east bank of Pontesbury brook, the original village defences are possibly fossilised in the village plan. The name, which appears in the form of Pontesburie in 1086, probably contains as its first element the Welsh *pant* ('a hollow'), thus meaning 'the earthwork in the valley'. An oval ring-road now known as Hall Bank in the north surrounds most of the older houses in the village. This ring-road almost certainly follows the line of a defensive earthwork. The church stands at the highest point of the village, roughly in the centre of the area bounded by the road (Fig. 4). Another possible Saxon defensive plan can be identified at nearby

[27] F. T. Wainwright, 'Aethelflaed, Lady of the Mercians, *The Anglo-Saxons,* Ed. P. Clemoes (1959); 'The Chirbury Excavation', *S.N.L.,* No. 10 (Feb. 1960).

[28] See p. 196.

[29] It has been suggested, however, that the *-bury* ending may refer to any earthwork, not necessarily just Saxon defences. Indeed it is probable that some at least of the oval-shaped villages are post-Norman Conquest, dating from a realignment of village following the building of a castle.

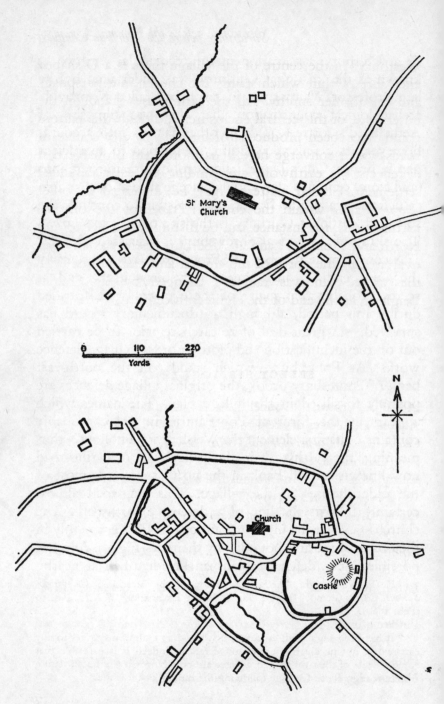

Fig. 4. Plans of Westbury (*top*) and Pontesbury
The plans show the oval alignment of roads which reflect early defences.

Westbury. In the centre of the village there is a D-shaped enclosure, within which stands the church, the parsonage and the former smithy. All the farmhouses stand on the outer edge of this central enclosure. Although this pattern could have been produced fortuitously by the course of roads which converge here, it is more than probable that it reflects the earthwork surrounding an early defended settlement. Similar patterns may be identified at other -*bury* villages within the county. Traces of the original fortifications, for instance, can be distinguished at Lydbury North and Clunbury; and at Alberbury there was an open oval area to the north of the church and castle ruins until the village-plan was radically changed by Sir Charles Leighton at the end of the eighteenth century.

SELECT BIBLIOGRAPHY

Angles and Britons, O'Donnell Lectures, Cardiff (1963).

Auden, T., 'Traces of Prehistoric Man', *T.S.A.S.,* Vol. 30 (1907).

Celt and Saxon: Studies in the early British Border, Ed. N. K. Chadwick, (Cambridge, 1963).

Chitty, Miss L. F., 'An Introduction to Shropshire Archaeology', *Arch. J.,* Vol. 113 (1956).

Chitty, Miss L. F., 'Notes on Prehistoric Implements', *T.S.A.S.,* Vol 43 (1926).

Collingwood, R. G. and Myres, J. N. L., *Roman Britain and the English Settlement* (Oxford, 1936).

Eyton, Rev. E. W., *Antiquities of Shropshire,* 12 volumes (1854–60).

Finberg, H. P. R., *Early Charters of the West Midlands* (Leicester, 1961).

Finberg, H. P. R., 'The Mercians and the Welsh', *Lucerna* (1964).

Hartshorne, Rev. C. H., *Salopia Antiqua* (1841).

The Irish Sea Province in Archaeology and History, Ed. D. Moore (Cardiff, 1970).

Noble, F., *The Shell Book of Offa's Dyke Path* (1969).

Rowley, R. T., 'The History of the South Shropshire Landscape 1086–1800', Oxford B.Litt. Thesis (1967, unpublished).

Stenton, F. M., *Anglo-Saxon England* (Oxford, 1943).

Victoria County History, *Shropshire*, Vol. 1, pp. 195–278.

Webster, G., *Wroxeter Roman City*, H.M.S.O. (1965).

Webster, G., and Dudley, D. R., *The Roman Conquest of Britain* (1965).

3. Shropshire in 1086

The Norman Conquest.   Settlement in 1086.

The Norman Conquest

TRADITIONALLY THE Norman Conquest has been regarded as a watershed in English history. In reality it is doubtful if the political and tenurial changes brought about by the exchange of Norman for Saxon landlords made any immediate impact on most of the Shropshire peasantry. Apart from the devastation of some western areas, the immediate influence on the landscape too was small. No English landscape study would be complete without some reference to the Domesday Survey of 1086. Despite the difficult problems of interpretation, this unique survey enables us to see something of the topography of eleventh-century Shropshire; and in many ways the coming of the Normans did mark the beginning of a number of long-term landscape changes.

Shropshire was the first of the Mercian shires to be named —in 1006—when it was recorded as the area to which King Ethelred fled. It was common for Saxon shires to adopt the name of the regional capital and Shropshire took its name from Shrewsbury, O.E. *Scrobbesbyrig*—'Scrobb's fortified place'. The difference between the present name of the town and that of the county is due to various changes having taken place in both forms, including the loss of the medial— *bury*—in the latter. The usual abbreviation for Shropshire, Salop—earlier *Salopescire*—is derived from a Normanised form of the English name. It has been suggested that the creation of the Mercian shires was a piece of deliberate planning which had not been completed by the time of the Domesday Survey. It is possible that the artificial Saxon hidage found in the survey was part of this plan.[1]

Shropshire, in 1086, was substantially different from the modern county. Large areas in the east were included under Staffordshire and Worcestershire, while in the south-west the Hundred of Wigmore in modern Herefordshire occupies what was once the greater part of the Shropshire Hundred of *Lenteurde*. Further north much of *Witentreu* Hundred was placed in Montgomeryshire in 1536. The whole of the Welsh border was in a fluid state and much of the Clun Forest in the south-west was not included in the survey at all. The degree of confusion in the border region can be measured by the unhidaged Welsh districts included in the Shropshire folios, principally *Cynllaith* and *Edeyrnion* which are recorded under *Mersete* Hundred. The inclusion of these districts, now well into Flintshire, may represent temporary Norman superiority there. The area which is now Montgomeryshire, however, was under precarious Norman control by 1086, and its acquisition indicated an understandable desire to hold the lowland areas and river valleys, which represented potential inlets into England. The divisions within the county were drastically reorganised soon after the Domesday Survey; new hundred boundaries were drawn up some time before 1158 and even the three hundreds which suffered little change in area were renamed.

After the Conquest, King William shelved the Welsh border problem by assigning the three border shires to three of his leading vassals. Shropshire was initially

---

[1] C. S. Taylor, 'The Origin of the Mercian Shires', *Gloucestershire Studies,* Ed. H. P. R. Finberg (Leicester, 1957). The Saxon shire appears to have been composed of two tribal districts, that of the *Magonsaetan*—'settlers around the Maund (Herefordshire)' and that of *Wreocensaetan*—'settlers around the Wrekin'. The Shropshire hide is generally thought to have been about sixty acres.

established as a county Palatinate under Roger de Montgomery. This was a short-lived attempt to create a buffer
state between Norman England and the Welsh. In the early
twelfth century this was amended and large parts of
western Shropshire were included in what were known as
the Marcher Lordships, principally the extensive honours
of Clun, Ellesmere and Oswestry. Technically these did
not revert to Shropshire until the Act of Union with Wales
in 1536, when Shropshire assumed roughly its present
form. The place-names English and Welsh Frankton in
north Shropshire distinguished the community which lay
in the Marchlands from that which was in the medieval
county of Shropshire.

Shropshire's border siting in the post-Conquest period
had an important influence on subsequent landscape
developments. Prior to the Conquest, Shropshire was almost
exclusively rural. Domesday records only two boroughs—
Shrewsbury and Quatford. The need for defended administrative and market centres, however, encouraged the plantation of a number of towns. Mostly these were developed
within the protective shadows of large stone castles, as
at Ludlow and at Clun. The plantation of new towns in the
county continued well into the thirteenth century, and
despite some failures, all market towns in Shropshire
began life as deliberate creations of this kind. On a smaller
scale some villages clearly were laid out within the baileys
of small castles. Plate 11 shows this arrangement at the
shrunken village of More, where the main street and regular
tenements can be traced on the ground. Virtually every
settlement in western Shropshire had an earth-and-timber
castle. Many of these castles survive today as small conical
mounds—one of the most characteristic earthwork forms
in the Shropshire landscape.

The coming of the Normans also brought about far-
reaching changes in the parochial structure. Only twenty-one

places in Shropshire were specifically attributed with a church in 1086. Most manors had only one church, but Shrewsbury's five reflected the importance of the Saxon town. Chirbury manor had two churches, one of which was St Michael's in Chirbury itself, the other was the daughter-chapelry at Church Stoke, now in Montgomeryshire; here we are dealing with an early example of a dependent chapelry. Chirbury parish was originally very large, constituting almost the whole Domesday Hundred of *Witentreu.*

Such Saxon minster churches often had a group of resident clergy who served the extensive parishes of pre-Conquest Shropshire. Writing of Clun before 1086, Eyton remarks "here was one of those great Saxon foundations whose parishes we hardly venture to define for fear of falling short of reality". These parishes covered tracts of forest and open heathland in west and south Shropshire. After the Conquest, Chirbury founded further chapels at Montgomery, Snead, Forden and Hyssington. This process of church and chapel foundation, which was of great importance in the development of the Shropshire landscape, is later dealt with in more detail. [2]

The church at Stokesay appears to have been founded from the neighbouring manor of Aldon, which in 1086 was a small but wealthy manor with a church and priest. Soon after Domesday, Aldon's ecclesiastical status appears to have changed and it became a dependent chapelry of Stokesay, providing an unusual and interesting change of fortune. This transfer almost certainly reflects the decision of the lord of the manor, Picot de Say, to build a castle and a new church at Stokesay; the doorway of the church here is Norman. Stoke-upon-Tern was already independent in

[2] Dependent chapels possessed only the right of baptism (granted principally for cases of infant mortality in large remote parishes), but the mother-church reserved rights of marriage and burial. See p. 79.

1086, when the manor was said to have a church and a priest. The mother-church was probably at Hodnet, but the link had been all but severed by the time of Domesday. Stoke-upon-Tern was known as North Stoke during the twelfth century to distinguish it from Stokesay, which was known as South Stoke. Both manors were tenanted by the de Say family after the Conquest, giving rise to the place-name Stokesay—*Stoke-de-Say*.[3]

In addition to the places where churches were specifically recorded, priests without churches were mentioned in a further twenty-nine manors; it is almost certain that such a reference implies the existence of a pre-Conquest church. This means that out of a total of 630 villages and townships, only fifty appear to have had churches. But Domesday Book is notoriously suspect in its record of churches—in fact thoroughly unreliable whenever it can be tested from other sources. It is therefore probable that there were far more than fifty churches in Shropshire at the time of the Conquest.[4] However, whereas prior to 1066 the majority of churches were built in wood, after the Conquest local stone was extensively used in the rebuilding of existing churches and the building of newly founded chapels. Traces of Norman architecture can be seen in just under a hundred Shropshire churches.

Before the Norman Conquest there were no regular monastic foundations in Shropshire, only a number of

[3] The Normans left a considerable legacy of personal place-names in Shropshire. Because of the confusion caused by the large number of places with common names such as Aston and Stanton, the names of the new Norman lords were often attached to the old Saxon place-names in order to distinguish their various manors. Thus we have such names as Aston *Botterell*, Aston *Eyre*, Albright *Hussy*, Hope *Bowdler* and Hope *Baggot*.

[4] For some discussion on this subject, see especially R. V. Lennard, *Rural England, 1086–1135* (1959), Chapter 10 on 'The Villages and Churches'. One documented case in Shropshire is Attingham, where the historian Ordericus Vitalis was baptised in 1075, but no church is recorded here in 1086. Also a number of churches that contain Saxon architecture are not recorded.

E

minster churches, of which Wenlock, rebuilt *c.* 1050 and dedicated in honour of St Milburge, was the finest. After 1066, however, there was a spate of new foundations; Wenlock was refounded (1079–82) and Domesday records, Earl Roger "has made the church of St Milburge into an abbey". Shrewsbury was founded in 1083 and Buildwas founded *c.* 1148. These earliest monasteries stood within a few miles of Watling Street and along the main arteries of communication in wooded regions just being opened up for cultivation. Both Wombridge and Haughmond (Plate 8) were sited in remote woodland clearings, outside the territory of any parish, and the sixty acres of assarted land included in Haughmond's original grant demonstrates the colonising nature of these early foundations. Buildwas Abbey, in keeping with many other Cistercian foundations, appears to have completely absorbed the Domesday manor and village of Buildwas.

Following these early creations, other priories at Chirbury and Alberbury in the late twelfth century were fashioned from Saxon minsters. Later foundations included a Hospitaller's house at Halston and a Templar's preceptory at Lydley in Cardington, and numerous small houses and cells. None of the Shropshire houses, except perhaps Buildwas (the only Shropshire house to figure in Pegolotti's list of monasteries supplying wool to Italian merchants in the thirteenth century), was of more than local importance, but their economic power did play a major part in the making of the medieval landscape.

There is some danger of overemphasising the monastic role in the Middle Ages, largely because of the uneven survival of documents relating to these institutions as compared with lay estates. There can be little doubt, however, that accumulated capital and continuity of tenure did mean that the monasteries were in the forefront of the attack on forest and waste. They developed specialised farming techniques based on far-flung granges and later in the Middle Ages they were involved in the development of industry.

The Domesday Survey gives us our first glimpse of woodland in the county. In many ways it is an unsatisfactory and incomplete record, but it does give some indication of the distribution of the surviving woodland in the eleventh century and is particularly useful for its references to animal parks or *haies*, of which there were over sixty in Shropshire.

The Shropshire Domesday appears to include only woodland capable of economic exploitation. Large areas of dense woodland and scrub in the south and west were therefore excluded: later sources demonstrate that throughout the county the claylands had carried a heavy woodland cover in the eleventh century. The progress of woodland clearance by 1086 is, however, silently recorded in those manors with a large arable hidage. It seems for instance that the area to the south-east of Shrewsbury along the Severn had already been largely cleared of woodland. Emstrey Manor was assessed at thirteen hides, Eyton on Severn at eight and a half hides, and Upton Magna, Uckington and Uffington each at five hides. An indication of continued post-Conquest woodland clearance in Shropshire is given by references to 'hospites', described by F. W. Maitland in *Domesday Book and Beyond* (1897) as "colonists whom the lord has invited onto his land". Such colonisers were recorded only in Shropshire and Herefordshire.

Domesday records far more deer parks (*haies*) in Shropshire than in any other Midland county. A *haie* was a small hunting park found normally in woodland areas completely enclosed with a pale, hedge or wall designed for the retention of red, fallow and roe deer. Later the term 'haye' often referred to any enclosed woodland, such as the Forest of Hayes in Westbury manor. Some hayes were maintained as

deer parks throughout the Middle Ages, others simply
disappeared without trace. Saxon hayes tended to lie away
from villages while later parks lay near to, or even incorporated, the manor house and the church. The place-name
'hay' or 'hayes', however, is still common in Shropshire,
normally associated with a single farm. Hay House lies on
the east bank of the Severn in Alveley parish. The original
seventeenth-century house, that possibly stood on the site
of a Saxon hunting lodge, has recently been destroyed.

At Corfton the haye, which in 1086 was 'for catching roe
deer', *Haia capreolis capiendis*, had become a royal chase
with its own forester by the late thirteenth century. A
document of 1293 notes the service of "a barbed arrow to
the king as often as he shall come to those parts to hunt in
his chace at Corfton". The park lost its hunting function in
the late Middle Ages along with many Shropshire deer
parks and by the end of the sixteenth century it had been
partially enclosed. The final extinction of the haye, however,
did not come until 1777 when Corfton Wood was enclosed
by Act of Parliament and divided into fields. Two other
hayes entered under Wenlock in 1086 can be identified as
'Kings Wood' and 'The Hurst' in Shirlett Forest, the first
of which is still known as the Old Park attached to Willey
Hall.

Following the conquest, considerable areas of Shropshire
were designated Royal Forest. A hint of this process appears
under the entry for Albrighton, where reference is made to
wood for fattening 100 swine, which had been placed in
the hands of the king.

Settlement in 1086

The Domesday Survey shows that the basic settlement
pattern of the county had been established by the eleventh
century. Place-names, however, are often retained when the

size and pattern of settlement has radically changed. The Domesday evidence must therefore be viewed both cautiously and critically as an introduction to Shropshire's settlement history.

Some 440 places mentioned in the survey are contained in the modern county of Shropshire, including Shrewsbury —the only place in the county for which burgesses are recorded, since the borough at Quatford in Eardington manor was said to yield nothing. A further 191 dependent unnamed berewicks are mentioned. Shrewsbury had fifty-seven berewicks, Morville seventeen, Ford fourteen, Worthen thirteen, Condover ten and Whittington eight and a half. Each of these berewicks represents a dependent-village or hamlet. In some manors, townships were not specifically recorded but were included under a blanket assessment. Thus the entry for Stoke St Milborough which was assessed at twenty hides, must have included the daughter-hamlets of Bockleton, Kinson, More, Cleedownton and Heath. Even manors with only a modest hidage could conceal a large number of dependent townships. Thus Burford, which is assessed at only six and a half hides, covered eleven dependent townships.

Not all the Domesday names appear on the modern map; most of the surviving names appear as hamlets, but some are attached to single farms. Thus Emstrey, a large manor in 1086, is today a farm in a loop of the Severn to the south-east of Shrewsbury. A few names disappeared altogether in the early Middle Ages and have yet to be identified. Among these are the manors of *Slacheberie* near Ellesmere, and *Neuetone* near Knockin which is not heard of after 1291.

A considerable number of settlements which today figure prominently in the county do not appear in Domesday. The main omissions are the new towns such as Ludlow, Bishop's Castle and Oswestry which were founded soon after 1086, while some places on the coalfield, such as Iron Bridge, do not appear until the eighteenth century. Despite these later changes, the distribution of Domesday names shows a general similarity to that of present-day settlement. It is only when individual villages and areas are examined in detail that really significant differences emerge.

The vills were more or less evenly scattered throughout the county, although some variation may be discerned. Settlements were most numerous in the Severn Valley, from the Welsh border to the Iron Bridge Gorge. In the southern uplands where heavy clay fills the valley bottoms, the settlements are strung out along the upper limits of clay. This is particularly noticeable on the lower slopes of the Long Mynd, and in Ape Dale, Hope Dale and Corvedale below the limestone escarpments. Lines of villages also encircle the infertile sandstone and volcanic rocks of the Clee hills, while the hills themselves stand out as empty spaces. In the northern plains, where the underlying sandstones are masked by clay and sands, numerous heaths and marshes remained to be colonised in the seventeenth and eighteenth centuries. Prees Heath and Whixall Moss are examples of such infertile areas where settlements were sparsely distributed.

There is little evidence to suggest the existence of much dispersed settlement even in remote upland areas. Occasionally, however, there are indications of isolated communities. In the south and west there were a number of extremely small manors. The single-virgate manor at Little or Lesser Poston, *Posseton*, overlooking Corvedale was probably a lone farm. Here one tenant was to render the church of St Michael, the chapel in Shrewsbury Castle, a bundle of box on Palm Sunday. All subsequent references to Lesser Poston suggest that it was an isolated farm.[5] Similarly, the

[5] The place-name ending *-ton* was usually attached to a community rather than an isolated farm. The earthworks found around Lesser Poston farm today may well belong to a pre-Conquest deserted hamlet. Virgate—a quarter hide.

hamlet of Marsh in Westbury parish (now occupied by Marche Hall) appears to have already been dispersed into scattered farms by 1086. Other instances of pre-Norman village mortality undoubtedly remain to be identified in Shropshire. It may also be possible to find examples of pre-Conquest scattered farms in the Welsh areas of the western foothills, but in general terms the dispersed farm was not an important element in the countryside until the thirteenth century. Domesday does, however, hint at the existence of isolated hunting lodges; for instance, when the King rode out to hunt at *Marsetelie* (Marstley farm in Habberley), the sheriff had to find thirty-six foot men as beaters.

The Domesday folios contain many references to 'waste' in Shropshire. Some forty-three vills were whole or partially waste in 1066. Their destruction appears to have been caused by the raids of Gryffth ap Llewelyn, Prince of North Wales, in alliance with Algar the outlawed Earl of East Anglia. By 1070 this number had increased to 121 when manor after manor which yielded a good income in 1066 is entered as 'waste' when its new holder received it. It is impossible to determine what proportion of these were due to the Norman invasion or what to Welsh attacks. Accounts by the Shropshire historian Ordericus Vitalis and others suggest that the Normans were particularly savage in their dealings with the Welsh; this remarkable increase in 'waste' settlements may well relate to unrecorded Norman brutality in the Welsh-speaking villages of Shropshire. On the other hand, there was certainly a good deal of Welsh retaliation. In 1069, for instance, Shrewsbury castle was besieged by the Welsh together with the men of Chester, and there were other major Welsh uprisings in 1077, 1088, and 1094. Some forty-five manors were still waste in 1086 while many others were only slowly recovering their old value. The devastated vills of 1070 had been evenly spread throughout the county, while those which were waste in 1066 and those of 1086 were mainly in the west.

Until recently writers have regarded this 'waste' as a temporary phenomenon, probably brought about by the intransigent Welsh, but leaving little permanent imprint on the landscape. However, the scale of the devastation, greater than in any other Midland county, has recently led to a reassessment of its long-term impact. It has been suggested that in the Vale of Montgomery, at least, such was the scale of the damage that many settlements did not recover and were eventually completely rebuilt in association with the construction of small castles.[6] There is room here for a closer topographical examination of those areas which were most severely affected.

SELECT BIBLIOGRAPHY

The Domesday Geography of Midland England, Ed. H. C. Darby and I. B. Terrett (Cambridge, 1954).
Eyton, Rev. E. W., *Antiquities of Shropshire.*
Victoria County History, *Shropshire,* Vol. 1, pp. 279–349 and Vol. 2 (forthcoming).

[6] D. J. Cathcart King and C. J. Spurgeon, 'The Mottes in the Vale of Montgomery', *Arch. Camb.,* Vol. 114 (1965).

4. Medieval Landscapes

Village and hamlet. Churches and chapels. Castles and manor houses. Mills and fishponds.

Village and hamlet

THE ORIGINAL UNIT of settlement in Shropshire was the nucleated village in the lowlands and the nucleated hamlet, consisting of half a dozen or so dwellings, in upland and marginal areas. Today, the isolated farm and scattered hamlet are more common than either village or hamlet in the south and west. Only in the eastern parts of the county do comparatively large village communities such as Claverley and Beckbury still survive. Many of the old market towns, however, such as Clun in the south and Ruyton-Eleven-Towns in the north, are only about as large as an average-sized Midland village.[1]

Bearing in mind all the subsequent changes it is often difficult to disentangle any clear medieval pattern within a village. Most rural settlements in Shropshire are simply clustered next to the church or chapel, often covering a comparatively small area. Indeed, many former hamlet sites are now occupied by a single farm. At Burley, for instance, a township in Stokesay manor, the site of the hamlet marked on a map of 1770 is now covered completely by a single farm and its outbuildings.

[1] Ruyton of the Eleven Towns, is the full name of the village. It acquired this curious name because it was part of a manor containing the eleven townships of Ruyton, Coton, Wykey, Shotatton, Shelvock, Eardiston, West Felton, Sutton, Rednal, Haughton and Tedsmore, the last five of which are now in the parish of West Felton.

Many communities are too small to conform to any recognisable pattern. The most characteristic hamlet shape is a loosely-knit cluster of houses on a ridge or knoll. Foothill settlements provide the most obvious examples of this type and hamlets such as Stapleton and Woolstaston at the northern end of the Long Mynd clearly fall within this category.

We have already seen how Saxon defences probably influenced the subsequent development of some villages. In other border settlements the construction of a post-Conquest motte-and-bailey castle affected the later village plan. At West Felton near Oswestry, for instance, the village developed around the edge of the castle bailey in a horseshoe shape and the road-pattern still reflects this. Since the early nineteenth century, however, the village has shifted to Telford's Holyhead road which runs a few hundred yards to the east of the medieval village.

Village greens are comparatively rare in Shropshire, although in eastern Shropshire there are a number of settlements such as Norton in Hales, Albrighton and Weston under Redcastle which still have greens. Such greens originally may have been associated with forest or heathland clearance, since a central green does imply an element of planning liable to be found in new colonising communities. Thus settlements in marshland areas often have well-defined village plans; Kynnersley and Preston upon the Weald Moors, for instance, have small village greens lying next to the church, while nearby Cherrington and Longdon-upon-Tern have linear plans.[2] A green at Minton, a village perched on the southern end of the Long Mynd, feels as old as the village itself. However, the green here may have resulted from a remodelling of the settle-

---

[2] Regular parish boundaries in the Weald Moors suggest the former existence of an extensive estate, which may have been systematically divided up and settled in the late Saxon period.

ment with the building of a castle here after the Norman Conquest (Plate 7). The remains of the castle lie to the south-east of the green.

Tugford, in the Corvedale, which in many ways is typical of the Shropshire village, has a green, now partly incorporated into the churchyard. The shape of the ancient village, which occupies a meander of the Tugford Brook, was largely determined by this green, around which all the houses used to stand. The green was undoubtedly of great antiquity and villagers enjoyed common rights upon it; attempts in the early seventeenth century to establish squatter-cottages here were quickly suppressed by the manor court. The squatters were ordered to pull down their cottages, which are still recognisable as house platforms on the green. Although common rights in the manor were abolished in 1815, the village green remained intact.

At Munslow, the village green did not survive parliamentary enclosure (1838), when it was auctioned for sixty pounds to pay towards the cost of the enclosure of Munslow Common.[3] The road-pattern still respects the former green, now occupied by houses. Marchamley village green was similarly dealt with following an Enclosure Act in 1808.

Finally a word of caution over green-villages. At Shipton, a large open area in front of the hall and church, surrounded by several half-timbered houses, appears to be a perfect example of a village green. The 'green', however, dates only from 1587 when Shipton Hall was built, at which time the old village was demolished in order to give a clear view from the house. The village was then rebuilt around this new green. The open area in the centre of Morville was cleared at about the same time, for the same reason,

[3] The presence of greens at Munslow and Condover, both administrative centres of hundreds, suggests that there may be some link between ancient meeting places and village greens.

and the green at Woolstaston was created on the site of a dung-heap in 1865.

Most crossroad-villages in the county are post-medieval, although some communities such as Muckley Cross in Acton Round parish grew up around inns in the late Middle Ages. Cross Houses in Berrington parish started life as a crossroad squatter settlement, and is now larger than any of the ancient settlements in the manor.

There are a number of linear villages in Shropshire, many of them appearing to incorporate an element of deliberate planning. At Hodnet, for instance, the main road running south from the church, along which the village is strung, probably dates from a charter of Henry III which granted a weekly market and an annual fair. And certainly this form of village at Knockin, Whittington, Baschurch and Ruyton is the result of medieval plantation. There are some villages where the linear form is probably of greater antiquity. In the south-east of the county beyond the Severn, there is a group of villages which have grown along the top of a series of sandstone ridges. Alveley, Romsley and Quatt all have a clear linear form. Associated with these settlements there is a distinct rectilinear road-pattern. At Romsley, a shrunken village, the houses lay along a road running parallel to a ridge-top road, and there are a series of deeply entrenched linking roads, indicating the antiquity of the pattern.

At Stanton Long, in the Corvedale, there is a good example of an ancient linear village. The place-name, which first acquired the 'Long' element in the twelfth century, is itself a guide to the old village shape. The village was called Stanton in 1086, as was the adjacent manor; the latter was called Castle Holdgate by the early twelfth century. Stanton Long was parochially dependent on the already declining village of Patton, head of the Saxon hundred of that name; during the following century

Patton was incorporated into Stanton Long and a new parish church was built there. As the ridge-top was already occupied by the village, the church had to be built on sloping ground to the north of the main settlement. Stanton Long is today very small and the original east–west road axis has been partly replaced by a road running southwards from Shipton, but even now the church lies uncomfortably in relationship to the shrunken hamlet.

Wistanstow lies directly on the Roman road running from Wroxeter to Leintwardine and has probably preserved its present linear plan since Saxon times. The partly Norman church lies directly on the Roman road and the village runs along the road to the north and south. Even the coming of the railway with a halt a quarter of a mile away from the church has not disturbed this ancient pattern.[4]

Churches and chapels

Medieval churches still form one of the most important features of the Shropshire rural landscape. In 1086 there were comparatively few churches in the county. These were mainly large missionary centres with canons who presumably used to travel throughout the extensive Saxon parishes. In the south of the county, stone churches were built during the ninth and tenth centuries and Wenlock had already established daughter-chapels in some of its widely dispersed manors, such as Barrow.

The building of churches and chapels in local limestone and sandstone was accelerated after the Norman Conquest. The example of such places as Shrewsbury Abbey, started by Roger de Montgomery about 1080, may have stimulated some of this activity. But more important was the tradition

---

[4] Lilleshall Abbey cartulary refers to a pre-Conquest church at Wistanstow. Wistan was a Mercian saint, martyred in A.D. 849, so the church may date from soon after that.

of stone building which new Norman lords brought over from France. Following the Conquest, virtually every existing church within Shropshire was rebuilt or restyled and a considerable number of completely new churches and chapels were founded.

Many of these churches and chapels show a high degree of architectural skill. In south Shropshire much of this work was wrought or inspired by the work of the Hereford School of Romanesque architecture. This school apparently began working in the early twelfth century at Shobden in Herefordshire. Shobden church has now been pulled down and the best surviving example of their work now is at Kilpeck. The style is amazingly vital, showing great inventiveness and technical skill. The elaborate decoration of doorways, windows and fonts includes much material taken from contemporary life, such as fighting warriors or animals and birds used in hunting. The architecture appears to be a mixture of Anglo-Saxon and Scandinavian, with motifs from the churches of the Pointon and Charente districts of western France, as well as demonstrating some Spanish influence. Indeed, one of the sculptors of the Hereford School had been to Santiago di Compostela with Oliver de Merlimond in the mid-twelfth century.[5]

Traces of the Hereford School work in Shropshire can be seen at Stottesdon, Aston Eyre, Tugford, Holdgate, Uppington and Much Wenlock. Their work was mainly executed for lay lords and they brought exotic architecture to small parish churches. Although much of their work in Shropshire has been destroyed and remains only in the form of an occasional font or doorway, their importance as an example to others should not be underestimated. The wealth of late Norman church architecture in Shropshire was undoubtedly influenced by the Hereford School and the vitality of late twelfth-century architecture found in Shrop-

[5] G. Zarnecki, *Later English Romanesque Sculpture* (1953), pp. 9–13.

shire monastic buildings certainly owes something to them.

One of the most interesting features about Shropshire churches is the amount of Norman architecture that has survived. Virtually complete and very fine examples of Norman chapels are to be seen at Heath and Linley (Plate 9), and square Norman towers are common throughout the county. The most spectacular are the low, squat, buttressed towers found mainly in the south-west of the county at places such as Bishop's Castle and Lydham.

The survival of so much Norman architecture can be attributed to the quality of the original buildings and to the later comparative poverty of the county. The Normans brought wealth and skill into the county, which led to the construction of these churches. Afterwards church-building largely reflected the county's economic fortunes. In the east, at places such as Tong, later prosperity did lead to large churches with fine interior ornaments. Elsewhere rebuilding was on a more modest scale; there was certainly no 'wool prosperity' to pay for the construction of later massive medieval churches. Indeed, the wealth gained from trading in wool and textiles is reflected only in secular buildings and the town churches of Ludlow and Shrewsbury.

Some reference should be made to the spread of daughter-churches in the twelfth century. The process of chapel-building was in some cases initiated by monasteries, in others by large and wealthy mother-churches. Typical of these was the minster church at Morville, which was the only Domesday church recorded in the whole Saxon hundred of *Alnostreu*. In the time of King Edward (the Confessor) the church of St Gregory at Morville was then served by eight canons. By 1086, however, there were only three priests (*presbiteri*) here; in the following century a considerable number of chapels were planted in the parish. Apart from completing Tugford chapel, which was a parish church by the end of the twelfth century, other chapels in

79

Morville parish were founded at Billingsley, Olbury, Taseley and Aston Eyre before 1140. This latter chapel contained a remarkable tympanum, showing Christ's entry into Jerusalem, considered by many to be the finest piece of Norman sculpture in the county. Further chapels in Morville parish were later founded at Aldenham, Underton and Astley Abbots. Significantly the chapel at Astley Abbots was endowed with some *assart* land suggesting that perhaps chapel creation on this scale was associated with woodland clearance.[6] The original chapel at Bridgnorth too was initially dependent upon Morville. Although all traces of the chapels at Underton and Aldenham have disappeared along with the hamlets they served, the remainder all later emerged as parochial centres.

In many other large parishes there was a similar burst of activity. St Mary's church at Shawbury founded chapels at Acton Reynald, Moreton Corbet, Grinshill and Great Wytheford. A certificate of Bishop Roger de Clinton dated 1140 tells of the time when these manors were without chapels and that he himself had consecrated three of them. This pattern of chapel foundation was repeated throughout the county. In the south-west there were extremely large parishes and little settlement, and chapels were planted in hamlets along the river valleys. A line of such chapels (later parish churches) follows the county boundary along the Teme valley at Bedstone, Bucknell, Stove and Llanfair Waterdine.

A considerable number of these chapels simply disappeared in the late Middle Ages, with the desertion and shrinkage of settlements. Duke in his *Antiquities of Shropshire* (1854) records some 105 lost chapels in the county. One of these at the deserted hamlet of Bold, in the parish of

---

[6] Assart, Old French *essarter*, means literally to grub up, and land which has been assarted has been claimed from forest or wasteland. *Assart* is often found as a place or field-name.

Aston Botterell, was later incorporated into the out-
buildings of the surviving farm, and was drawn by the
Reverend Williams in one of his valuable watercolours of
Shropshire churches at the end of the eighteenth century
(Plate 10) (which are now kept at Shrewsbury Public
Library).

The siting of a church or chapel is often of great significance; for instance, an isolated church containing medieval
architecture is almost always an indication of the existence
of settlement-desertion or shifting. Or a church occupying
the central or highest point within a village may date from
the beginning of that settlement, and one on the edge, as at
Stanton Long, may be a latecomer.

One feature about many Shropshire churches that
deserves further study is the church which lies within a
circular churchyard. Something like forty per cent of
churchyards in south Shropshire are round. When such a
churchyard occupies the highest point within a village it is
difficult not to link this with defensive siting, possibly of
pre-English origin. At Cardeston and Church Pulverbatch,
for instance, the church and circular churchyard occupy
classic sites on low mounds surveying the surrounding
area. Very frequently, the banks are built up and there are
traces of an outer ditch. At Abdon, where an excavation was
undertaken to examine this phenomenon, the churchyard
had obviously been extended since the Middle Ages as it cut
across a thirteenth-century long-house.

Not all churches in the county lie right in the village;
indeed some are completely divorced from the communities
they serve. At Leebotwood, for instance, the church lies
some 600 yards to the west of the present village and although there is no obvious reason for this, it has been
suggested that the glacial moraine on which the church now
stands was probably chosen as providing a more secure
foundation than the alluvial soil found in the village centre.

F

Castles and manor houses

During the immediate post-Conquest period a considerable number of motte-and-bailey castles were constructed in the Welsh border. In the western part of Shropshire virtually every village has the remains of one of these small fortifications. They were normally in the form of a circular mound (motte) with an attached defended courtyard (bailey). Initially, most castles were built of earth and wood, although some like Ludlow had a large stone keep instead of a motte. The majority were small, but some like Clun had stone buildings and very impressive defences.

There is no evidence for the existence of motte-and-bailey castles in the county prior to 1066, although it is possible that there were mottes at Ewyas Harold and Richards Castle in Herefordshire before the Conquest. Immediately after the Conquest, work began on castles at Shrewsbury, Holdgate and Oswestry and soon after that castles at Ludlow, Bishop's Castle and Clun were started. At Shrewsbury fifty-one houses were destroyed and a further fifty made waste by the construction of the castle. In new towns such as Clun, fresh sites were chosen, and at Ruyton-Eleven-Towns where the castle ruins lie within a few feet of the church it looks almost as if the two were contemporary. In many of the smaller villages the siting of castles next to the church must have caused considerable disruption. At Holdgate, the castle and church were contemporary, and the village, recorded as being waste in 1086, was probably laid out afresh at this time. A steep-sided circular motte with a shallow ditch lies immediately to the east of the church. The remains of a fine thirteenth-century stone castle, which occupied the bailey, are now hidden at the back of the sixteenth-century farmhouse.

Over 150 motte-and-bailey castles have been identified in

Shropshire. Many of the castle mounds are eroded, partly destroyed or tree-covered and in some cases all trace of the attached bailey has vanished. The ditches of a large proportion are silted up or have been filled, often to the foot of the mound on all sides. Mottes are similar to prehistoric *tumuli*—indeed they have often been labelled as such on maps, in that they are often small enough to be ploughed away. There are several cases where mottes have been completely removed, Hardwick in his 'Materials for a History of Shropshire' cites two such eighteenth-century examples at Shipton and Munslow in the Corvedale. Garbet in his *History of Wem* (1818), tells of the partial destruction of Wem castle; the mound here was "about eight yards high with a level plain at the top, now about forty yards in diameter, encompassed with a foss eight yards broad. Mr Wilson sunk the hill six feet and took up several large steps on the side opposite to the church. Mr Henshaw . . . the present occupier has carried off several loads of stone and by frequent ploughing still lessens the height of it."

The motte-and-bailey castle was extremely effective both for attack and defence and rather like the Roman fort it could be quickly built within enemy territory. The Norman determination to control all the western valleys resulted in the construction of mottes well within territory that is now part of Wales. A good example of this is at Hen Domen, a motte-and-bailey which lies near to, and was possibly the forerunner of, the present town of Montgomery. Four years after the battle of Hastings, King William gave Roger de Montgomery, his kinsman and close friend, the Honour of Shrewsbury, with territory which extended beyond Offa's Dyke to the Upper Severn. On the edge of this territory Roger built a timber castle on a ridge of Boulder Clay overlooking the river and the ancient ford of *Rhyd-Whiman,* in an area of 'waste' used by three Saxon *thegns* as a hunting ground, and nostalgically named it after the seat of his family. This castle was to be a base for launching attacks into central Wales, and in 1074 the *Annales Cambriae* has the laconic entry 'from Montgomery Hugh (Roger's son) devastated Cardigan'. Hen Domen castle was finally abandoned in the thirteenth century when it appears to have been replaced by the stone castle at Montgomery. The name 'Hen Domen', a Welsh term meaning 'Old Mound', must have been given to the site when it deteriorated to the earthworks we can now see.[7]

It has been suggested that a number of timber castles lying to the east of Offa's Dyke in the Vale of Montgomery form a distinct group (Fig. 5). These castles, which are typified by tall mottes with small tops, appear to date from the end of the eleventh century.[8] This area, which was then in the hands of the Corbet family under Earl Roger, was 'waste' after the Conquest, and this homogeneous group of castles may well have been established as a part of a resettlement plan. It is certainly true that apart from the castles themselves, the hamlets of Marton, Wilmington and Dudston have other topographical similarities. Basically all have a straight road running eastwards from the castle. At Marton, in particular, this alignment coincides with a kink in the road, which could well represent a change in the old road-pattern at the time of the replanning of the 'new village'.[9] There is a similar situation at Pulverbatch, in the northern foothills of the Long Mynd, where the church and castle lie in different townships, Church Pulverbatch (locally known as Churton, an abbreviated form of Churchtown), and Castle Pulverbatch. Strangely enough, the church occupies a hilltop site and stands at the junction of the roads running northwards from the Long Mynd and

[7] P. A. Barker, 'Hen Domen, Montgomery: Excavations 1960–7', *Chateau Gaillard III European Castle Studies* (1969).

[8] D. J. Cathcart King and C. J. Spurgeon, op. cit.

[9] Marton Castle has recently been destroyed, *S.N.L.*, No. 35 (Dec. 1969).

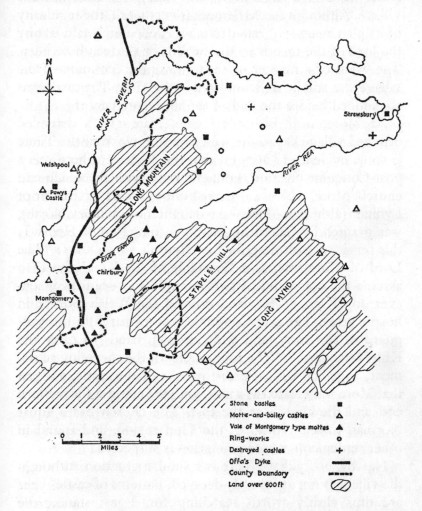

Stone castles ■
Motte-and-bailey castles △
Vale of Montgomery type mottes ▲
Ring-works ○
Destroyed castles +
Offa's Dyke ▬▬▬
County Boundary ▬ ▬ ▬
Land over 600 ft ▨

0 1 2 3 4 5
Miles

Fig. 5. Castles in western Shropshire

eastwards from Huglith. At Castle Pulverbatch the impressive remains of a large motte-and-bailey still dominate the
village. Although the settlement is very small, the regularity
of its plan again suggests that it was deliberately laid out by
the lord of the manor in the twelfth or thirteenth century.
The grant of a market in 1254 shows the economy of the
village was still being stimulated at this time. The castle was
abandoned before the end of the thirteenth century.

At More, near Bishop's Castle (Plate 11), a defended
deserted village lies to the west of a ring-work castle. There
is some evidence to suggest that the settlement here was a
post-Conquest creation, contemporary with the castle and
church. More, which was carved out of the Saxon manor of
Lydham (although More was a daughter of Lydbury North),
was granted by Grand Serjeantry in the reign of Henry I;
this service is best described by Eyton's words thus: "The
Lord of More was, as a Constable of the King's host, to
assume the command of two hundred foot-soldiers whenever any King of England crossed the Welsh Border in
hostile array. The said Constable was to march in the van-
guard of the army, and with his own hands to carry the
King's standard."[10] The topography of the surviving settlement, together with the earthworks of the castle, suggest
that More was created as a unit, with the castle at the western
end and the church at the east. The church has a squat
Norman tower, typical of the Clun region, and found in
other settlements where plantation is suspected.

Nearby, at Lydham there is a similar situation, although
the village is not as severely decayed. Patterns of castle-types
are thus clearly worth searching for. For instance, the
Fitzalen castles in south-west and north-west Shropshire
were clearly linked. Elsewhere there is no clear relationship

[10] Eyton, op. cit., Vol. 11, p. 284. In 1086 the Bishop of Hereford's estate
at Lydbury was extensive—fifty-three hides. It was later named Lydbury
North to avoid confusion with another of the Bishop's estates at Ledbury in
Herefordshire.

between the castle and its village. In many western manors, the castle acted as the manor house during the early Middle Ages, but in other cases it is doubtful if the castle was ever permanently occupied. At Woolstaston castle, for instance, an excavation produced no evidence of any permanent buildings.[11]

Most of the small motte-and-bailey castles were redundant by 1225, and those which were not rebuilt in stone in the thirteenth century fell into decay. Once conditions along the border became more settled many lords built new manor houses away from the old village. Castles at places such as Shrewsbury and Bridgnorth, which had once been in the front-line of defence against the Welsh, were left to decay in the late thirteenth century and an account of Clun Castle in 1272 tells of the need to repair the roof and the bridge, and that the buildings in the bailey, a grange, a stable and a bakehouse were in a weak state. It is true that some stone castles survived to be garrisoned during the Civil War, but their strategic importance had almost completely disappeared by the end of the Middle Ages.

An illuminating sixteenth-century account of Corfham Castle in the Corvedale records:

> Cofham hath been a manor of great fame, and had in it a castle compassed about with a mott and a strong court wall, strong towers, whereof one doth remain called Rosamund's Tower, but can't long stand for it is uncovered and the lead taken away. The foresaid courts was also compassed about able to withstand any suddain invasion, but nowe all decayed, ruinated and destroyed.[12]

[11] R. T. Rowley, 'Excavations at Woolstaston', *S.N.L.*, No. 29 (Dec. 1965).

[12] S.R.O. 1093/Box 40D Transcript of Corfham manorial documents. Rosamund's Tower was named after Fair Rosamund, Henry II's mistress, who was born at Corfham and was buried at Godstow Nunnery in Oxfordshire.

Today nothing remains of this once formidable castle or its village except for overgrown earthworks.

Although most castles had been abandoned by 1300, many manor houses still maintained some form of defence, normally in the form of a moat. When these manors were sited away from the village, the moat was simply a means of keeping out wild animals or vagrants. Indeed, the move away from the community must have represented a major break in the early Middle Ages; understandable fear and superstition apart from elementary caution would have provoked the construction of a defensive moat. It is doubtful, however, if most fortified manors were ever intended for serious fighting. Some of them, such as Stokesay, occupied particularly vulnerable sites. And the association of certain family names with these manors suggests that there was an element of fashion in the building of fortified manor houses in the thirteenth and fourteenth centuries.

Stokesay castle, one of the earliest fortified houses of England, is today perhaps the best known medieval monument in Shropshire. Together with the adjoining church the castle forms one of the most perfect pictures of rural serenity in the whole of Britain (Plate 12). Licence to crenellate (fortify) Stokesay was granted in 1291 to Lawrence of Ludlow, one of the greatest wool merchants of his day. Much of the visible fortification is medieval, but Stokesay could never really have been defended against serious attack. The castle was simply built as a fine manor house which was walled and surrounded by a moat. Stokesay stands more as a monument to the wool exporters of Shropshire than to the turbulent currents of border warfare.[13]

The other well-known surviving fortified manor is Acton Burnell Castle, built, between 1283 and 1286, by Robert Burnell, who travelled in Wales when castle-building was

[13] J. T. Smith, 'Stokesay Castle', *Arch. J.,* Vol. 113 (1956).

Plate 12 Stokesay Castle and Norman church with the millpond in the foreground. In the background is the silhouette of Norton Camp wood.

Plate 13 The ruins of the late thirteenth-century castle at Acton Burnell, with the so-called Parliament Barn behind and Acton Burnell Hall, which is largely early nineteenth century. The small church of St Mary lies next to, and is roughly contemporary with, the castle

Plate 14   The earthworks of the deserted hamlet of Pickthorn, showing the old street-pattern and house-platforms. The half-timbered farmhouse and outbuildings in the background represent the vestiges of the hamlet.

Plate 15   Moreton Corbet Castle, which incorporates a medieval keep, is largely late sixteenth century. In the background the medieval church represents all that is left of the village, which was moved with rebuilding of the castle.

at its height, and probably picked up the idea of a fortified dwelling then. For like Stokesay, despite its outward appearance, Acton Burnell Castle had a thoroughly domestic function. The two stone gable walls of the so-called Parliament Barn which lie some 100 yards from the castle possibly represent the remains of an earlier manor house (Plate 13).

It is significant that the Burnell family were involved with rebuilding of two other fortified manor houses in the county. Robert Burnell rebuilt Holdgate Castle in stone in 1280, and the Burnells were also associated with Cheney Longville, a little-known but most interesting castle lying just to the north of Craven Arms. Licence to crenellate here was not granted until 1395, by which time the manor house had certainly replaced the nearby ring-work. The regular alignment of the little village of Cheney Longville and its relationship to the earlier castle suggests that it too was originally a planted village. It does not appear to have been particularly successful since in the mid-twelfth century it was recorded that "the vill was at the time so impoverished, that even a stranger would not have given £15 for it".[14]

Mills and fishponds

It is difficult today to appreciate the former importance of running water in the everyday life of the community. Up until the eighteenth century, streams provided the only source of constant energy for turning mill-wheels to grind corn, to beat wool in fulling mills and later to blow bellows in blast furnaces. In the late Middle Ages, however, windmills appear to have been quite common, particularly in the north of the county.

The water-mill, together with the church and castle, was an integral part of village topography over the centuries.

14 Eyton, op. cit., Vol. 11, p. 370.

The construction of a mill produced important landscape changes, at first confined to its immediate surroundings. The banks, with ponds and weirs, leats and the redirection of streams and roads, and often the establishment of a near-by bridge are all obvious examples emphasising the re-shaping of the immediate topography. The excavation and embanking involved gave a permanence to the site of a water-mill in a way not applicable to church, manor house or windmill. At Tugford the mill stands on the opposite side of the brook to the Norman church of St Catherine's. Its deeply engraved mill-runs and pools suggest that it occupies the same site as the mill recorded here in the Domesday Survey. The mill and its channels loomed large in village life, and manor court rolls illustrate the long and continued discipline necessary to keep the waterways in good order.

In Shropshire, a county possessing numerous small streams and rivers, there was considerable activity along the valleys. A mill at Acton Round was built for the Earl of Arundel in 1312. The following account[15] gives a good idea of the landscape implications of building such a water-mill:

For making the walls	14s.	3d.
For the mason for building the walls and digging the stone	33s.	3d.
For Rich. Crumpe for the same	5s.	8d.
For making 430 laths for the same mill	10s.	3d.
For buying iron and making russes for mill wheel	9s.	7d.
For buying two mill stones	24s.	
For carriage		6d.
For cord		1½d.
For wax		1d.
For thatch covering	1s.	6d.

[15] S.P.L., MS. 7531.

For a basket		3d.
For 1 plate		3d.
For digging the pond for 4 days	2s.	2d.
By way of payment for digging the mill ditch to the pond for 14 days	16s.	½d.
Labour for 5 hours for 18 days	9s.	4d.
For 42 hours labour at the same place	9s.	
For 2 carpenters for 3 days to cart away timber		12d.
Stipend for carpenters for 8 days		16d.
	£6 18s.	7d.

Acton Round mill ceased to function in the mid-nineteenth century, but the mill buildings and its associated earthworks can still be seen. Such earthworks are common in Shropshire, sometimes they are found next to the earthworks of abandoned fishponds. In the south of the county, in particular, every effort seems to have been made to fully utilise the streams, so that a mill-run would be taken off the main stream immediately below the upstream mill. These old mill-races can often be identified by the lines of willow trees that follow them and now stand as straight boundaries cutting off meanders.

Larger villages and towns normally had several mills. In the early fourteenth century there were at least fifteen watermills in Shrewsbury operated by the burgesses, quite apart from those worked by the abbey. Indeed, at this time, the mills in Shrewsbury were frequently a source of dispute between the townspeople and the abbey; the latter claimed, under the grant of their founder, the exclusive privilege of grinding all the corn used in the town and the sole right of possessing mills within its limits. Eventually, it was agreed that the mills in the suburbs should be destroyed, and those within the town were to be maintained by both parties in common.[16]

Additionally, many communities operated fulling mills from the thirteenth century onwards. References to fulling mills, or Walkmills as they were known, are preserved in place-names, such as Walkmill Brook in Woolstaston and Walkmill in Wentnor, and in the west the place-name *Pandy* —Welsh for fulling mill—is occasionally found. The ruins of a fulling mill on the River Teme at Ludlow survived until the late nineteenth century.

Although many medieval corn mills had disappeared by the sixteenth century, a considerable number survived into the nineteenth century and the first edition of the Ordnance six-inch map (1873) marks many mills which were still operating. A few of these have survived, but only a handful have preserved their mill-wheels and grinding equipment. One of these, at Bouldon in the Corvedale, has retained its equipment, which includes an iron bucket-wheel, cast appropriately in Coalbrookdale. The mill-wheel has, however, not turned for over a decade. A considerable number of tall brick-mills are still to be found on streams in northern Shropshire, but all of these are now motor-powered.

During the Middle Ages many mills operated alongside fishponds, and these too were an important element in the medieval landscape. The most ambitious fishpond complexes belonged to monastic houses, such as those at Buildwas and Haughmond. Some fine fishponds (now dry) can be seen at Great Oxenbold, which up until the Dissolution was a grange belonging to the Prior of Wenlock. Often the outlying earthworks attached to the ruins of monasteries represent industrial works, agricultural buildings as well as fishponds and would well repay careful

[16] Rev. C. H. Drinkwater, 'The Abbot of Shrewsbury versus the Burgesses thereof in the matter of the Mills', *T.S.A.S.*, Vol. 18 (1894). There were also three horse-operated horizontal mills and a windmill in the town then.

study. There were, however, fishponds on lay-estates and a group of seven have survived at Middleton Scriven.

There is some evidence to suggest that some fishponds were later used as furnace-ponds; possibly the *vivary* mentioned at Stirchley in 1209 was later converted into a pond for the ironworks there. It is also tempting to think that the medieval fishponds in Shirlett were used for the iron-furnaces at Willey. These ponds were later landscaped into Willey Park, demonstrating that ponds are one of the most versatile elements in the landscape.[17]

There were a considerable number of fishponds in the marshy areas of northern Shropshire. At Sandford, for instance, the road from Newport to Whitchurch was diverted in order to extend a fishpond in 1330. The pool which is still water-filled lies to the west of the castle mound at Sandford. The planted medieval town at Newport, first heard of as *Novus Burgus* in the twelfth century, owes its siting to the importance of local fisheries. Appropriately, the burgesses held their ancient liberties by the purveyance of fish to the king's court. A map of 1641 shows the ancient *vivary* marked as Newport Pool, dammed on the east by the enbanked road leading out of the town (see Fig. 17). In 1833 the Shropshire Union Canal Company built a branch canal from Norbury to Wappenshall on the Shrewsbury Old Canal. The old fishpool was then incorporated into a barge basin and wharf.[18]

[17] The ornamental ponds on the River Tern at Attingham share the same history. See Chapter 6 for further discussion.

[18] E. Jones, 'Historical Records of Newport, Co. Salop', *T.S.A.S.* Vol. 7 (1884).

SELECT BIBLIOGRAPHY

Barker, P. A., *The Medieval Pottery of the Welsh Border from the Conquest to 1400* (Shrewsbury, 1969).

Cranage, D. H. S., *The Churches of Shropshire* (1894).

Eyton, Rev. E. W., *Antiquities of Shropshire*.

A Guide to the Shropshire Records, Salop County Council (1952).

Pevsner, N., *Shropshire* (1958).

Renn, D., *Norman Castles in England* (1968).

S.N.L., Nos. 1–39 (1957–60).

Victoria County History, *Shropshire*, Vols. 2 (forthcoming) and 8 (1968).

5. Forest Landscapes

Colonising the woodland. Royal Forests. Shirlett Forest. Morfe Forest. Clee Forest.

Colonising the woodland

WOODLAND IN SHROPSHIRE is now confined largely to escarpments and areas generally unsuitable for agriculture. Indeed, only about seven per cent of the county is wooded today with most of the timber now in the south, much of it under the Forestry Commission. The Shropshire countryside does, however, appear to be well endowed with trees as you travel through it. We owe the wooded appearance of the landscape partly to post-medieval enclosure, which produced small fields and large hedges, and partly to the early iron industry, which encouraged the plantation of coppice land for charcoal blast furnaces.

The story of settlement and agriculture must be seen against the background of the clearance and colonisation of primeval woodland. Before the appearance of Neolithic man dense forest covered much of Shropshire. Only the heaths and mosses in the north and the highlands in the west were relatively open. Even the sand, gravel and alluvium that attracted early man originally carried an open tree cover. Settlement before the Saxons was limited to the open uplands and the lighter soils of the river terraces; and as far as we can see little impact was made on the forest until the seventh century. Saxon place-names give us some concept of the original extent of woodland. *Ac* (oak) and *ash* are common place-name elements in Shropshire. Place-names

also reflect clearance techniques—*brant* or *brent*, indicating
the burning of woodland, was a common medieval field-
name in parts of the county. Brandwood or 'Burntwood' is
a shrunken hamlet in Myddle parish which was probably
won from the forest by fire.

Within Shropshire there are a variety of ancient forest
regions possessing distinctive features; it is convenient to
call these 'forest landscapes' or more properly landscapes of
woodland clearance. Little is known of woodland clearance
prior to 1086; apart from place-names the process went on
unrecorded. We can only imagine the gigantic effort that early
settlers made, in clearing virgin woodland for their villages
and fields. We have already seen that the Domesday Survey
is not particularly enlightening, except in its record of those
manors with large arable hidages, particularly in the Severn
Valley, where a good deal of clearance had already been
achieved. During the Middle Ages the process of woodland
clearance is much better documented. We know that by the
sixteenth century little natural woodland remained except
in the region of Oswestry. Clearance was often stimulated or
executed by monasteries and great inroads were made not
only into manorial woodlands, but also Royal Forests.
Most large foundations relied heavily on the establishment
of granges, Buildwas Abbey, for instance, had ten in Shropshire and another three outside. The nearest of these to the
Abbey grange farm now lies next to the new power-station
at Buildwas.

The extent of monastic involvement in assarting, from an
early date, can clearly be seen in south Shropshire. Soon
after the foundation of Shrewsbury Abbey, Henry I in-
formed his Shropshire foresters that Shrewsbury Abbey was
to have pasture rights and wood for making houses from
the Royal Forests within the county. In 1230–1 the Abbey
was granted a total of 220 acres specifically for assarting on
Brown Clee hill. References to assarting by other monas-

teries are common throughout the twelfth and thirteenth centuries, for instance in 1199 the Knights Templar of Lydley asserted forty acres in the Forest of Botwood.

The monasteries also tried to build up large pastoral estates. Amongst the most successful was Haughmond Abbey, which in the early Middle Ages acquired grazing rights for its horses on the Long Mynd and established a large estate known as the Manor of Boveria. Betchcott and Leebotwood, originally within the manor, had been described as barren tracts in the twelfth century. Clearance, largely based on granges, brought much of the area into agricultural use by the end of the Middle Ages and there is even some suggestion that the monks provided loans to settlers and colonisers on the estate.

The work of clearance and settlement in most manors, however, was carried out by freeholders. In some cases, clearance was carried out from post-Domesday hamlets. Wheathall in Condover parish, for instance, now consisting of two farms and three cottages, was first recorded in 1209 and appears to have been a late woodland colonising settlement. Originally the hamlet stood around a green which is perhaps indicative of deliberate colonisation. There are several *assart* elements in the names of the Wheathall open fields and of their constituent strips and furlongs. The Wheathall Farm itself contains the remains of a cruck truss; in Shropshire, cruck houses were normally associated with the emergence of wealthier peasants and yeomen in the late Middle Ages. The comparative wealth demonstrated by medieval colonising settlements in the woodlands can be compared to that of prosperous sixteenth- and seventeenth-century farms found on the edge of the Shropshire Mosses.

Over much of southern Shropshire, medieval colonisation produced the first isolated farms. Many of these were surrounded by a moat for protection against wild animals and the occasional vagrant. The isolated dwelling was a departure from centuries of village and hamlet settlement. It must have been a considerable break for farmers to leave the communal security and companionship of the village for a lonely farm in the woods. This fear was not completely without foundation, for wolves were recorded at Langley in the Long Forest in the late thirteenth century. Thus we find the majority of moated farms in Shropshire outside nucleated settlements. The name 'Woodhouse' refers often to a moated, isolated woodland settlement. There are no fewer than thirty-nine places known as Woodhouse in Shropshire, and several of these still have a moat or traces of one; a series of farms, many of them moated, lies along the Rea Valley to the west of Shrewsbury. A group in Pontesbury parish have the self-descriptive names of Little Hanwood, Moat Hall, Woodhall and Woodhouse. These developed as freehold estates from the twelfth century onwards under tenancies of the Barony of Longden.

Royal Forests

After the Norman Conquest much of Shropshire was designated Royal Forest. 'Forest' in this context was a legal term applied to particular areas in which only the Crown or its assign had hunting rights. The establishment of such Forests, including villages and their fields, did not involve any expropriation of private property, but merely imposed a special code of Forest Law on its inhabitants. And although the Forests of Wyre, Morfe, Brewood and parts of the Long Forest were thickly wooded, Royal Forest was not necessarily tree covered. The Stiperstones and Clee Forests consisted largely of areas of semi-open heathland unfit for agriculture. Almost all Condover Hundred lay within the Long Forest and Mount Gilbert Forest covered all of *Recordine* Hundred. Indeed, at their height in the late twelfth century, more than half the county was under Forest Law— collectively known as the Forest of Shropshire.

The administration of such a massive Forest proved impossible and large areas were disafforested in the thirteenth and fourteenth centuries and this often led to considerable confusion. In the Long Forest much of the woodland disafforested at the end of the thirteenth century was almost immediately enclosed into manorial parks. and accordingly at this time a considerable number of grants of 'free warren' were made. In real terms this simply meant a transfer of hunting rights from the Crown to the manorial lord.

During the early Middle Ages the Forests served as reservoirs of timber for building border castles, towns and monasteries. In 1256 William de Harcourt is reputed to have felled 6000 oak trees and 300 acres in Tong Wood near Lizard Grange. Tong had just been taken out of Brewood Forest. When Abbot Faritius (1100–35) rebuilt his Abbey at Abingdon in Berkshire, we are told that "For all the buildings which the Abbot made he caused beams and rafters to come from the district of Wales . . . For he had six wains for this purpose, and twelve oxen to each of them. Six or seven weeks was the journey, coming and going, for it was necessary to go as far as Shrewsbury." Timber from Shropshire used in the south-west of England was sometimes referred to as 'walschborde'.[1]

Shirlett Forest

Shirlett Forest remained partly under royal control until the sixteenth century. This Forest, which must originally have joined Wyre Forest to the south, Clee Forest to the west and Long Forest to the north, lay within the arc of the River Severn to the north of Bridgnorth. All that remains of

[1] L. F. Salzman, *Building in England* (1952), p. 245.

Shirlett today is a small area of woodland lying largely within Willey Park. Timber from Shirlett was despatched throughout Shropshire and the border counties in the thirteenth and fourteenth centuries, and it seems probable that Shirlett was in fact the *Shire Forest*, representing the residue of the early Norman Shropshire Forest. Shirlett, in fact, means 'share of the shire'. In 1233 two of the King's carpenters were sent to Shirlett "to make bottices to fortify Montgomery Castle when the need arises", and ten years later oak trees were sent throughout the county as "the men of Llewellyn are in many places rising". A survey of Shirlett Forest in 1235 noted the great amount of recent timber felling and recorded "the custody is good as regards oak trees and underwood, except that great deliveries have been made by order of the King to the Abbeys of Salop, Buildwas and Wenlock . . . There is small abiding of beasts except in coming and going from other Forests."

The process of medieval woodland settlement can clearly be seen at Spoonhill Wood, originally part of Shirlett Forest, where there are a number of decayed forest townships. Wenlock Priory was originally responsible for founding four woodland hamlets here in the early Middle Ages, later known as Monkhall, Mason's Monkhall, Harper's Monkhall and Woodhouse Field. By the end of the thirteenth century, they were in the hands of freeholders. At Mason's Monkhall the traditional three-field system was operated by only three freeholders, Roger Styme, Henry Attewoud and William the Mason. During the fourteenth century the holdings at Mason's Monkhall were consolidated and the hamlet contracted to a single farm. By 1600 all four were isolated farms (Fig. 6).

Morfe Forest

Across the Severn a slightly different forest landscape is to

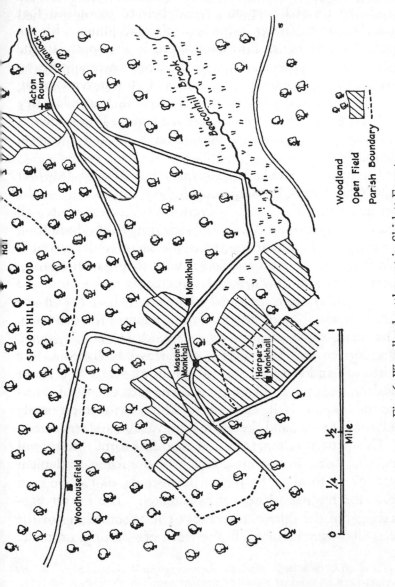

Fig. 6. Woodland settlement in Shirlett Forest

A reconstruction of medieval settlement and fields in Spoonhill Wood, originally part of Shirlett Forest, based on a map dated c. 1700.

be found in the area of the old Morfe Forest. This Forest originally formed part of a great belt of woodland that stretched from Kinver in Staffordshire and joined with the great Worcestershire Forest of Wyre in the south. In the Middle Ages settlement within the Forest area appears to have been restricted, although extensive clearance was being carried out from neighbouring manors such as Claverley and Worfield, but to the south of the ancient Forest there is a landscape of shrunken villages and moated medieval farms.

The modern parishes of Romsley and Alveley, together with Glazeley, Billingsley and Highley to the west of the Severn, and Arley and Wolverley in Worcestershire, all share the *ley* ending (O.E. *leah*—clearing) thus indicating the original extent of forest, when the Saxon settlers arrived. We find that the mother-villages with their Saxon clearing names represent the original settlements and Coton and Kingsnordley were secondary hamlets. Settlement in the area took the form of isolated farms, many of them moated. The place-name element *green* found in Thurleygreen, Doddsgreen and Hartsgreen, all farms established in the thirteenth and early fourteenth centuries, refers to a forest clearing and not a village green. The area empty of farms around Coton Hall and Little Coton was traditionally ancient demesne, and therefore not available for settlement.

This pattern is repeated in a modified form throughout the old Morfe Forest area. Much of the forest settlement was in the form of individual farmsteads, as can be seen from the high incidence of *cot* suffixes.[2] The Forest proceedings of the thirteenth century tell us something of the men who were involved in the work of assarting, normally

---

[2] It is often difficult in modern place-names to decide whether the *-cot* derives from an original plural or singular form. In Shropshire, however, the survival of such places as Coton derived from the plural, suggests that Farncot and Dalicot are singular forms.

in half or single acres newly planted with oats. Their very names conjure up a picture of pioneers—William atte Mor, Robert atte Ok, Robert atte Lee (whose name is still preserved in Lee Farm near Dalicot) and Hereward de la Syche (Sytch Farm). Although the Forest theoretically remained subject to Forest Law throughout the Middle Ages the map of 1582 rather pathetically shows that the majority of woodland had been cleared (Fig. 7). This was drawn as evidence in an enquiry about grazing rights and shows the Forest consisting largely of saplings and stumps, and a survey of 1556 records only fifty-two acres of wood here. Much of the cleared land within the old Forest was not initially cultivated and became common waste. The remnants of waste and woodland, left after medieval assarting and Tudor destruction, were finally enclosed in 1812. The resulting pattern of regular fields, often with quickset hedges, can be clearly seen, as for example, along the stretches of straight enclosure road between Six Ashes and Bridgnorth. The regular pattern contrasts with the parts of the Forest earlier settled with winding deep-cut lanes and irregular fields, elements of a more ancient landscape.

Clee Forest

Clee was one of the smaller Shropshire Forests, no more than 24,000 acres, and it remained directly under the control of the Crown for only a short time. The Clee ceased to be true Royal Forest in 1155, but it was later operated on the lines of a Royal Forest by the Cliffords from Corfham Castle. Its history, however, illustrates some aspects of landscape-history which are significantly different from the true wood-land Forests. The Clee Forest, constituting Brown Clee hill and its surrounding area, was almost certainly originally joined with the Long Forest to the north and Shirlett Forest to the east. The name Brown Clee does not appear

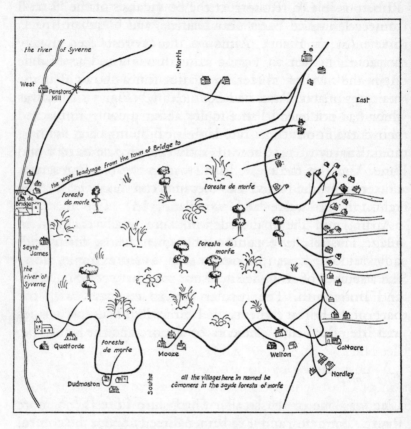

The river of Syverne

North

West

Penstons Mill

East

the waye leadynge from the town of Bridge to

vil̃d de Bridg

foresta de morfe

foresta de morfe

Seynt James

the river of Syverne

foresta de morfe

foresta de morfe

Quatforde

foresta de morfe

Mooze

Welton

Gattacre

Nordley

Dudmaston

Southe

all the villages here in named be cõmoners in the sayde foresta of morfe

Fig. 7. Plan of Morfe Forest, 1582
Copy of map of Morfe Forest in 1582 (P.R.O. E.178/4428) drawn as
evidence in an enquiry about grazing rights. The map shows that little
woodland remained in the Forest by this date. The original is very
faded and the names north of Gattacre are illegible and consequently
are not shown on this copy. The original is coloured and measures
25 by 27 inches. There is no scale on the original map.

until the fifteenth century, before which date the hill and Forest were known as 'Les Clives'.[3]

It is possible to reconstruct the boundaries of the Forest from ecclesiastical parish boundaries, which radiate from three most prominent points on the Brown Clee, giving each foothill-township a proportion of wood and wasteland on the hill. Where these boundaries run as straight lines they presumably reflect unexploited woodland or heath, which had not been subject to any tenurial control prior to their creation or at any rate had not hitherto been demarcated. Earnstrey Park, now in Abdon parish, was part of the Forest and the medieval 'haye' there probably represents a Saxon park, the boundaries of which can clearly be identified on the ground today.

Apart from the manorial woodland attached to each village, most of the remaining timber was cleared during the early Middle Ages, principally by Wenlock Priory and Shrewsbury Abbey. In 1465, when a new fence was required for Earnstrey Park, the timber had to be bought outside the Forest and by the time Leland visited the area about 1540, he observed, "There is no great plenty of wood in Clee Hills."

A most interesting document of 1612 called 'A Description of Clee' demonstrates the persistence of the common rights of all the townships that had lain within the ancient Forest. Common rights on Brown Clee included agistment and pannage (grazing rights for livestock), turbary (right to cut and collect turfs) and estovers (right to take wood for repairs and fuel). These rights, however, were reserved for those townships that actually lay on Brown Clee, the inhabitants of the old Forest area being allowed only common rights of considerably less importance. In return

[3] The name is probably derived from O.E. *claeg*—clay. Brown was later added to distinguish this hill from neighbouring Titterstone Clee and is an obvious allusion to the reddish-brown soils of the area.

for these privileges, the 'out-commoners' were subject to a modified form of Forest Law and in particular they were to refrain from disturbing deer found among their crops.

The out-commoners had to follow very precise routes from their townships to the grazing areas on the Clee. These roads were known as 'driftways', 'straker' ways or 'outracks' (see Fig. 3). Many of them are deeply entrenched and can still be traced as sunken or 'hollow'-ways. The routes were still in use in the seventeenth century when it was claimed "the driftways are long and tedious because the strakers were to drive the lands and commons belonging to other lordships before they could reach Clee soil."[4] The name 'outrack' is still given to a sunken road in Ditton Priors leading to Brown Clee, and other outracks survive on the Long Mynd and in other hilly parts of the county.

An interesting footnote to this story was that at the time of parliamentary enclosure (1809), Thomas Mytton, lord of Earnstrey, tried to claim extensive allotments on Brown Clee as 'lord of the Clee Chace'; in reality this was an attempt to claim rights from the Royal Forest which had been disbanded some six centuries earlier.

SELECT BIBLIOGRAPHY

Baizeley, M. C., 'English Forest in the 13th Century', *T.R.H.S.*, Vol. 4, 4th ser. (1921).

Eyton, Rev. E. W., *Antiquities of Shropshire*.

Rowley, R. T., 'The Clee Forest, a Study in Common Rights', *T.S.A.S.*, Vol. 58 (1966).

Victoria County History, *Shropshire*, Vol. 1, pp. 483–93, and Vol. 8.

Yates, E. M., 'Dark Age and Medieval Settlement on the Edge of Wastes and Forests', *Field Studies*, Vol. 2, No. 2 (1965).

[4] The term 'straker' probably refers to the method of calling the inhabitants of Forest by a horn. (M.E. *strake* means to blow a horn as a summons.) Gough in his *History of Myddle* refers to 'streaking' in connection with similar movements of animals to commonland.

6. Deserted Villages and Hamlets

THERE IS A natural tendency to regard villages and hamlets as permanent features of the rural landscape. Pioneer work by Professor Hoskins in Leicestershire and Professor Beresford in his book *Lost Villages of England* has shown, however, that there are quite literally thousands of 'lost' and shrunken villages in England. Many of these were deserted during the later Middle Ages, but desertion brought about by enclosure and emparking continued into the nineteenth century. In some areas, depopulation is still responsible for the gradual shrinkage of rural settlements, particularly those hamlets lying well away from towns and the main lines of communication.

At the time Beresford wrote his book on deserted villages the true nature of the medieval settlement pattern in Shropshire had not been properly explored. The system of daughter- or dependent-townships extending throughout Shropshire was not fully understood, and as a result of this only one deserted village is recorded in the original county list.[1] Since then considerable numbers of 'lost' villages and hamlets have been identified. The degree of shrinkage and desertion in Shropshire can best be gauged by an analysis of Ford Hundred, where out of the seventy Domesday hamlets, nine have been deserted and thirty-three have

[1] Caus is the settlement named for Shropshire, and this in fact was a failed medieval town plantation. Current county lists of known or suspected deserted villages are kept by the Secretary of the Deserted Medieval Village Research Group, Mr J. G. Hurst, 67 Gloucester Crescent, London, N.W.1, who will also be interested to hear of any new or suspected sites. The revised edition (see Select Bibliography) gives a total of nine, still admittedly incomplete.

shrunk to single farms. Indeed only twelve hamlets have survived as nucleated settlements. Some Shropshire settlements were abandoned as a result of direct action by lords of manors, Allcot in Acton Burnell and Ramshurst in Frodesley are examples of this, but gradual reduction was a much more common occurrence. The two main reasons for shrinkage were firstly the movement of population out of hamlets to isolated farmsteads on the fertile clay and woodland areas, particularly during the late Middle Ages, and secondly the rise of the large farm in the eighteenth century, rendering superfluous such houses in ancient hamlets which were not converted into labourers' cottages.

Desertion and shrinkage of rural settlement in the county was almost always closely associated with enclosure. The compact nucleated village, surrounded by strips in open fields, was economically sensible in the Middle Ages, since each tenant was within easy reach of his own scattered holding. But with the creation of enclosed farm-holdings often some distance from the old village, the situation changed. The farmer remaining in the village was at a disadvantage, and as soon as possible rebuilt his farmhouse within his own enclosed fields. In Shropshire, enclosure spanned several centuries, and accordingly the readjustment of settlement was a slow process. Because of the slow rate of shrinkage the identification of sites is often very difficult, and to some extent the search for the traditional deserted village is spurious, as in most parts of the county virtually every settlement was larger at one time.

There are, however, a number of sites which declined gradually and where there are clear earthworks. A series of these has recently been identified from the air by Dr St Joseph. A particularly good example is Pickthorn near Stottesdon, a typical Shropshire deserted hamlet contained within a single modern field (Plate 14). Although Pickthorn was an independent manor in 1086, originally it was probably a township of the large Saxon Manor of Stottes-don. As late as 1571 there were still eight tenements at Pickthorn, but like the seven medieval townships of Stottesdon, the hamlet appears to have been gradually reduced to a single farm.

As for the reasons behind the abandonment of villages, there is little to support the popular view that the Black Death (1348-9) was responsible, despite the very high mortality of Shropshire clergy at the time. Pestilence was, however, a factor in weakening the village structure. In the year following the Black Death many manors were said to be reduced in value because of plague and a few hamlets do appear even to have succumbed completely; for instance, Yeye, a small township in Stanton Lacy manor, is last recorded in 1350 as being ruinous. Similarly, Broomcroft, a township in Kenley parish, had been depopulated by 1363, when it was said to be uncultivated because of lack of tenants. It is obvious, however, that many manors were declining before the Black Death, and the plague was in most instances only partly responsible for desertion.

A valuable source of information about village mortality in Shropshire is contained in the *Assessment of the ninth* (1341) which adjusted the parish assessment originally fixed in 1291. The assessors tell a story of hardship almost universal throughout the county. Even allowing for exaggeration, the *assessment* does shed some interesting light on depopulation in Shropshire. In almost every parish there was a substantial reduction. At Upton Cressett, for example, the assessment dropped from £3 6s. 8d. to 17s. because, it was stated, the land lay untilled and "the tenants of the same have withdrawn because of penury". Reasons given for the reduction in other parishes included high taxation, pestilence among cattle and sheep, bad harvests and the destruction of crops by storms.

Nor is there much evidence to show that periodic attacks by the Welsh had any permanent effect on settlement in the border area, although they probably did retard economic development in a number of western manors. At Westbury, for instance, Thomas Corbet of Caus was engaged in constant warfare with his relative Griffith ap Gwenwynwyn throughout the thirteenth century. In 1405–6, following Owen Glendower's rebellion, the townships of Caus, Marsh, Vennington, Westbury and Yockleton, which had been burnt down, were excused taxation. Indeed, some of the houses thus destroyed in Minsterley had not been rebuilt by 1445. There is one reputed instance of a hamlet having been destroyed at this same time which never recovered; Burfield, today an isolated farmstead, was originally a township in the manor of Tempsitur, some two and a half miles west of Clun near to Offa's Dyke. Allegedly the township and chapel at Burfield were laid waste by Owen Glendower about 1400, and thereafter it was known as "the decayed township of Berfield".[2] In this instance the Welsh attack may have been the crowning blow to an already weak village, but on the whole periodic warfare appears rarely to have been responsible for total desertion.

It is not possible yet to draw an overall picture of village mortality within the county, nor is it possible to draw up comprehensive distribution maps as has been done by the Deserted Medieval Village Research Group for counties such as Northamptonshire and Oxfordshire. Much work remains to be done on the identification and recording of sites. Desertion does, however, appear to be particularly common in the extreme south of the county, where, as yet, there has been little research; but almost certainly sites are to be found in all parts of the county. Yet one can see from those areas that have been studied that there is great

[2] T. Salt, 'Ancient Documents relating to the Honor, Forest and Borough of Clun', *T.S.A.S.*, Vol. 9 (1887).

variety in the nature of settlement desertion and shrinkage in Shropshire. Sites vary from a field-name, as at Marston in Diddlebury parish,[3] to a considerable earthwork site surrounding an isolated church, as at Abdon; or most common of all they are farmhouses, as at Stitt, in the parish of Ratlinghope.

In recent years a number of sites in the county have been destroyed. One of these at Braggington in Alberbury was excavated prior to its being levelled in 1963. The earthworks of Braggington lie at 400 feet a quarter of a mile north-east of Braggington Hall on a north-facing slope of the foothills of the Breidden. A small stream, which demarcates the Welsh border here, runs eastwards at the foot of the slope, and banks and leats suggest that a mill once stood on it. Braggington is first recorded in 1255; the place-name, however, with its -*ington* ending implies a Saxon settlement. It is thus possible that the Saxon hamlet of Braggington was abandoned after the Norman Conquest and refounded a century or so later. The relationship of the deserted village to the surrounding ridge-and-furrow is also unclear, much disturbance having been caused by later drainage. The ridges in the north seem to be ending in the typical reversed S as they meet the main ditch. There is, however, no headland and therefore no obvious turning place for a plough team. It is probable that the ridges here and on the west side have been cut across by the village. If this is so the medieval village was planted on ancient arable land, clearly indicative of a break in the continuity of settlement. Such tantalising questions cannot, as yet, be answered. There was a population of sixteen Welsh tenants at Braggington in 1301 and it seems to have been occupied by Welsh families throughout the Middle Ages.

[3] The site of Marston is in a low-lying part of the Corvedale, hence the name (Marsh-town). It is last heard of as a small hamlet in the late fourteenth century.

Excavations here revealed a long-house occupied with little change from the fourteenth to seventeenth centuries. Braggington was abandoned before 1650 when work started on Braggington Hall. As we shall later see, villages were frequently flattened and moved to ensure greater privacy for country houses. The kink in the road to the north-east of Little Braggington suggests the road was diverted at the same time.[4]

In south Shropshire an interesting group of deserted and shrunken hamlets has been identified on and around the Clee Hills. A particularly dense concentration is to be found on the plateau around Brown Clee. These appear to have been marginal arable settlements which were gradually deserted as the area turned towards a more pastoral economy. Desertion rarely appears to have been abrupt, and gradual shrinkage associated with farm amalgamation, which occurred later in central and western parts of the county, began here in the fourteenth century.

One of the abandoned settlements in the area is aptly named Cold Weston. Like many of the neighbouring deserted hamlets, all that remains of the medieval settlement is an isolated church, surrounded by sunken roads and house platforms which undoubtedly mark the site of the old hamlet. Cold Weston appears to be an example of bad siting, lying as it does at 800 feet on a north-facing slope. The village was in decline before the Black Death; in 1341 the parish was assessed at 4s. 8d. compared with £5 3s. in 1291. The assessors stated that there "had once been abundance of cattle here", but they had decreased because of the murrain which had hit the region. The account continues, "the chapel is in a waste place and the living had been presented to four parsons within the year

---

[4] P. A. Barker, 'The Deserted Medieval Hamlet of Braggington', *T.S.A.S.*, Vol. 58 (1968). The site of a medieval settlement next to Sutton chapel, near Shrewsbury has recently been destroyed through the building of a housing estate.

but none of them would stay, and there are only two tenants living by great labour and in want, and others have absconded". After this date there was never a nucleated settlement on the site, and the number of houses in the parish gradually declined. In 1544 there were eight families living in the parish, by 1672 this had decreased to five. A visitation of 1793 tells a typical story of rural depopulation, "there was formerly a parsonage, three farmhouses and six small dwellings, of these four have recently been taken down . . . Mr. Davies' property was in three farms now consolidated into only one." Today there is a single farmhouse, Cold Weston Court, and two cottages within the parish.

At the deserted village of Heath, nearby, more visual traces of the medieval landscape have survived. The almost perfect Norman chapel is the centrepiece of the site (Plate 9); in the surrounding fields there are extensive earthworks belonging to the old village, representing the roads, houses and the fields of the medieval community and in the field to the north of the chapel there is a stone-lined well. The documentary evidence for Heath is slender, but it does demonstrate a gradual decline from seven taxable families in 1327; the extent of the earthworks here, however, suggests a considerably larger medieval settlement. By 1770 there were only four dispersed tenements at Heath, but a plan of the chapelry at that date still bears the imprint of the medieval landscape (Fig. 8). This map shows that the medieval road pattern had survived and that the earthworks of the village to the north of the chapel were called Moat Meadow, clearly referring to medieval earthworks which later inhabitants must have thought were intended to be water-filled. The 'Wynet' open field had maintained its name and can be identified on the ground today in the form of curving ridge-and-furrow. The fishponds, which in 1241 were valued at one mark, were still there and their banks are still clearly visible. Heath Park, originally a deer park, appears as a compact enclosed holding.

Finally, in this group of deserted villages comes Abdon, which has a slightly more involved history than the other sites, and also serves a warning against the oversimplification of settlement history. The isolated church of St Margaret lies at 800 feet on a ridge of Devonian sandstone. The earthworks here are more spectacular than at most Shropshire deserted villages. In the field to the east of the church there are a number of distinct house platforms with an intersecting pattern of hollow-ways and on one side the village earthworks are bounded by ridge-and-furrow (Fig. 9). A scattered settlement consisting of two farms and two cottages in a hollow about a quarter of a mile to the south of the church represents the residue of the community. The fragmentary documentary evidence suggests that Abdon, like Heath, declined slowly during the later Middle Ages. It differs, however, from its neighbours because the site was partially reoccupied in the sixteenth and seventeenth centuries, when its inhabitants were employed in the mines and quarries on Brown Clee. During the late eighteenth century, however, Abdon was fated to be deserted yet again, for with the decline of the Brown Clee extractive industries, the villagers moved away. After a visit to Abdon in 1793 Archdeacon Plymley observed "some houses have been taken down and several seem to have fallen down."

Abdon is one of five Shropshire deserted villages where there has been excavation (the others are Braggington, Bury Walls, Sutton, and Detton);[5] here they revealed the base of a thirteenth-century stone house lying immediately to the south of the present churchyard (Site 1). This

[5] S. Stanford, 'A Medieval Settlement at Detton Hall, Shropshire', *T.S.A.S.*, Vol. 58 (1967). Despite the destruction of much of the medieval occupation levels, the pottery evidence suggests that the village was deserted about 1300.

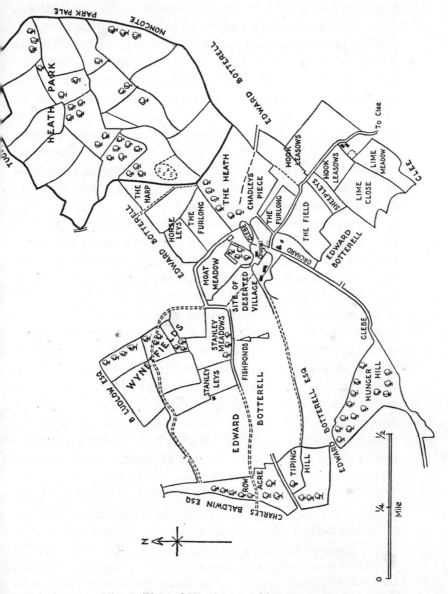

Fig. 8. Plan of Heath township, 1771
Site of deserted village, 1771, based on a survey in the Craven collection
(S.P.L. MS. 2481).

proved to be a long-house built on the sandstone bedrock, which, having been altered on at least three occasions, was finally abandoned in the late thirteenth century.[6] There was no occupation in this part of the village after 1300 and no evidence of any earlier Saxon settlement was recovered. A second excavation (Site 2) provided evidence of the later industrial occupation when the base of an eighteenth-century outbuilding was uncovered. It now seems certain that the medieval village was concentrated around the church and that the later industrial settlement lay on lower, more sheltered ground, some 100 yards to the south-east of the church.

The desertion and deliberate movement of villages went on into the nineteenth century. The creation of planned estate villages on the edge of parkland, particularly in the east of the county, suggests deliberate movement in association with landscaping. We know that Atcham virtually disappears in the eighteenth century as a result of the extension of Attingham Park; other examples are discussed later.

Finally, reference should be made to the comparatively recent abandonment of small settlements that grew up around industrial workings during the eighteenth and nineteenth centuries. In the Shelve district, for instance, there are several examples of communities of smallholders grouped together near to the lead mines. Since the abandonment of these mines early in this century, several of these

6 'Long-houses' were a common form of peasant dwelling in Shropshire throughout the Middle Ages, and indeed a standing long-house dating from the late fifteenth or early sixteenth century has been identified at Tir-y-Coed, Kinnerley. J. T. Smith, 'The Evolution of the English peasant house to the late seventeenth century', *J.B.A.A.*, Vol. 33, 3rd ser. (1970).

Fig. 9. (*opposite*) Plan of earthworks, Abdon deserted medieval village Plan of earthworks, showing site of excavations. Although there has been considerable disturbance, the line of the main streets can be clearly identified as well as some houses with their attached enclosures. An area of open-field ridge-and-furrow lies in the middle of the earthworks.

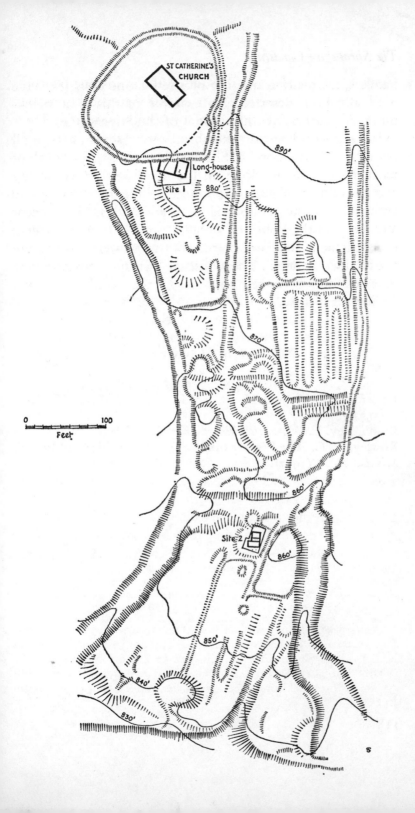

ST CATHERINE'S
CHURCH

Long-house
Site 1   890'

880'

870'

0   100
    Feet

860'

Site 2   860'

850'

840'

830'

S

hamlets, normally consisting of a few stone cottages, have gradually been deserted. An example of this is at Blackmoregate, just below the summit of the Stiperstones.

Instances of desertion and shrinkage of settlements of all periods are common in Shropshire, but a great deal of work remains to be done on the identification, recording and surveying of sites. Undoubtedly the most profitable approach to the subject is that adopted in the recent Volume 8 of the Victoria County History, *Shropshire*, where the settlement structure of parishes in western Shropshire is examined in detail. The landscape historian must examine deserted and shrunken villages in the context of total settlement history.

SELECT BIBLIOGRAPHY

Beresford, M. W., *The Lost Villages of England* (1954).
Beresford, M. W. and Hurst, J. G., *Deserted Medieval Villages* (1971).
Eyton, Rev. E. W., *Antiquities of Shropshire*.
Rowley, R. T., 'The History of the South Shropshire Landscape'. *S.N.L.*, No. 1 (1957).

7. Parks and Country Houses

Medieval deer parks.   Country houses and their parks.

Medieval deer parks

ONE OF THE most important elements in the Shropshire landscape is the country house and park. During the sixteenth century the park changed both in form and function. Previous to this a park was part of the lord's demesne, simply consisting of an area of woodland and pasture enclosed by an earthen bank, often with an inside ditch. The bank was topped by a wooden paling which was occasionally replaced by a quickset hedge or stone wall and the enclosure would be broken only by gates and deer leaps. The primary purpose of the medieval park was to keep deer for hunting; it differed from the forest, chase and warren in that it was the only one that was completely enclosed. Most wealthy lords aspired to a park, which was either adjacent to or, more normally, some distance from the manor house.

A few of these parks, such as Earnstrey on Brown Clee, can be traced back before the Norman Conquest, but the majority were created in the thirteenth and fourteenth centuries. At that time the Crown issued hundreds of 'grants of free warren', which resulted in the monopolisation of hunting rights by the lord within his newly created park. In many cases deer parks were carved out of disafforested areas of Royal Forest such as the Long Forest. Occasionally, however, the creation of such parks disturbed agriculture and communications. In 1275, for instance, Sir Odo de

Hodnet enclosed two roads which ran through the centre of Hodnet Park, and re-routed them around his new park. Such detours can often be clearly identified on the ground today.

The fashion for creating deer parks declined rapidly during the late Middle Ages when many parks simply deteriorated, the boundaries were left to collapse, and in many cases hunting ceased altogether. In the sixteenth and seventeenth centuries, some old parks were cleared of their woodland and enclosed; subsequently they were divided between freeholders or consolidated into a single farm. Thus medieval hunting gave way to a more economic use of the land. Heath Park, for instance, was enclosed into a farm in the mid-sixteenth century and given the name Heath Park Farm; the boundaries of the park can still be traced in the field boundaries (see Fig. 8). Where such a 'park' name survives it is usually an indication of the existence of a former medieval deer park. At Tilstock, where the park was cleared and enclosed in the late sixteenth century, a remarkable survey has survived showing the farmers Greene, Chawner and Gregorie each clearing his respective area of trees (Fig. 10). The plan even shows the farmers carrying axes over their shoulders, as well as the stumps of felled trees. This process was repeated many times throughout the county.

Apart from place-names and boundaries some hunting lodges belonging to former parks have also survived. The fourteenth-century farmhouse at Upper Millichope has traditionally been regarded as a hunting lodge, but probably the most striking example is Frodesley Lodge, which stands gaunt and alone at 650 feet on the northern slopes of Hoar Edge, an escarpment running two miles to the north-west of Wenlock Edge.[1] It was probably built as a hunting lodge

[1] Hoar Edge was an ancient boundary of the Hereford diocese, and probably marks the division between the Saxon *Magonsaetan* and *Wreocansaetan* kingdoms.

Plate 16 Attingham Hall, built 1783–5, with the River Tern on the right. Possibly the most elegant country house in Shropshire.

Plate 15. Blake Mere, with the town of Ellesmere and Oteley Hall (1826–30). The Ellesmere Canal lies in the foreground.

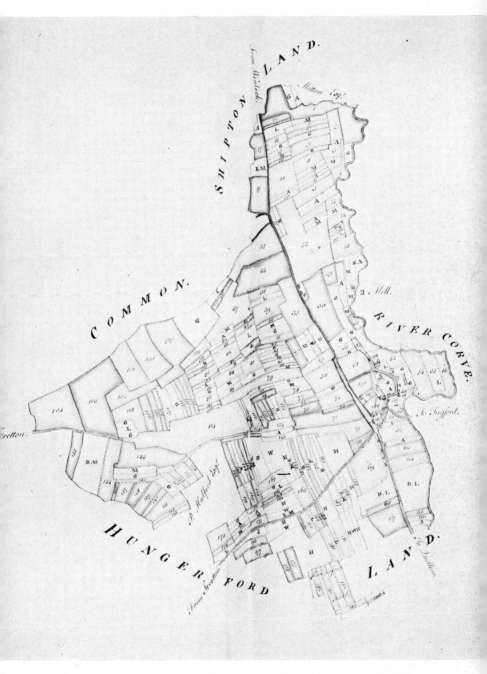

Plate 18 The township and open-fields of Broadstone in Corvedale in 1770. The fields were enclosed in the early nineteenth century; following enclosure the village declined.

Plate 19   Remains of bell-pit coal mines at Lubberland on Catherton Clee in south Shropshire. The regular fields of parliamentary enclosure in Silvington parish contrast strikingly with squatter encroachments, some of which form islands in the middle of the waste common land.

in the early seventeenth century when the lord of Frodesley was carrying out improvements in Frodesley Park. The park was eventually divided into fields *c.* 1787, although the park-pale can still be traced in field boundaries, and to the south of Park Farm the stone wall built around the park in 1609 is still standing. Fields called Big and Little Deer-house Leasow lie within the wall. Many medieval parks did not survive into the sixteenth century; indeed Saxton's 1577 map of the county marks only twenty-three enclosed parks and several of these, such as Kenwick Park near Ellesmere, were enclosed soon after this.

Country houses and their parks

During the sixteenth century many of the old hunting parks were broken up and brought into cultivation. At the same time a new form of park and house was emerging. The confiscation of monastic estates in the 1530s produced a redistribution of land-ownership on a scale unknown since the Norman Conquest and made considerable areas of land available for emparking. Along the foot of Wenlock Edge, this process resulted in the establishment of a series of country houses with small parks at Shipton Hall (1587), Lutwyche Hall (1587) and Larden Hall (1607). Much of the newly emparked land was on good soil in the lowlands and valleys and not confined to the sourest and driest soils like many earlier parks. The creation of landscaped parks introduced a completely new factor into the Shropshire countryside; for the first time land was being used principally for aesthetic rather than economic purposes since land that had previously been farmed was enclosed into new parks. At Longnor, for instance, ridge-and-furrow within the park-pale demonstrates that this land was once arable. Although some Shropshire parks, such as Hawkstone, do reflect and incorporate their immediate environments,

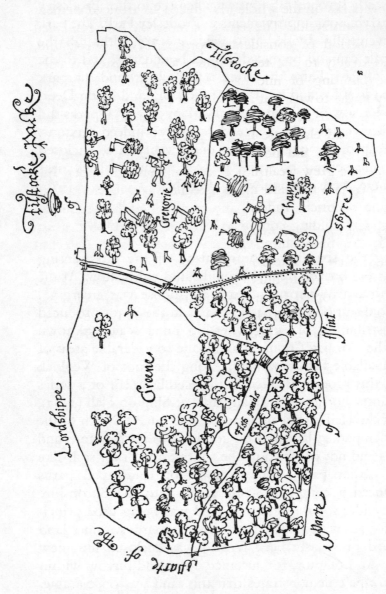

Fig. 10. The enclosure of Tilstock Park, *c.* 1600

Copy of original plan (S.R.O. 212/Box 466) showing the division and enclosure of Tilstock Park between the farmers Greene, Gregorie and Chawner, who are busy clearing their areas of woodland.

the new parks on the whole introduced an artificial element into the countryside. The release of monastic land coincided with a period of considerable prosperity in Shropshire, related largely to the textile trade, which expressed itself in the building of fine mansions and public buildings, mainly in the towns, but also to some extent in the country.

In the towns it was the clothiers who built the most expensive and elaborate houses and it is worth observing that the houses did not change from timber to stone as these people grew wealthier, but from stone to timber. For it was possible to build more ostentatiously in wood than in stone or brick. Indeed, the tradition of half-timbered vernacular building continued into the eighteenth century in northern Shropshire. Country houses of the sixteenth century, such as Pitchford Hall and on a smaller scale Sibberscot in Pontesbury, use techniques and decoration deliberately copied from town houses. It is also of some interest to note that brick, which arrived late in the county anyway, is first used in country houses, Plaish Hall probably being the first example. Not far away, there is another remarkable Elizabethan brick building possibly encasing an earlier medieval structure at New Earnstrey Park. The very early use of brick in these isolated parts of the county clearly demonstrates a long-forgotten prosperity.

A fine, but sadly neglected, early brick house still stands at Upton Cressett, not far from Bridgnorth. This house is dated 1580, and the turreted gatehouse is earlier, *c.* 1540; the truly remarkable feature of the hall, however, is a splendid medieval wooden hall, encased in Tudor brickwork. This is certainly a feature of many smaller buildings in the county, but it is unusual to find it happening so early and on such a grand scale.

The first reference to Upton Cressett Park was in Wolsey's Inquisition of Enclosures (1517), when it was alleged that Thomas Cressett had emparked forty acres of arable land at Upton. The village of Upton was deserted then, or possibly slightly later in the mid-sixteenth century, with the rebuilding of the house and the extension of the park. The road running south-west from Bridgnorth was stopped and there apppears to have been some landscaping. Later the park was enclosed, Upton Park Farm and Upton Lodge being the only reminders of its former existence. The decaying gate-house still stands near to the Norman church, surrounded by scrub and the earthworks of the former village. Together they create a nostalgic and striking picture of earlier prosperity and grandeur.

Another ruined house of about the same period, which has managed to maintain much of its dignity, largely through the help of the Inspectorate of Ancient Monuments, is at Moreton Corbet, near Shawbury. Moreton Corbet Castle incorporates a medieval keep, but has extensive Elizabethan additions, dated 1579. Much of this still remains and architecturally it must originally have been "amongst the most impressive and consistent designs in the country".[2] The façade is articulated throughout in the French way by attached Tuscan columns and gives an impression of real splendour rarely achieved in Shropshire houses (Plate 15). Around the castle can be seen the earthworks of the medieval defences and village of Moreton Corbet. In 1503 there were still thirteen 'messuages in Moreton towne' but the village appears to have been deserted at about the same time as the rebuilding of the 'Castle', when a park was created and the road diverted. Most of these country houses had a park of some sort, but even at this date parks were still utilitarian. Parkland was used extensively for grazing and in some instances for crops. Highly formalised and sophisticated landscaping was not introduced on any scale until the eighteenth century.

If we look at two examples of seventeenth-century parks

[2] Pevsner, op. cit., p. 205.

we can obtain some idea of this functional nature of parkland. Firstly, a map of Longford Hall (1682) to the south-
west of Newport shows that the landscaping was really
limited to a small area of formal gardens in front of the
house.[3] There were avenues of trees leading from the house,
but these did not interfere with the enclosed paddocks. Some
medieval fishponds were re-used as ornamental ponds and
it is worth noting that the church stands isolated to the north
of the hall and probably formed the centre of the old village.
Both the hall and church were rebuilt at the end of the
eighteenth century.

Aldenham, near Morville, has a similar history. The park
appears to have been laid out at about the same time as the
rebuilding of the hall in 1691. The driveway, almost half a
mile in length, gives a grand but deceptive impression of the
extent of the park; this device manages to convey an
impression of grandeur that is found in other Shropshire
houses. At Linley Hall, near Bishop's Castle, for instance,
the drive extends for nearly a mile and is completely
divorced from the rest of the park.

In Aldenham Park there were coppices for the iron
industry as well as normal arable fields (Fig. 11). Indeed a
map of 1725 marks a 'furnis' quite close to the house, and
it has been suggested that the siting of the house and park
may be due to the presence here of early ironworks. Today,
apart from the drive, much of the park has been disbanded.
But the early eighteenth-century entrance and wrought-
iron gates in front of the long drive, with the hall silhouetted
at the end, give an impression of wealth and splendour out
of all proportion to the size of the building and its
grounds.

During the eighteenth century, both country houses and

---

[3] S.R.O. Longford Estate (Luke family) papers. The County Record
Office has a fine collection of seventeenth- and eighteenth-century estate
maps, including several country parks.

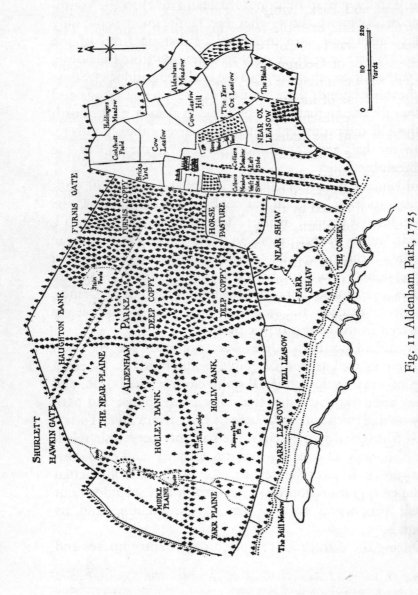

Fig. 11 Aldenham Park, 1725

Plan of Aldenham house and park (S.R.O. 1093/Box 160) showing farming land and coppice wood for near-by charcoal furnaces. On the left-hand side of the plan there is a series of pools

their parks became more ambitious and impressive. Attingham Hall and Park, lying immediately to the east of the Severn, is a fine example from this period (Plate 16). The present hall was built for the first Lord Berwick in 1783–5 to the design of George Stewart and was altered by John Nash at the beginning of the nineteenth century. It was the grandest house of its time in the county, and certainly one of the most representative Georgian buildings in the area. Nash also built the Italianate villa at Cronkhill which was probably 'The Villa in Shropshire' exhibited at the Royal Academy in 1802.

It has been suggested that the original siting of Attingham Park was influenced by the presence of an earlier ironworks here, as at Aldenham, Willey, and possibly other parks in the county.[4] The Tern Forge stood from 1710 to 1757 on the River Tern in what is now Attingham Park. It is recorded in the 1717 list of ironworks compiled by Fuller as producing 300 tons of iron goods per annum; yet virtually no trace of it remains beyond a few lumps of slag on the bed of the Tern at that point. Indeed, it is obvious that all trace of the ironworks had gone within a dozen years of its closure. This is all the more surprising in view of the scale of the works. A letter of 1713 records how, within three years of the start of operations, there was already "a mill for Rowling of Brass plates and Iron hoops and Slitting of bar iron into Rods for making of nails . . . a Wire Mill, forge and a furnace for Converting of Iron into steel." In addition, workshops and housing had been built for forty men and their dependants. Following the closing of the works, however, in 1757, the housing and workshops were demolished to get rid of squatters who had quickly moved into the vacant premises.

Abandoned industrial structures sink back into the

[4] R. Chaplin, 'Discovering Lost Ironworks', *The Local Historian*, Vol. 2, No. 2 (1970).

landscape quite as rapidly as deserted villages and it seems quite probable that Humphrey Repton used some of the ponds and pools here for his landscaping in the late eighteenth century. Perhaps the eloquence of the landscape gardeners has often deceived us about their real contribution to parkland scenery. Certainly it would have been easier to use existing landscape features such as furnace pools rather than to create completely new ones.

Repton, who was employed to improve the park here in 1789, expresses the aspirations of the Georgian landscape gardeners in his *Red Book* (1797-8), which is still kept at Attingham Hall. In his criticism of Attingham Park prior to the alterations, he complains that there were no trees to assist perspective and divert the eye towards the house. Also that barns and other outbuildings which were visible detracted from the hall. Amongst his suggestions for improvement were the plantation of trees to hide the parkpale, the diversion of water, the construction of bridges and the setting of hedges. His general idea was to contrast wide natural views using the Wrekin and the Welsh mountains as a backcloth against beautiful miniatures or set-pieces. Some, but not all, of Repton's improvements were carried out; but the importance of the *Red Book* lies in its concept of landscaping.[5]

The present approach to the house from Atcham dates from soon after 1807. About this time a number of cottages on the north side of Watling Street were demolished and the line of the Uffington road altered so that the park could be extended. Before this the main entrance was midway between Atcham and Tern bridges, but this did not meet with Repton's approval when he worked on his *Red Book*

[5] Humphrey Repton also improved Ferney Hall (1789), Condover (1803), Hopton Court (1803) and Longnor Hall (1804). The only other landscape gardener of note to work in Shropshire was Lancelot Brown who improved Tong Castle (1765) and Oakly Park (1772-5). Tong Castle, designed by Brown, was pulled down in 1954.

for Attingham. He was concerned by the proximity of the
house to Tern bridge and suggested extending the park
across the road and building a pair of lodges, one on each
side of the road, at the eastern extremity of the park "so that
we shall induce the stranger to conceive that he passes thro'
the park and not on the outside of it". This idea was inspired by the existence of a turnpike cottage which Repton
visualised as being remodelled as a classical building worthy
of a nobleman's park. Only one of these lodges survives, that
on the north side, which served as the entrance to the former
east drive to the house. It was presumably designed by Nash.

Apart from reinforcing the planting in the park and intro-
ducing shelter-belts round it, Repton's main contribution
was to make the River Tern play a greater part in the landscape. He suggested the building of a weir to the south-east
of the house to maintain the water level in the upper reaches
of the river and a cascade which should be visible from the
house. This still exists, but not situated as Repton recom-
mended. He also constructed another weir below Tern
bridge so as to create above it a much wider river that would
be visible from the house. However, his idea of making the
bridge more monumental was not adopted, nor was his
suggestion that a spire should be added to the tower of Wroxeter Church some two miles to the south-east of the house!

Towards the end of the eighteenth century there was a
movement towards more dramatic park landscapes. A
striking contrast to Attingham is to be found to the north
of Shrewsbury at Hawkstone which, incidentally, was the
seat of the Hill family, a branch of which was responsible
for the building of Attingham Hall. The grounds of Hawkstone are exceptionally happily situated for any improver
who wanted a rugged parkland, i.e. for the later Georgian
rather than the mid-Georgian ideals of landscape. The ridge
of sandstone cliffs, falling precipitously away south-west
and south of the house and being guarded by sudden

1

isolated crags, could not be more dramatic. Moreover, when the improvements began, there was already a ruined medieval castle here, the Red Castle perched on its rock as no painter could have invented it. We have descriptions of the whole large and felicitous scheme as it originally was, including walks of over ten miles, rocks compared with the ruins of Palmyra, the wax effigy of the ancestor of a neighbour in the grotto, a hermitage complete with a hermit 'generally found in a sitting posture', a vineyard laid out like a fortification with turrets, walls and bastions, an Elysian Hill, an Awful Precipice, a menagerie, a Gothic greenhouse, and so on. All these features dated from before 1784. After that date others were added including 'A Scene in Switzerland', 'A Scene in Otaheite' and an obelisk. Dr Johnson visited Hawkstone in 1774 and pronounced it to be a place of 'terrific grandeur', but rather churlishly concludes "The house was magnificent compared with the rank of the owner!"[6] Hawkstone Park is still a remarkable place; although some of the original attractions have disappeared, there are still a number of follies within the splendid sandstone scenery.

During the nineteenth century there were few new major attempts at landscaping and after 1850 no new country houses were built. One of the last to be erected on the grand scale was a neo-Elizabethan mansion, Otley Hall (1826–30), built overlooking Ellesmere and using the meres as part of the landscaping (Plate 17).

The importance of the creation or extension of landscaped parks on the contemporary landscape cannot be overestimated. Many villages were abandoned, moved and radically changed because of emparking, and there are numerous examples of major and minor road diversions throughout the county brought about by park schemes from the sixteenth century onwards.

6 *A Description of Hawkestone* (1840).

The park at Acton Burnell offers a particularly interesting example of the continuous influence on landscape development exerted by such a park. Acton Burnell has the appearance of an estate-village on the western edge of the park. The original medieval deer park was created by Robert Burnell at about the same time as he built the castle at the end of the thirteenth century. There is reason to believe that before the formation of the park, Acton Burnell village lay to the west of Lynall Brook, nearer to the original line of Watling Street. This would explain the western projection of the parish boundary at this point. To the west of a thirteenth-century moated site there was a field called Townend in 1845. At the north-west corner of Townend Field a small and irregularly-shaped field called Little Meadow seems out of place in a part of the parish which was formerly common-field land, and may mark the site of the original hamlet. The building of the castle and the church on the edge of the park may have led to the abandonment of the old village and the creation of a 'new' planned village (Fig. 12). The present pattern of settlement has changed little since the seventeenth century, for apart from a few council houses the existing houses are nearly all seventeenth-century timber-framed farmhouses or eighteenth-century stone cottages. The addition of 'rustic' features in the nineteenth century has given Acton Burnell the appearance of an estate-village. In most cases this was achieved by rough casting and by the application of rectangular hood-moulds above doors and windows.

During the eighteenth and nineteenth centuries, there were considerable additions to the park, including a small common near Hollies Coppice, added *c.* 1759 and, with the rebuilding of the hall in 1814, the park was extended northwards. The old Acton Pigott road was stopped and a new road built to the north of the village. Within the park, the lodge, a Gothic folly, and a grotto lined with shells were

131

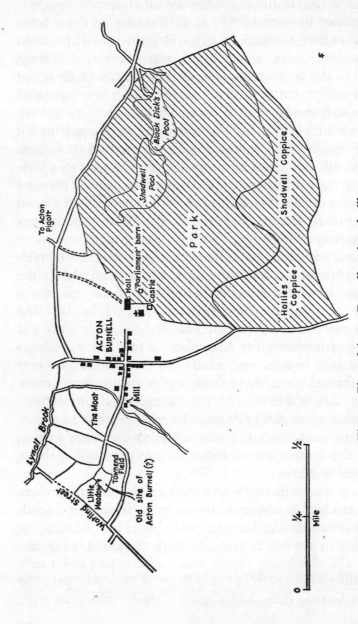

Fig. 12. Plan of Acton Burnell park and village

Based on the tithe map, this map shows the probable site of the original settlement in Little Meadow and the later village and park.

built in the mid-eighteenth century; the two ornamental lakes are probably the fishponds recorded here in 1292.

A similar situation is found at Bitterley, not far from Ludlow, where the mainly Early English church lies next to Bitterley Court, a Jacobean house with a Georgian façade. In the landscaped grounds of the park evidence of the old village can be seen in the form of house platforms and sunken roads. The modern village of Bitterley lies some half-mile to the west of the church and court and it can be clearly seen that the road-pattern has also been changed to serve the new village and avoid the park, although the number of footpaths converging on Bitterley Court may reflect the ancient road-pattern. The move at Bitterley must have taken place in the seventeenth century as no park is marked here on early county maps.

Kinlet Park lies a few miles to the east. Here, in the early eighteenth century, a massive park was created, the village extinguished and the road diverted leaving the house and church (part Norman) in the park. Later a small estate-village was built well away from the house and church. Other instances of such movement would not be difficult to find, since emparking appears to have been fashionable, at this time particularly in the south of the county. Indeed, in most cases, it is impossible to imagine the creation of such parks without considerable upset to existing farms and fields. Post-medieval landscaping can be linked with family names such as the Corbets, who destroyed or moved villages for parks at Longnor, Acton Reynald, Moreton Corbet and Adderley.[7]

Few of these moves are well documented and for the most part they appear to have passed without disturbance. One particularly interesting late piece of landscaping resulting in desertion was at Acton Reynald, originally

[7] Adderley, Shavington and Calverley form an interesting group of parks in the north-east of the county; they were the basis of an extensive Saxon estate held by Nigel the Physician in 1086.

a township of Shrewsbury. In the early eighteenth century there were thirty-five farms, cottages and tenements there (Fig. 13). By 1810 the hall had been extended, a park created, the old road abandoned, a new turnpike skirting the park constructed, and the village abandoned without trace. The only hint we have is Blakeway's *History of the Liberties of Shrewsbury*, written in the early nineteenth century. "He determined himself here . . . on a healthy eminence, commanding a noble view to the extremity of the county, even to the distant Clees, though much destructed by an *unsightly village* . . ."[8] He went on to write that the park had lately been extended and greatly improved by the present baronet. Thus the motive for the abandonment is made clear in his condemnation of the old village, but no record of the extinction of the village appears to have survived.

It is a sad truth that the great country houses with their splendid parks are now a landscape luxury. Today few people can afford to run them as family houses, and more often than not, where they have not been taken over by a school or other institution, the parks have been broken up. Happily Attingham Park and a few more are in the hands of the National Trust, but others such as Condover Park have not fared so well and have been divided into building plots for 'superior' residences. Thus are the dreams of privileged Tudor landowners translated into the jargon of twentieth-century salesmanship.

SELECT BIBLIOGRAPHY

Pevsner, N., *The Buildings of England—Shropshire*.
Prince, H., *Parks in England* (1967).
S.N.L., Nos. 1–39 (1957–70).
Victoria County History, *Shropshire*, Vol. 8

[8] Bodleian Library, MS. Top. Salop. C.6, printed in *T.S.A.S.*, Vols. 16–21 (1892–7).

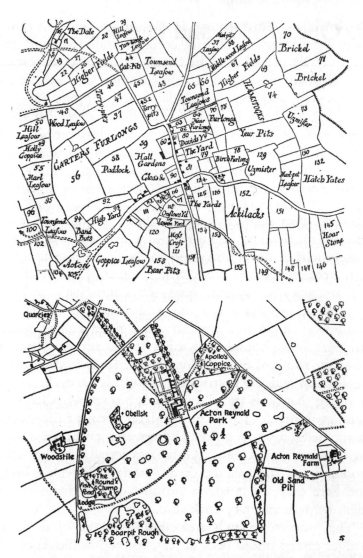

Fig. 13. Plans of Acton Reynald, c. 1780 and 1884
Maps to show the extinction of Acton Reynald village between the middle of the eighteenth century (map based on S.R.O. 322/Box 74) and the first edition of the six-inch Ordnance Survey, 1884. One of the few features common to both maps is the parish boundary in the north-east.

8. Open-Fields and Enclosure

The open-fields.   Early enclosure.   Enclosure and agricultural improvement.

SHROPSHIRE REMAINS overwhelmingly a farming county and it is the fields and their hedges which still constitute the greater part of the countryside. In the flatter northern parts of the county the large regular fields, mainly the product of parliamentary enclosure, give the countryside an open appearance, while in central and southern Shropshire, continuous undulating country has given rise to smaller irregular fields, bounded by thick hedges and sunken lanes, often the result of early enclosure. The landscape appears to be wooded and the visitor may justifiably be deceived into thinking that he is travelling through open woodland. For here, as in much of western England, most of the trees lie in the hedgerows, coppices and coverts, and little concentrated woodland remains. Only occasionally, in the Stiperstones region, for instance, do dry-stone walls replace hedges and here they are mostly a product of squatter encroachment or parliamentary enclosure.

The processes which created this mosaic of fields and hedges can be traced back at least to the Middle Ages. The enclosure of open arable fields, as well as the enclosure and improvement of heath and fenland, accelerated in the sixteenth century, when it began to reflect the changing agricultural needs of a growing and an increasingly urban-orientated culture.

The open-fields

The open-field system was basically one of communal farming, but not common ownership. The tenants within a manor held widely dispersed strips of land in the three open-fields. Under this system the fields were cultivated in rotation, one field lying fallow every year. In some parts of England the open-field system can be traced back to before the Norman Conquest; traditionally the Laws of Ine (A.D. 688–94) are regarded as the first reference. Tangible traces of the pre-Conquest farming system, are, however, difficult to find.

There is some evidence in Shropshire to suggest that the three fields evolved from an earlier two-field system. The usage 'old field' may even refer back to an infield/outfield system. Under this system the 'infield' was permanently under cultivation, while the large 'outfield' was only cultivated periodically. It would seem natural for marginal hill settlements to begin with this method, rather than adopt a fully functioning three-field system. In the late Middle Ages a number of Shropshire manors had 'old' open-fields. At Smethcott, the Old Field and Lynch Field lay next to the church and the old village (now deserted); a third field called Stocking Field lies next to the new hamlet settled about 1300—'stocking' means 'a piece of land cleared of stumps'. References to other 'old fields' are to be found elsewhere in Shropshire; at Bromfield, for instance, Old Field is now part of Ludlow golf course, while at Chetton, near Bridgnorth, the area of the Old Field is clearly demarcated by a cluster of small irregular enclosures. In many parts of Shropshire the open-field names clearly demonstrate their origins as clearings; at Myddle, for instance, the fields were called Gorsty, Broomhurst and Woodfield.

There has in the past been some confusion about the

nature and extent of open-field farming in Shropshire. This has arisen largely because of the manner in which the open-fields were enclosed, normally by private agreement rather than by Act of Parliament. In the central-Midland counties, there were hundreds of Acts to enclose the open-fields while in Shropshire there were only seven (covering a mere 0·3 per cent of the total land area). This has led several writers to the conclusion that there was little open-field farming in the county.

Our picture of open-field Shropshire is not clarified by eighteenth- and nineteenth-century agricultural writers and topographers, who showed unusual reticence in their comments upon Shropshire's landscape. Arthur Young on a visit to Shropshire in 1785 merely remarked approvingly on "the Wrekin cut by enclosures three parts of the way up". While Bishton in the first Board of Agriculture Report (1794) on Shropshire simply notes, "the county did not contain much common field".[1] Accordingly it is necessary to look to older estate maps and documentary sources for any detailed account of enclosure and the survival of open-fields in Shropshire. A considerable number of seventeenth- and eighteenth-century estate maps in the Shropshire County Record Office and Shrewsbury Public Library clearly show remnants of the old strip system in the form of scattered parcels of land. In Volume 8 of the Victoria County History, it is demonstrated that in western Shropshire every village and township, however small, at one time possessed its own three-field system. Elsewhere in the county the story is much the same. H. L. Gray in his book, *English Field Systems*, written as long ago as 1915, recognised Shropshire as an open-field county and remarked that "only in the predilection for naming fields with reference to adjoining townships is there any variation from the

[1] A. Young, *Annals of Agriculture*, Vol. 4 (1785); J. Bishton, *General View of the Agriculture of Shropshire* (1794).

norm". A typical example of this is at Harley where the open-fields were called—the field towards Wigwig (or East Field), the field towards Blakeway (or West Field), and the field towards Cressage(or North Field). One possible reason for confusion over the field-system in Shropshire is that open-fields existed alongside enclosures from the late Middle Ages onwards. In many cases by the seventeenth century enclosed farmland was more extensive than the open-fields. A survey of the townships of Mawley and Prizeley in Cleobury Mortimer of 1582 records only eighty-two acres in the three open-fields compared with 314 acres of enclosed fields.

A valuable technique for examining the extent and nature of the open-fields is to study the relationship of ridge-and-furrow to datable earthworks or monuments. Ridge-and-furrow represents fossilised open-field strips in the form of distinctive regular ridges giving fields a corrugated appearance. Frequently there is a marked curve in the form of a reversed S. This *aratral* (plough) curve, as it is known, is normally only found in medieval strips and as a rule distinguishes genuine open-field strips from later land-drainage ridges. Shropshire is not particularly rich in good ridge-and-furrow, except along the alluvial terraces of the Severn. Elsewhere in the county the ridges tend to be narrow. This may result from a comparatively short period of open-field farming in some areas, but also reflects a concentration of open-field agriculture on the lighter soils, which do not maintain large ridges very well. A light cover of snow or even ground-frost, however, is often sufficient to demonstrate the existence of ridge-and-furrow in most parts of Shropshire. The snow collects in the furrows, thus throwing the ridges into relief.[2] Some strips have been

[2] This phenomenon is of value in the examination of earthworks of all periods, but especially deserted medieval settlements where the earthworks are often very shallow or appear to be very confused. (See Fig. 9.)

ploughed out completely, as can be seen in the remarkable air photograph of ridge-and-furrow crop-marks at Wroxeter (Plate 3), the darker lines marking the old furrows.

I know of no successful attempt to date ridge-and-furrow in Shropshire, but if we extend our vision just beyond Offa's Dyke into Wales and look at Hen Domen in Montgomeryshire, we can see an instance of pre-Conquest strip-farming. Here it has been demonstrated that the motte-and-bailey castle clearly rests on top of ridge-and-furrow.[3] The manor of Montgomery was 'waste' in 1066, and work started on the castle in 1071. Presumably the ridge-and-furrow represents part of the 'waste' arable, and presents us with irrefutable evidence for pre-Norman open-field farming in the area.

Apart from ridge-and-furrow, the open-fields manifest themselves in the landscape in other subtle ways. At Clee St Margaret near Brown Clee, the lines of the strips of Stanley Field are clearly mirrored in a series of parallel hedges to the north of the village. Nearby at Stanton Long lines of oak trees clearly reflect the old strip pattern. At Craven Arms, a nineteenth-century railway settlement, strips of one of the open-fields of Newton township were used as a basis for its layout. Thus the curving line of Albion Terrace mirrors the line of a strip from the open-fields (see Fig. 26, p. 253). Similarly, much nineteenth-century development at Market Drayton and Little Drayton was carried out within the framework of the old open-fields.

Early enclosure

Even in the Middle Ages there were hedges and fences in the Shropshire landscape; as early as 1321 an enclosed croft called 'Olderugges' was recorded in Stoke St Milborough. Much assarted land was clearly not absorbed into the open-

[3] P. A. Barker, *Chateau Gaillard III,* op. cit.

fields, and was enclosed in irregular fields with names such as 'gorsty', 'rough', 'stoney', 'woodhouse' and so on while the open-fields continued to operate. Within the open-fields, however, there appears to have been little enclosure until the sixteenth century, except around deserted or shrunken villages. At Cold Weston, on Brown Clee, the enclosure of the small open-fields, and their amalgamation into a single pastoral holding, occurred in the fifteenth century following the abandonment of the hamlet.

Elsewhere the traditional open-field system was buttressed by the manorial courts. At Shipton, for example, in 1553 a court order directed that "everyone doe plow the land so that the rainwater may run thereof". At Cleobury North in 1600 it was recorded that the three fields were Stablefield (oats), Oakwoodfield (corn) and Haymas field (fallow), and as late as 1657 the Corfton court directed inhabitants to keep their cattle out of Dogsdytch field until after the corn harvest. Indeed the manor court of Market Drayton continued to refer to the neglect of common obligations in the town fields right up until the end of the eighteenth century.

The first major record of enclosure was Wolsey's Inquisition (1517–18), an enquiry into the nature and extent of the enclosure of arable during the previous thirty years. Altogether in Shropshire it was claimed that some 1765 acres in seventy villages were enclosed, involving the displacement of 344 people. On the whole these enclosures appear to have been small. A typical case concerned the Prior of Wenlock, whom it was alleged, had enclosed thirty acres of arable at Purslow and then converted them into pasture. In so doing he caused two ploughs to be put down and brought twelve persons to poverty. Purslow, once head of the hundred of that name, is now a shrunken hamlet, a mile or so to the west of Clunbury.

In south Shropshire there appears to have been a considerable amount of enclosure in the foothills, where arable land was converted to pasture. It was at this time that the townships of Kinson, Bockleton, Downton and More in Stoke St Milborough shrank to isolated farms, bringing with them an enclosed pastoral landscape. Today the fields in this area are smaller and more irregular than in areas of later enclosure, and the hedges tend to be thicker and higher. By the end of the sixteenth century the county must already have been largely enclosed, for Shropshire was excluded from the last Act (1597) relating to depopulation because "it was best treated as a pastoral county". During the seventeenth century some enclosed parts of the county, particularly around Oswestry and Ellesmere, began to concentrate on dairy produce and out of eighteen livestock markets in Shropshire at this time no fewer than seven specialised in cattle.[4]

Enclosure and agricultural improvement

During the seventeenth and eighteenth centuries the remaining parcels of open-field arable were exchanged and hedged. This was largely accomplished by freeholders drawing up agreements to exchange and enclose land among themselves. In south Shropshire, for instance, the Baldwin family was particularly active and a document of 1630 notes that they had "set about with quickset" their recently exchanged lands in the Corvedale. And throughout the county enclosure was generally achieved without disturbance or resentment by means of a multiplicity of friendly exchanges. Richard Gough in his *History of Myddle* refers to recent enclosure of land in the Myddle Wood Field, when telling of a chase during the Civil War. Everywhere throughout northern and central Shropshire, manorial

[4] *The Agrarian History of England and Wales, 1500–1640*, Ed. Dr J. Thirsk, Vol. 4 (1967), p. 492. These were at Shrewsbury, Oswestry, Whitchurch, Ludlow, Bridgnorth, Wem and Newport.

records tell of the gradual eclipse of open-field strips and the creation of hedged fields. By the time John Ogilvy wrote his road book *Brittania* (1675) less than one fifth of Shropshire was still open-field compared to sixty or seventy per cent in other Midland counties. The final vestiges of the open-fields did not, however, disappear until the nineteenth century. The persistence of open-field farming in some areas can be linked with absentee landlords or poor farming techniques. But there does seem to be some geographical significance in the survival of open-fields in the flatter north-eastern parts of the county. In the western and southern hilly districts only small pockets of open-field strips survived into the eighteenth century, and indeed in many townships here enclosure had been completed by the end of the Middle Ages.

Shropshire differs from most Midland counties in that even where open-fields had survived until the end of the eighteenth century, they tended to be enclosed by agreement, often in a piecemeal manner, rather than by Act of Parliament. Only seven Acts were brought forward for the enclosure of open-fields in Shropshire. These were for Donnington (1773), Melverley, Kinnerley, Edgerley and Tir-y-Coed (1784 and 1789), Shifnal (1794) and finally Sheinton (1813). Enclosure here was undertaken so that the Earl of Darlington might create a large centralised farm, but the total area of open-field and meadow enclosed was only seventy-five acres; this was merely a clearing-up operation.

At Tugford a 1770 survey shows that although there had been considerable enclosure, one of the open-fields having been completely enclosed, there were open-strips in two surviving fields; at this time there were nine farms, three small holdings and ten cottages in the village. The largest farm, occupied by Silas Jones, was 185 acres consisting of sixty different parcels of land, many of which were less than one acre. The surviving open-fields were very small; Morehead Field was only eleven acres divided into fifteen strips and Lower Field was fifteen acres divided into twenty-nine strips. The final enclosure of the open-fields was achieved in the early nineteenth century when there was a re-organisation of farm holdings following the enclosure of common land in the parish. The nearby township of Broadstone on the other hand was still completely unenclosed at this date (Plate 18). Enclosure here was quite rapid and led to the shrinkage of the township in the early nineteenth century, and with the construction of a turnpike road by-passing Broadstone the settlement virtually disappeared.

The survival of open-fields in the county appears to have depended, partly at least, upon the inactivity of certain landlords. On the Craven estates considerable areas remained open until the early nineteenth century when there was a radical change in farming organisation engendered largely by the lengthy French wars. There are survivals, however, which are more difficult to explain. Several market towns kept their open-fields well into the eighteenth century; Bridgnorth was still working its three fields, Highfield, Conduit Field and Hookfield, in 1739 and Market Drayton was still surrounded by open-strips as late as 1779, as the remarkable town survey of that date demonstrates (Fig. 14). Open-fields at Ludlow and at Wellington also survived well into the century and at Shifnal, as we have seen, the open-fields were not eclipsed until 1794. It is possible that these town-fields were being worked largely as market gardens in the eighteenth century, but here is an obvious area for future research.

The gradual extinction of open-field agriculture cannot be completely divorced from the radical reorganisation of agriculture within the county. Apart from the enclosure of arable this resulted in the enclosure of considerable areas

Fig. 14. Plan of Market Drayton town and open-fields, 1787
Town plan (S.R.O. 327/1) showing the regular planned settlement of Market Drayton with its
intact open-field system.

of common land and marshland; the amalgamation of, and rationalisation of, farm holdings; better drainage, improved farming techniques and the wholesale rebuilding of farmhouses and outbuildings.

This activity was, in part, caused by the protracted Napoleonic wars which meant that all available land had to be farmed as effectively as possible. But there may be another reason why these changes came so rapidly in Shropshire. By 1801 almost half of Shropshire's population were no longer directly concerned with production of foodstuffs. Shropshire was well ahead of its time, for at the beginning of the nineteenth century, seventeen per cent of the population lived on and were occupied in the Shropshire coalfield, and a further twenty-five per cent lived in Shrewsbury and the other market towns. It would not be true to say that all these people were completely divorced from farming, but there was a rapidly rising population which was not self-sufficient. For example, by the end of the eighteenth century the Darby ironworks in Coalbrookdale were employing 1000 men. The industrial prosperity of this area was largely responsible for an extraordinary increase in population in the coalfield parishes between 1750 and 1800. Madeley parish, for example, grew rapidly as the following table shows:[5]

Jan. 1782	440 houses	560 families	2690 persons
Mar. 1793	754 houses	851 families	3677 persons
Mar. 1801	943 houses	943 families	4758 persons

This great local increase in population and the encroachment of industry on land capable of food-production made these parishes dependent on external supplies of corn, meat and milk. The demand for milk, and for fodder for the hundreds of horses, ponies and mules employed in the coalfield and in the entrepôt trade of the Severn, set a

[5] J. Plymley, *General View of Agriculture of Shropshire* (1803).

premium on pasture and meadowland of any description in the area. Some farmers, like Sergeant Roden of Benthal, found it profitable to reclaim the slag and spoil heaps. Edward Harries, looking over Roden's farm in 1795, remarked, "He has improved two large rough pastures, with several coal-pit mounts in them into valuable watered meadows."[6]

It was probably in the field of improved estate management, however, that the greatest changes were made. Loch, in his *Account of the Improvements on the Estate of the Marquis of Stafford*, published in 1820, writes graphically about the Lilleshall estate prior to its improvements:

the occupiers of land in each township resided together in the same village. Their houses and farm offices consisted of those strong-built, half-timbered buildings—more picturesque in their exterior appearance than commodious in their internal arrangement. Behind each house was placed the garden and hemp butt, and then a few closes of their best land. The remainder of their farm was scattered in every direction over the township. The closes were extremely small and of the most irregular shape. The fences both for their number and their breadth, occupied a large proportion of the land. The crookedness of the ditches, by keeping the water stagnant, added to, rather than relieved the wetness of the soil. [Numerous] lanes of communication winding backwards and forwards from field to field, occasioned a still further loss of ground, capable of cultivation. It is impossible in riding over the estates, to mistake the land which is so occupied. Its wornout condition, and the general slovenliness of its culture, points it out at once.

The proposed remedy for these ills was to enlarge and

---

[6] E. Harries, *Annals of Agriculture*, Vol. 26 (1795), p. 381.

reshape the fields, often creating completely new boundaries. The estate was drained with a regular system of channels and new buildings were constructed. In addition, common land was enclosed and improved and the squatters, who on the foothill commons were able to continue their semi-legal occupation, were 'brought under control'. These methods were applied elsewhere in the county; Harries considered that the number of farms in Shropshire had diminished by about one third over a period of thirty years (1770–1800); and Plymley (1803) wrote that the size of farms had increased in all parts of the county as two, three or even four farms were put together.

By the early years of the nineteenth century few areas of strip-farming remained—open-field farming was a thing of the past. Those few open-field strips that had survived were barely noticed against the background of an enclosed landscape. It is interesting, however, to see that as late as the first edition of the 25-inch Ordnance Survey Map (1888) small parcels of open-field strips still survived in places such as Harley.

In 1794 Bishton had complained about the inconvenience "of the property being detached and intermixed in small parcels" and "having the farm buildings in villages", and one of the results of enclosure and improvement was to create farms lying in their own consolidated holdings. During the eighteenth and nineteenth centuries dozens of large square brick or stone farmhouses were built well away from the old villages. Frequently these replaced farms that had previously been in the villages, thus further weakening the ancient settlement structure. In parts of Shropshire, enclosure was the final blow to many hamlets. The shrinkage of hamlets such as Lowe, Trench and Newton, all townships of Wem, to single farmsteads, dates from this final phase of enclosure. The area to the south-west of Wem is now one of shrunken hamlets and eighteenth-century farms with names such as New House, Woodlands and Grove. Finally a word on the dating of hedges. It has recently been suggested that it might be possible to date hedgerows from the number of tree species found within them; working on a rough scale of one species for every hundred years. In Shropshire, however, this theory cannot be readily applied as there has been a tradition, extending back over several centuries, of planting a number of species when building a hedge.[7]

SELECT BIBLIOGRAPHY

Dodd, P., 'The State of Agriculture in Shropshire, 1775–1825', *T.S.A.S.*, Vol. 55 (1956).
Fussell, G. E., 'Four Centuries of farming systems in Shropshire: 1500–1900', *T.S.A.S.*, Vol. 54 (1953).
Gonner, E. C. K., *Common Land and Enclosure* (1912).
Hardwick, William, 'Materials for a History of Shropshire (1832–38)', unpublished MS. William Salt Library, Stafford.
Howell, E. J., *The Land of Britain—Shropshire* (1941).
Orwin, C. S., and C. S., *The Open Fields* (1954).
Plymley, J., *General View of the Agriculture of Shropshire* (1803).
Tate, W. E., 'A Handlist of Shropshire Enclosures', *T.S.A.S.*, Vol. 52 (1948).
Victoria County History, *Shropshire*, Vol. 8.

7 M. Hooper, 'Dating Hedges', *Area*, 1970.

9. Enclosure of Common Land

Cottagers and squatters. Parliamentary enclosure. Upland commons. Moss and mere.

THE ENCLOSURE OF the open-fields cannot be seen in isolation from the general improvement in agricultural techniques and the enclosure of common land. This was possibly the most dramatic post-medieval landscape development in the county, resulting in the improvement of thousands of acres of open heath and mossland. 'Common' is strictly a legal term used to cover a variety of landscapes, ranging from lowland mosses to highland moor. They share the name 'common' because they were normally areas of uncultivated land on which manorial tenants enjoyed certain grazing and gathering rights.

Generally the lowland commons coincided with areas of exceptionally light soils, often podsols, and before they could be cultivated profitably they often required considerable improvement. In some cases they represented the remnants of once extensive forest areas. Morfe Forest, which by the eighteenth century was no more than a scrub-heath, was co-extensive with an outcrop of Bunter Pebble beds (see Fig. 7). In the north of the county, heaths such as Prees lay in the area of 'hungry' soils, which originally carried an open woodland cover, but prehistoric man, attracted to the lighter soils in the area, changed the vegetation regime by repeated burning.

Considerable areas of common land survived into the nineteenth century in Shropshire. In some cases this was

due to the hostility to enclosure displayed by tenants en-
joying common rights; elsewhere, there was no clear
lead because of a complex of smallholdings and sometimes
the commons were simply left alone because of the inactivity
of an absentee landlord. The enclosure of common land
in Shropshire was a protracted affair, which started in
the Middle Ages and was not completed until the
late nineteenth century. Indeed, even today nearly
14,000 acres of common land have survived and remain
open.

Cottagers and squatters

Before examining more organised attempts at enclosure we
should first look at the unofficial activities of the squatters
—groups of settlers who made a considerable impact upon
the Shropshire landscape. From the sixteenth century
onwards landless and unattached groups of people began to
settle in humble dwellings on the edges of heath and moorland. The squatter movement had much in common with
earlier medieval assarting, and in some ways can be seen
simply as a continuation of this process on to the upland
heath areas. Such was the extent of squatter settlement in the
north during the early seventeenth century that Garbet in
The History of Wem (1818) records that the manor and parish
were "overcharged with divers poor cottages". They
erected small one-storey cottages normally half-timbered in
the north and stone in the south. Some were even built of
turf, such as those recorded on Pontesbury Hill in 1793,
but naturally enough none of these has survived. Attached
to the cottages were irregular enclosures of up to three acres.
Although normally the squatters clustered around the edge
of the commons, Dr St Joseph's photograph of Lubberland
common on Catherton Clee Hill shows a splendid example
of how the squatters settled 'island' encroachments well

into the common and later these have been joined together (Plate 19).

The squatters were normally there on the sufferance of the lord of the manor, although in some cases on the Clee hills and the Stiperstones cottagers were enticed on to common land by lords who needed labour for their nearby quarries and mines. Usually they were required to pay an annual rent of 6d. or 1s. Many squatter cottages have survived and can be seen ringing the area of enclosed common or encircling an existing common; normally, however, the original cottages have been encased or completely rebuilt in brick or stone. The first documentary record of squatters dates from the early sixteenth century, but they may well have begun their activities earlier. One of the first known references to squatter-cottages was at Kenley in 1537, where by the end of the sixteenth century there were twelve cottages on the common. At the time of enclosure in 1793 the rector of Kenley received an allotment of thirty acres as glebe and he divided this into ten lots "to accommodate the poor families of the common who had the largest families".[1] Evidence of the Kenley squatters still remains in the form of irregular enclosures and small stone cottages, many of them in ruins. Elsewhere cottagers fared a little better and Bayston Hill, now effectively a suburb of Shrewsbury, started life as a squatter settlement.

Cottages were often built near to extractive industries and many of the squatters were part-time coal-miners, lead-miners, or quarrymen. Annscroft, to the south-west of Shrewsbury, grew up in the early nineteenth century, when it was almost exclusively occupied by miners working at the Moat Hall Colliery. No houses stood there in 1802, but there were about nine by 1827 and the settlement had almost reached its present size by 1841. There was also extensive squatter settlement on the edge of marsh and mossland

[1] Victoria County History, *Shropshire*, Vol. 8, p. 95.

prior to enclosure. A small group of squatters' cottages, near to West Felton, known ominously as Grimpool (now called 'Grimpo'), was typical of such settlements. Today most of the old cottages stand empty and derelict.

Parliamentary enclosure

We must now look at more regulated attempts at enclosure by Act of Parliament. There were over seventy acts dealing with open common land in Shropshire. It is significant that thirty-seven of these acts were brought forward during the period of land-hunger of the French wars. Not all eighteenth- and nineteenth-century enclosure in the county was parliamentary, but the movement certainly acted as a stimulus. The first Act related to Newport Marsh and was passed in 1764; the final Act, concerning upland common in Llanfair Waterdine, was not passed until July 1891.

During the French wars open common land was viewed unfavourably by agricultural commentators. The prevalent attitude towards the commons is reflected in this extract from Bishton's *Report on Shropshire* (1794):

> The idea of leaving them [the commons] in their un-improved state to bear chiefly gorse bushes and fern is now completely scouted except by a few who have falsely conceived that the enclosing of them is an injury to the poor; but if these persons had seen as much of the contrary effects in that respect as I have, I am fully persuaded their opposition would at once cease. Let those who doubt go round the commons now open, and view the miserable huts and poor, ill-cultivated, impoverished spots erected or rather thrown together and enclosed by themselves . . .

The process of enclosure is best observed by examining

an omnibus award. In 1795 an Act was passed to enclose 2550 acres of land in north Shropshire; it was concerned with waste and common land in the townships of Prees, Darleston, Fauls, Mickley, Willaston, Moreton Say, Longford, and Stanton upon Hine Heath. Three commissioners, Henry Bowman, Valentine Vickers and Arthur Davies, were appointed and were on oath to carry out their duties "faithfully, impartially and honestly . . . without favour or affection to any person whatsoever". Public notice was given in church of the meetings, and all claims made were scrutinised and could be objected to. If need arose legal opinion could be taken on doubtful claims.

A surveyor was appointed to "form roads which had to be at least forty feet wide". These had to be completed within two years of enclosure. Such enclosure roads in Shropshire were largely limited to heathy upland and lowland moor, particularly in the north and east of the county. The old tracks were closed and new roads constructed in the enclosed area; these were wide and straight. The enclosure roads did not follow geographical features, but were systematically and often geometrically laid down by the commissioners. Consequently, short stretches of enclosure road contrast strikingly with the older roads; often the meeting place of the two types of road is marked by an awkward turn. Enclosure roads were a statutory width, normally forty feet, but varying with the status of the settlements they were linking. Rural depopulation in some areas has meant that some roads run between isolated farms. Accordingly, the metalled area of the small road necessary occupies only about half of the available area. Thus many enclosure roads in remote rural areas are characterised by wide grass verges (Plate 20).

The expenses of enclosure, except for fencing, were met by selling part of the commons. In all, the enclosure cost just over £3000—£1 3s. 6d. an acre—on top of which fencing for the new allotments had to be paid for by individual allotment holders.

The commissioners then divided the lands among the freeholders. First they gave Sir Richard Hill and his brother John "one full fourteenth part and also all pools and fisheries thereon", in lieu of their joint manorial rights over the common. The poor and the squatters were hardly considered and their common rights were completely extinguished. All squatter settlements made more than twenty years before were given outright to the lord. Later encroachments were to be allotted to him as part of his share as lord of the manor. From the number of squatters' houses that remain, there does not seem to have been any great destruction of cottages in Prees, but there was in Moreton, Longford and Stanton. It was not popular to pull down a cottage, and when purchasing a piece of land with a cottage on it one prospective buyer insisted that the cottage and cottager be removed before he even considered buying.

Next came the power to exchange and consolidate land in these and adjoining parishes, a power which was used to exchange three 'doles' owned by the parson, totalling about two acres and lying right in the middle of Squire John Hill's land. These were relics of the open-fields, for they represented the old balks for dividing furlongs. This provision also enabled Sir Andrew Corbet to reshuffle his very strictly tied estate and to sell a large part of it.

Following the Act there was a considerable amount of enclosure by agreement, and altogether another 1000 acres in Hadnall and Marchamley Woods, Ightfield Heath and Cotton Wood were privately enclosed. This substantial piece of legislation resulted in a landscape of large regular fields, enclosed with hawthorn hedges and wide straight roads over a large area of north-east Shropshire. Apart from a new road-system, straight drainage ditches were dug and new farmhouses created. Although parts of the north

Shropshire heathland have now partly reverted to waste, most of the region is comparatively prosperous. The overall effect of parliamentary enclosure was to convert an area largely made up of heath and moor into one great dairy farm. Often the only indication of former heathland is given by bracken and ferns growing in the hedgerows.

Parliamentary enclosure was frequently used to tidy up old piecemeal enclosure. Comparison of a series of maps of the part of Shirlett Forest that lay in Acton Round near Much Wenlock is instructive (Fig. 15). In 1625 the area,

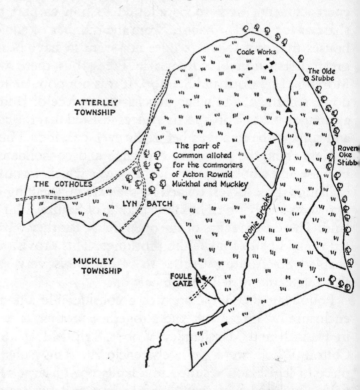

Fig. 15. Enclosure of common land in Acton Round
Plans showing progress of encroachment of enclosure: 1661 (S.R.O. Forester Collection) (*above*), 1725 (S.R.O. 1093/Box 159) (*top, opposite*) and 1838 (tithe award).

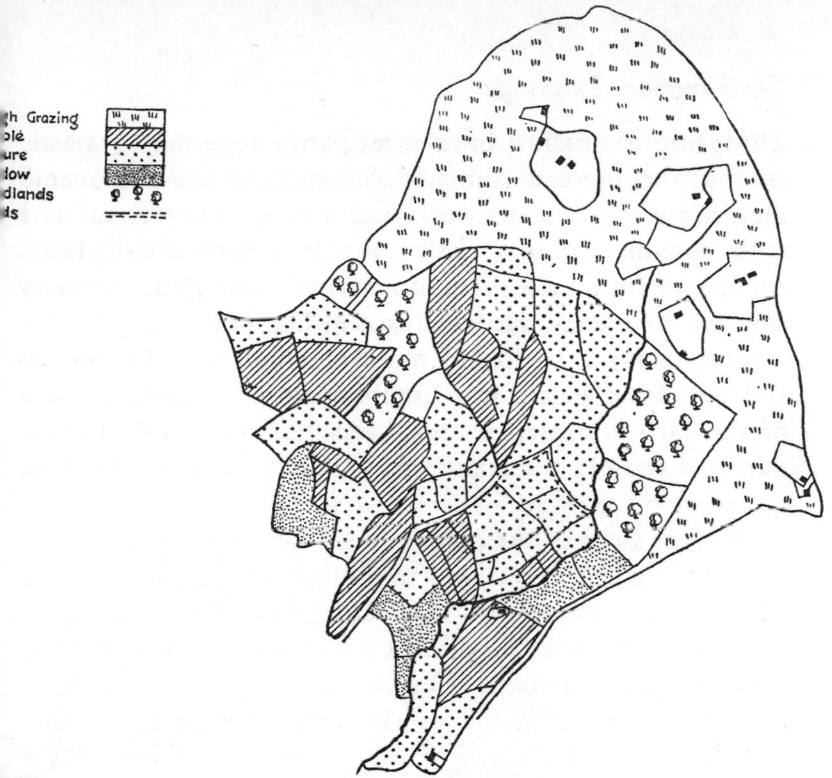

h Grazing
blé
ure
low
dlands
ds

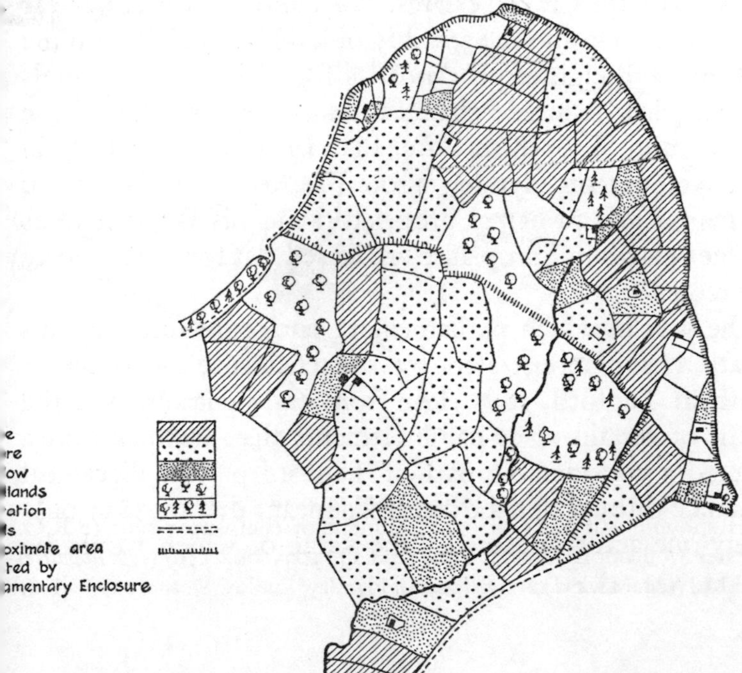

e
re
ow
lands
ation
s
oximate area
red by
amentary Enclosure

which had originally been wooded, was open rough grazing, common to the townships of Acton Round. At this time there were a few squatter encroachments, mainly associated with coal-mining. By 1725 there had been considerable encroachment on the common, and two coppices had been planted for use by the local iron industry. In 1814 an Act was passed for the enclosure of the remainder of the common and by 1838 the area was totally enclosed, although some of the ancient squatter enclosures had survived. Today, much of the old common area has been reafforested, thus completing the cycle.

In other parts of the county parliamentary enclosure had a catalytic effect upon land utilisation and farm holdings. The introduction of an Enclosure Act appears to have stimulated the rationalisation of farming on some estates, notably those of Lord Craven in southern Shropshire. A series of estate maps of the 1770s demonstrates that fossilised open-fields and widely dispersed holdings were common on the Craven estates. The continuation of 99-year leases after 1800 and the stability of land tenure between the sixteenth and eighteenth centuries found in Craven rentals suggest that tenurial changes here were behind those elsewhere in Shropshire. After his visit to Stanton Lacy in 1793 Archdeacon Plymley wrote "Lord Craven is lord of the manor and principal proprietor, but his farms here as in other places in Shropshire are leased out for lives at very low rents."[2]

The way in which parliamentary enclosure resolved this situation is demonstrated by the enclosure of Balaam's Heath in Tugford. It is clear from early charters and the extent of certain place-name elements that heathland once covered a considerable part of Tugford parish. Piecemeal clearance throughout the centuries meant that by 1815 only ninety-one acres remained, "the value of which would be

[2] B.M., Add. MS. 21018, Archdeacon Plymley, Ludlow Deanery visitation.

considerably increased if it were enclosed".[3] In the award
Lord Craven was allotted seventy-three acres and the
remainder was divided between the other six freeholders of
Tugford. Lord Craven's allotment was a large central block
which would have left the heath looking very much as it
had before; however, the old roads and bridleways were
stopped and new roads created. Once initial enclosure had
been achieved, Craven proceeded with other important
agrarian changes. The Craven allotment was fenced and a
large surrounding area was rearranged. By the 1840s the
newly enclosed area of Balaam's Heath had been divided by
Craven between two principal landholders and was mainly
arable. The enclosure of Balaam's Heath and the con-
sequent rationalisation of holdings resulted in the virtual
extinction of the hamlet of Baucott; there were only two
tenants here in 1841, compared to eight in 1770.

A series of Acts (1801–20) were passed to improve the
Lord Stafford's estates in eastern Shropshire, particularly in
the Weald Moors. During improvements executed under the
Act, a young permanent surveyor, under the guidance of
Telford, was appointed, and many miles of private and
public roads were repaired. James Loch in his *Account of
the Improvements of the Estate of the Marquis of Stafford* (1820)
states, "parishioners were employed in quarrying cinders
and slag from the Donnington iron works and the material
conveyed on rails constructed for the purpose." The roads
were kept in repair by the landlord's own workmen and the
tenants charged with the expense. The resulting landscape
is one of distinctive regular flat fields, large isolated
brickfarms with occasional shelter-belts of mixed woodland
to help prevent soil erosion. Here, as in the region of the
north Shropshire mosses, the roads stand on ridges. The
comparatively late prosperity of the area resulted in villages
such as Preston, Kynnersley and Cherrington being rebuilt

[3] S.R.O. Dep. plans, B.37.

in the eighteenth and nineteenth centuries, and accounts for the later brick-built parish churches found in the area.

Upland commons

During the nineteenth century considerable areas of upland common were enclosed, largely by Act of Parliament. Some areas were enclosed and cultivated, but the majority were simply demarcated to demonstrate ownership and remained visually unchanged.

Despite a series of Acts, passed to enclose the Clee hills, much open common remains there today. In 1809 an Act was passed to enclose the common land in Abdon and Stoke St Milborough on Brown Clee.[4] To meet the expenses of enclosure, something like a third of the allotments were put up for public auction and realised £3803. Most plots were bought by local farmers; one exception to this was Samuel Childs, a squatter coal-miner, who bought a small allotment next to his encroachment. It appears from contemporary accounts, however, that the Clee miners were generally impoverished and dependent upon their harvest earnings to supplement their wages.

The effects of parliamentary enclosure on the landscape can be seen on the ground today. The lots sold by auction were hedged with quickset bushes, frequently interspersed with small trees and a few with dry stone walls; in the late nineteenth century most of the remaining open allotments were fenced and the grazing land improved. This has resulted in a striking contrast along the parish boundary between Stoke St Milborough which has improved pasture up to 1300 feet, and Clee St Margaret which has remained open rough grazing. Clee St Margaret was never enclosed, probably because there was a multiplicity of smallholders in the parish. Further awards for enclosing on Brown Clee

4 S.R.O. Dep. plans, B.21 and B.22.

appeared in 1813 (Netchwood Common) and Ditton Priors (1841).

Despite the theoretical extinction of common rights of grazing arising from enclosure, the summit of the Brown Clee remains one of the largest areas of open common in Shropshire. Freeholders are supposed to graze their animals in certain specified areas, but the wild nature of the country makes this impossible in practice. One positive result of enclosure was to push the frontier of farming up the slopes of the hills where it has remained to this day.

In the middle of the nineteenth century considerable areas of upland common in the old Clun Forest were enclosed by Act of Parliament. Between 1845 and 1891 some 20,000 acres were affected. These acts covered some of the remotest country in Shropshire, for instance in 1847 "a tract of unenclosed Common Land in the Honour or Lordship and Forest of Clun" amounting to 8600 acres was enclosed, and in 1858 a further 3580 acres was the subject of an Enclosure Award (Plate 21). As a result of Acts passed in 1852, 1865 and 1880, over 2000 acres in the parish of Llanfair Waterdine alone were enclosed. And the final Act concerning Shropshire completed the enclosure of the parish in 1891. This area, still forming part of the wildest and most exciting countryside in Shropshire, is now traversed by fences, hedges and stone walls dating from enclosure. Over the past decades the Forestry Commission has been particularly active in this area of south-west Shropshire and many hillslopes in the Clun region carry a cover of coniferous woodland.

Not all upland commons, however, were enclosed by Act of Parliament. Some commons in western Shropshire, notably Bromlow, Meadowtown and Hope in Worthen parish (over 600 acres), were quietly enclosed by agreement in the first half of the nineteenth century. On the first survey for the Old Series Ordnance Survey (1816, for this part of Shropshire) these commons were open. By the 1840s they had been converted into a pattern of straight-hedged fields some with new smallholdings, others in large blocks attached to established farms. Hope Common, in particular, consisted of a dense pattern of twenty-four smallholdings on only 110 acres. The commons in those townships held by a single estate, such as Rorrington in Chirbury Parish (400 acres) and Gatten in Ratlinghope (385 acres), remained in the sole use of large farms. Under such strong landownership it was therefore easy for ancient common rights to be replaced by alternative terms in new farm leases. Since then the landowners have been free to let their uplands for forestry as well as for grazing.

Finally, reference should be made to the surviving commons. There are sixty-one in Shropshire totalling 13,798 acres. The largest of these is the Long Mynd. The whole area of 6550 acres, over ten square miles, is common land and most is good sheep-run (Plate 21). Immediately to the east of the Long Mynd in the central north–south valley of Shropshire is the resort town of Church Stretton, which grew up largely in the post-railway era. From here extensive use is made of walks passing up and on to the Long Mynd. Consequently the common has considerable amenity value, a value which is likely to increase greatly in the foreseeable future.

Apart from the Clee common, the remainder tend to be small, normally less than 100 acres, and some, such as the Shruggs on Nesscliffe hill, are only a quarter of an acre in all. They normally represent land that has escaped enclosure because it is too poor, or because of tenurial problems, or simply because it was too small to warrant an enclosure agreement.

Moss and mere

The Shropshire meres and mosses consist of a series of water and peat-filled hollows in the glacial drift which covers the Shropshire–Cheshire plain. These sites tend to occur in clusters in various parts of the region, the most important being the group around Ellesmere and Whitchurch on the border between north Shropshire and the detached part of Flint called Maelor Saesneg. Often they were bordered by more conventional heathlands, from which they differ by virtue of the fact that when improved they often became agriculturally productive, and the process of drainage and enclosure that went on from the sixteenth century in northern and eastern Shropshire has produced a distinctive landscape type. The north Shropshire mosses are now largely given over to dairy farming with some arable fields on the better drained sands and gravels.

Forest clearance in the area proceeded, on the drier soils at least, from Neolithic times. A great deal of Middle Bronze Age material has been recovered from the Shropshire peat mosses, both in the north of the county, and in the Weald Moors. These antiquities normally lie underneath the peat, which formed almost certainly during the wet phase of the late Bronze Age onwards.

Little historical work has been carried out on the Shropshire mosses and we can certainly learn more of man's early influence on the landscape from these deposits than from documents. The mosses almost certainly originally carried an open wood cover. During the improvement of the mosses, fir-wood stumps and trunks were frequently found; oaks, for instance, were discovered in the peat at Dudleston Heath in 1602. And prior to enclosure Brown Moss was covered with thickets of birch and furze. Until the second half of the sixteenth century, when peat cutting, drainage and reclamation became extensive and systematic, the true mosses and valley fens appear to have remained largely undisturbed. They were the haunt of hunters and fishermen; Eyton quotes a survey of 1309 which includes the following description:

> The *stagna* (meres) of Ellesmere, *Culghmere* (Cole Mere), *Croulesmere* (Cross Mere), *Swotlemere* (Sweat Mere), *Chetelmere* (Kettle Mere), *Poulesmere* (possibly Newton Mere), *Blakemere*, and *Whitemere* and other meres, with a weir at Warchet, were worth, in respect of the fisheries thereof, £13 6s. 8d. per annum, and not more because the tenants fished when they pleased, except in the month of May, in Ellesmere-mere.[5]

And there are several references to medieval hunting and trapping activities in the area. Little information has survived about early attempts to drain the mosslands, although a survey of Ellesmere manor of 1280 includes a reference to 563½ acres of assarted land, indicating extensive colonisation in the area.[6] Numerous traces of moated farmsteads, such as Highfield and Northwood near Wem, are to be found in these damper areas of north Shropshire, and undoubtedly many other farmsteads in this region were originally moated. Elsewhere in the county we have seen that moated farms were normally associated with medieval colonisation. It is reasonable therefore to associate these sites with the period of freehold-farming expansion in the thirteenth and early fourteenth centuries.

In time these areas adjoining the true mosslands became comparatively prosperous. The moated farms were replaced by a series of fine half-timbered houses, such as those on the south-eastern side of Whixall Moss; Alkington Hall and Bostock Hall (sixteenth century), Sandford Hall and Lowe

---

[5] Eyton, op. cit., Vol. 10, p. 244.
[6] 'Extent of the Mannor of Ellesmere 1280', *T.S.A.S.,* Vol. 23 (1899). The place-names Abbey Green, Stanley Green and Paddolgreen, all contain the medieval clearing element 'green'. 'Heath' is another common clearing element found in the area.

Hall (seventeenth century) and Northwood Hall (eighteenth century) all lie within a few miles of each other. This pattern of fine country houses, many of them half-timbered, is found extensively in Cheshire, but is also repeated in Shropshire around the Baggy Moor with houses such as Wycherley and Ellesmerc itself at Oteley[7] (see Plate 17). Such early improvement was concerned largely with marginal land adjoining the meres and mosses. When cleared and cultivated they proved to be extremely fertile.

In north-west Shropshire, in the vicinity of the meres and mosses, despite the medieval colonisation, there was dense forest until the early sixteenth century. However, between 1550 and 1650 there was rapid clearance especially in Wem, Myddle and Whitchurch lordships; the process was accelerated by the demands of eager landlords who encouraged glassworks in the late sixteenth century and sold wood to ironmasters from the late 1620s.[8] The clearances provided new pasture and with it the need for more winter feed and consequently for meadowland. Attention therefore turned to the inhospitable mosses as a source both for fuel and meadowland. Peat-cutting on a large scale appears to have begun at about the same time as regulated attempts at enclosure. Cutting began in the area of Wem Moss about 1560 and at Brown Moss, near Whitchurch, by 1572; the pools on the latter site appear to have been caused by denudation of the peat to drift level.

One of the earliest recorded accounts of mossland enclosure concerned a typical marsh-common (the Dogmore)

---

7 J. Peake, *Ellesmere* (1889). An etching of the old Oteley Hall shows it to have been an extensive half-timbered mansion. It was pulled down about 1770.

8 J. Lawson, 'Historical investigation of lowland basin sites in Shropshire', *Proceedings of a Meres and Mires Conference, Attingham Park, Dec. 1965*, Ed. P. Oswald and A. Herbert. Glass required a considerable quantity of timber for fuel. Recently a series of glassworking sites have been identified in this area, notably at Ruyton-Eleven-Towns, Whitchurch and Cheswardine.

lying a mile to the south of Prees on the edge of Prees Green. In 1539, Rowland Lee, Lord Bishop of Lichfield and Coventry, and President of the Council of the Marches, sold about 200 acres of Dogmore to Sir Richard Brereton of Cheshire. The land was typical waste:

> the same was allways in wynter and in somer also so myry and depe of watter that no cattall coulde fede or pasture thereon, nor any profit coulde be taken thereof, onles it were a very harde frost in the wynter tyme that some of the tenants of Press wolde cut and fell certen woode and pooles [poles] ther and so dragge the same upon the Ise with ropes throughe the grounde for other wise they coulde not carry it off.

Brereton proceeded to enclose, and in all spent about 1000 marks in the purchase and the "stockyng, dytching and mending of the Moore". But the tenants of Prees were at once up in arms, as they considered the more common land, although it had been leased as long ago as the thirteenth century, but had reverted to waste and was listed as one of the decayed lands of the manor. The tenants, however, had a masterful man to deal with in the bishop and when they made an affray on one Thomas Taylor, a servant of Sir Richard Brereton, the ringleaders were sent to Montgomery Castle. Roger Bromley continues the story, when "ryding with the said late Bysshop Rowland at about such tyme, as about the nomber of fourtie wyfes of Prees came and mett hym to th' entent to complayne [about the loss of their husbands?] as he supposeth. And one of them rudely began to take his horse by the bridell whereat the horse sprang aside and put the said Bysshop in danger of a fall." Eventually Bishop Rowland persuaded the tenants to allow him "to let Dogmore to whom it lysted him to lett the same". But this was only after an action in the Court of the Marches, which had ordered the land to be "meted and bounded", and referred the dispute to the Manor Court.

Despite further argument, Sir Richard had peace for eight years and completely reclaimed the land, so that it was then worth forty marks a year compared with 12d. formerly. He built two houses and gathered some good "croppes of hoppes and saffaron" by 1549, when, in the words of Reignold Bingham "being tennant to Sir Richard", and "dwelling on one of the tenements erected by him upon Bogmore", he was "expulsed thereof by the tennants of Prees to the number of 100 persons urged on by Master Banaster in Great Rowte and by them the same house was ov'thrown and pulled down and the saffaron and hoppes ther growing they did distroye and spoyle and cutt up the quicke sett ther". Brereton apparently recovered possession, for eighteen months later "Sir Richard Brereton with John Dode Esquire the Justice of the Peax in the Shire" went "to Dogmore to appease a great tumults of the Tennants ther gathered together . . . but Dode declared . . . that he went not thether with him", as he "was dysseasid of a styche". It is surprising how ill the very thought of 100 able-bodied rioters can make one feel. Ironically enough, Mathew Harward, the leader of the rioters, was rewarded by the manor tenants for his efforts to prevent the enclosure, by a grant of twenty acres of waste for him to enclose.

Eventually Brereton had his claim upheld by the Star Chamber and was later able to sell the improved estate for £1000. Later a small cottage settlement grew up, and although rather shrunk, still survives today. Dogmore was later subject to parliamentary enclosure, which removed many of the small enclosures and created a landscape of regular hedges, ditches and roads. Nearby, Lawrence Bannister, high steward of Wem in 1586, "by ditching, draining, and stocking, made divers parcels" of the Old

Pool Marsh "firm land which he enclosed for his own use or set to undertenants".

A less turbulent story of enclosure is told of Tetchill Moor on the Duke of Bridgewater's estate near Ellesmere in the early seventeenth century. Mr Gosse, one of the participants in the agreement, wrote that prior to enclosure the moor was "a great waste of mosse and morishe ground overflowed with water and overgrown with alders and other underwood of no great value". He went on to say that it was so rotten, that a man could in most places thrust a spear in it and find no bottom. After Gosse had noticed that some pieces on the edge of the moor had become good meadow following enclosure he decided to dig a ditch to drain the land and lease it. Eventually some 450 acres out of 730 acres were improved. Gosse claimed that when the alders and brush were cut, the land proved to be very good, both for corn and grass, while the lower ground was good meadow.[9]

One of the major problems involved in this type of improvement was the shrinkage and lowering of the ground surface resulting from drainage. Gosse himself writes, that following the initial cutting the moor sunk "a full yard". Windmills proved too fickle and it was not until the use of the steam-engine in the nineteenth century that recurrent flooding could be avoided.[10] Even so, much of the land is now sunk to such an extent that the roads and even the drainage channels stand well above the adjacent fields.

In eastern Shropshire an extensive tract of marshland known as the Weald Moors was subject to attempts at improvement from the mid-sixteenth century onwards.

[9] S.R.O. (Bridgewater Collection), Ellesmere and Tetchill papers.

[10] Windmills were certainly used to drain marshy arable land; both Prees (1517) and Ellesmere (1602) had open fields called 'Windmill field'. The fact that a windmill is portrayed in a fifteenth-century stained-glass window at St John's Chapel, Ludlow, suggests that they were not an uncommon sight in Shropshire.

Plate 20 A straight parliamentary enclosure road at Hopton Wafers near Cleobury Mortimer, dating from 1866. Note the wide verges and ferns growing in the hedge, a legacy from when the area was open common land.

Plate 21 Regular parliamentary enclosure on Hopesay hill in the foreground, with the Stretton hills in the background. This area was enclosed in 1858. Several of the fields have reverted to rough grazing on the higher ground.

Plate 22 The town plan of Clun, 1883 (first edition 25-inch Ordnance Survey). The ancient settlement lay around St George's church, while the medieval planned town was developed, together with the castle, in the bend of the river. High Street seems to have been the first element in the plantation. There has been little post-medieval expansion here.

Plate 23   Air photograph of the deserted medieval town at Caus, Westbury parish. The remains of the stone castle are tree-covered, while the outer defences of the town run parallel to the road in the foreground.

Plate 24 A vertical air photograph of Ludlow, clearly showing the regular planned nature of the settlement, together with the castle and town walls. Note the colonisation in the High Street to the east of the castle. Outside the town walls on the east there has been some suburban and industrial development.

The Weald Moors were mosslands based on glacial drift and historically were occupied by small villages lying on higher land between the damp open marshes. A series of maps deposited in the Shropshire Record Office show that a complicated system of rivers and streams, with artificial channels or strines, was already in existence by 1600. A picture of the Weald Moors before these improvements is given by George Plaxton, a rector of Kinnersley in the middle decades of the seventeenth century. He writes:

> All that vast morass was called Weald Moor, or Wild Moor, i.e. the Woody Moor . . . and I have been assured from aged people that all the Wild Moores were formerly so far overgrown by rubbish wood such as alders, willows, salleys, thorns, and the like, that the inhabitants commonly hang'd bells about the necks of their cows that they might the more easily find them.

These moors were the last remnants of this 'morass' to be enclosed. The remainder, "that great tract, formerly called *Vasta Regalis*", had by Plaxton's time, "by draining, become good pasturage". He adds, "it yields great quantities of hay though much of it is of such a nature that it will dry up a new milch cow, starve an horse, yet it will feed an ox to admiration". Immediately prior to enclosure and improvement the Moors could be grazed for part of the summer season only, and were inundated after a heavy rainfall.[11]

The total impression made by the Sutherland maps is that in the sixty years following the dissolution of the monasteries considerable piecemeal efforts were being made by the new landowners, such as the Levesons and Eytons, to improve their estates and deal with the problems of

[11] Rev. George Plaxton, 'Some natural observations in the Parishes of Kinnardsley and Donnington in Shropshire', *Philosophical Transactions*, Vol. 25 (1673).

drainage. They were responsible for improvements connected with Black Dyke, New Piece Ditch and Hooke Ditch; and the creation of many smaller strines on the newly-divided moors. It was this system which in the nineteenth century was improved by substituting a few large channels for many small ditches.

The enclosure of Whixall Moss, which lies mainly in Cheshire, was also undertaken in several stages, initially by agreement and later by Act of Parliament. Here a considerable area consisted of open heath and mossland and enclosure has resulted in a remarkable landscape of small enclosures, narrow lanes, and scattered red-brick houses. And as in most areas of dispersed late settlement, small brick Nonconformist chapels are common. Articles of Agreement (a forerunner of the Enclosure Award) were drawn up for the drainage and enclosure of Whixall Moss in 1704. A further attempt to enclose the remaining area (some 887 acres) was made when the Enclosure Act (1823) was passed. This, too, was not absolutely successful, and some of the enclosed land later reverted to fenland, and indeed the whole of the mossland area is still dotted with numerous pools as well as the surviving meres.

One of the last major improvements carried out in the county concerned the low-lying valley of the River Perry to the north of Ruyton-Eleven-Towns. Previously this region had been inhospitable and barren. On Rocque's Map of Shropshire (1752) Baggy Moor, as it was known, was the most extensive remaining area of marshland in the county. But after an act was passed (1861), the river was dredged and straightened and all weirs, dams and fords along it were removed. Consequently some 1290 acres in the parishes of Baschurch, Hordley, Stanwardine, Weston Lullingfields and Stanwardine in the Fields were improved. New straight drains and enclosures were laid out and the area is today one of prosperous mixed farming.

On the whole, the true meres were less susceptible to exploitation, except as fisheries, and information about them is scanty. It is clear that former meres near Ellesmere, now Pikesend Moss (Pyklesmere in 1302) and Whattall Moss, have changed by natural succession. At the latter site a dug-out canoe, probably of the early Iron Age, was found at the base of the peat. However, drainage has occurred where conditions were suitable. Between 1553 and 1619 a pool of 200 acres near Wem (in the region of Lower Pools Farm) was drained and converted to meadow. Richard Gough in his *History of Myddle* tells of the drainage of Heremeare (now Harmer Moss) when "Sir Andrew Corbett and Mr Kelton caused this meare to be loosened and made dry and converted it to a meadow and pasture."

Changes have also been made in the levels of several other meres. There are ornamental plantations with exotic conifers and rhododendrons about the shores of some, and activities such as fishing and sailing are beginning to have an impact on the bird population. About four fifths of the peatland acreage of North Shropshire is now wholly reclaimed and under pasture, including a former market-gardening belt on the fringe of Whixall Moss. None of the mosses has escaped at least partial drainage and burning. Of those still waste a few, for instance Whattall and Pikesend Mosses, are afforested, and the Whixall–Fenn's Moss area is exploited by an efficient peat-cutting industry. The black peat is now cut for domestic use only and it is the white peat that is finding an expanding horticultural market.

SELECT BIBLIOGRAPHY

Garbet, *History of Wem* (1818).

Gough, R., *History of Myddle*. New edn. with Introduction by W. G. Hoskins (1968).

Hill, M., 'The Wealdmoors, 1560–1660', *T.S.A.S.,* Vol. 54 (1953).

Hoskins, W. G., and Dudley Stamp, L., *The Common Lands of England and Wales* (1963).

Howell, E. J., *The Land of Britain—Shropshire.*

Pannet, D., 'Commons of the Stiperstones area', *Bulletin Shropshire Conservation Trust,* No. 17 (1969).

Plymley, J., *General View of the Agriculture of Shropshire.*

Sinker, C. A., 'The North Shropshire Meres and Mosses: A background for Ecologists', *Field Studies,* Vol. 4 (1962).

Sylvester, Miss D., *The Rural Landscape of the Welsh Borderland* (1969).

Tate, W. E., 'A Handlist of English Enclosure Acts and Awards', *T.S.A.S.,* Vol. 52 (1958).

Whitfield, J. R. W., 'The Enclosure Movement in North Shropshire', *T.C.S.V.S.,* Vol. 11 (1939).

10. Towns

New towns.   Ludlow.   Bridgnorth.   Shrewsbury.

OUTSIDE THE COUNTY town of Shrewsbury there has
been little suburban development in Shropshire and many
of the old market towns are no larger than many Midland
villages. For although the Industrial Revolution had its
origins in Shropshire, the county did not experience the
urban explosion found in other industrial areas during the
nineteenth and twentieth centuries.

Today many of the market centres are static or even in a
state of decline. Bishop's Castle, for instance, which was
until recently the smallest English borough, with a population of just over 1200, lost its municipal status in 1965.
Of the ancient towns only Shrewsbury, still acting as a
regional capital for central Wales and the Marches, and
Bridgnorth, rapidly developing as a commuter centre for
the industrial West Midlands, continue to grow. In the
eastern part of the county a massive new town called Telford
will weld together the dispersed areas of early industry in
and around the coalfield towns of Dawley, Madeley and
Wellington.

The Domesday Survey clearly demonstrates that the
Saxon occupation of Shropshire was esssentially rural,
since only two boroughs are recorded. Following the
Norman Conquest, however, there was a spate of urban
plantations in the Welsh borderland. Some of these towns
were extensions of already existing market centres, others
were completely new creations. What is very clear is that

with the possible exception of Shrewsbury, town life had to be artificially stimulated and that 'organic' towns did not exist in the region. In the eleventh century, places such as Ludlow, Bishop's Castle and Bridgnorth simply did not exist. And villages which today are relatively insignificant, such as Lydbury North, Morville and Stanton Lacy, were the market and ecclesiastical centres to which people looked. Conversely, places which did not even appear as settlements on modern one-inch Ordnance Survey maps, such as Patton and Corfham, were the administrative capitals of extensive Saxon hundreds.

We are conditioned into thinking of villages and particularly towns as permanent and stable features of our countryside. The experience of suburban development and the creation of new towns since 1945 should, however, tell us that settlement is rarely, if ever, static. Villages, towns and cities are constantly readjusting to changing economic conditions.

New towns

We have already seen that there was an element of deliberate plantation in villages during the early Middle Ages, and this undoubtedly reflected the activity in the new towns. In many such towns the nature of their origins can be traced in their regular plans. The reasons for town plantation in this area were both strategic and economic. Many new towns such as Ludlow were developed as military and administrative centres within the shadow of Border castles; others, such as Newport, appear to have been created purely for commercial reasons, in order to stimulate trade.

One plantation that appears to have started as a strategic settlement under the wing of a Border castle was Bishop's Castle in the foothill region of south-west Shropshire. The castle was erected about 1127 in the western part of the

18,000-acre parish of Lydbury North, now a small village three miles south-east of Bishop's Castle. The town seems to have been planted some time in the late twelfth century, and by 1285 there were forty-six burgesses here. This plantation was not as successful as that at Ludlow and the town has not grown outside its basic medieval plan: a simple grid of streets on the ground, falling steeply to the south of the castle. By 1291, rents from Bishop's Castle yielded five pounds compared with three pounds only from Lydbury North. The church of St John Baptist, created originally as a chapel of Lydbury North, lies half a mile to the south of the site of the castle at the end of the High Street (Fig. 16). The precarious position of these border towns was demonstrated by John Fitzalan's occupation of Bishop's Castle for sixteen weeks in 1263; during which time it was claimed he wrought such havoc as to destroy the wealth of the whole vill for six years to come.

A little to the south of Bishop's Castle, another plantation, Clun, suffered similar attacks. We hear that before the battle of Radnor (1195-6), Prince Rees had besieged Clun Castle and eventually reduced it to ashes. The attempt to stimulate a town here probably dates from the rebuilding of the castle in stone. A charter for a three-day fair here was granted in 1204; by 1272 there were 183 burgages at Clun and, significantly, it was noted that twenty-two of these had been created out of assarts. The plantation was not an unqualified success: a rental of *c.* 1300 records that some sixty burgages were lying empty and yielded nothing. Unlike Bishop's Castle, which was a completely new creation, Clun was already an important manor in 1086. Plate 22 clearly shows that the old centre was around St George's church, while the new town was built in a rectangular plan to the north of the River Clun, in a situation reminiscent of that of Ludlow's. Although there is no record of walls here, the town plan suggests that they once existed. Around

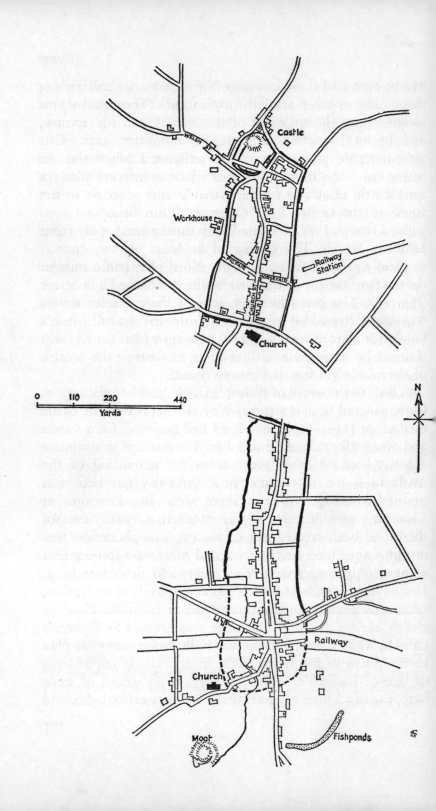

the church too there are traces of earthworks conceivably belonging to some ancient fortification. There can be little doubt about the antiquity of the name Clun, and recently it has been suggested that it may belong to that small group of pre-Celtic place-names; the settlement here takes its name from the River Clun, but its close proximity to the prehistoric trackway suggests that it may well be a very ancient foundation. Like Oswestry, Clun occupies a site close to Offa's Dyke and the Welsh border and for centuries was a meeting place for the two nations.

Oswestry itself was another fortified plantation founded in the late twelfth century by William Fitzalan; a borough charter was granted in 1228, when it was stated that the burgesses "received messuages from my bailiff for the improvement of my market". Oswestry was originally planted in the manor of Maesbury, but very soon after it took over not only the manor but also the hundred of *Mersete*. The town-plan shows that the castle, mentioned as early as 1086, was the first settlement here; the line of the bailey defences can be traced in the horseshoe shape described by Willow Street, Cross Street and Leg Street; the bailey was later infilled , but one of the roads was called Bailey Street. St Oswald's church and the regular market street settlement appear to make up a secondary planned unit. Not very far away the small towns of Ellesmere and Wem were also planted near to castles and in the later Middle Ages both had town walls. A careful topographical study of all these towns would certainly be revealing. In

Fig. 16. Town plans of Bishop's Castle (1883) (*top*) and Shifnal (1888) The regular settlement of both towns reflects their origins as planned towns. Plans based on the first edition of the six-inch Ordnance Survey. Note that in both cases the earlier churches are divorced from the main settlement.

some cases the castle and associated town probably formed an integrated contemporary plantation.

Another less successful attempt to create a fortified town was made at Caus near Westbury, where the new town was named after the Norman district of Caux, from whence the father of the founder, Roger Fitz Corbet, had originated. It was sited at the eastern end of the Long Mountain, commanding the valley road from Shrewsbury to Montgomery. The ruins of a castle with its outer fortifications now have to be disentangled from the undergrowth and nothing except earthworks remains of the borough. The town was created by Robert Corbet in 1198, and by 1349 there were fifty-eight burgesses living here; in the mid-fifteenth century much of the remainder of the town was burnt down during the rebellion of Sir Griffith Vaughan; by the time of a survey in 1521 the castle was recorded as being in "grete ruyne and decay". Caus was essentially a strategic Marcher borough which lost its function when more settled times came, when it was, in the words of Professor Beresford, "like a prehistoric monster crushed beneath the weight of its own armour" (Plate 23). In the thirteenth century a similar attempt, at Richards Castle (now just over the border in Herefordshire), to create a town in an extended outer bailey of the castle was a complete failure, although the earthworks of the decayed settlement can clearly be traced by the ruins of the castle and the church (which incidentally has a detached tower).

These western plantations were all, at least partially, strategic in character, but elsewhere in the county most new towns were created for purely economic reasons. The revenues and tolls which came from the towns were an obvious incentive to lords, Church and Crown alike, and there is any amount of evidence to show that many plantations were speculative ventures. One of these at Newport (originally *Novus Burgus*) in eastern Shropshire was a completely fresh creation planted in an area known as Bois Marais—'the wood in the marsh'. It was granted a borough charter by Henry I at the beginning of the twelfth century. The town lies in an area of ponds and meres and the economic origins of the settlement are suggested by its obligation to carry fish from the vivary to the royal household, and by the three fishes *naiant in pale*, that make up the town's arms. The church is appropriately dedicated to St Nicholas, the patron saint of fishermen. The imposing church stands in the middle of a long, broad market place that has regular burgage tenement blocks running off it at right-angles (Fig. 17). Initially, the church was dependent on the mother church at neighbouring Church Aston, now virtually a suburb of Newport. The old parish boundaries demonstrate, however, that the town was carved out of the extensive Saxon manor of Edgmond.

Other successful market town plantations were stimulated by monasteries. At Market Drayton, for instance, the Cistercian Abbey of Combermere (in Cheshire) expanded an existing village in the mid-thirteenth century. The town plan clearly reflects the deliberate nature of the settlement here (see Fig. 14). Similarly, Wenlock Priory developed Madeley, partly out of forest assarts, during the thirteenth century. By 1300 it was a flourishing community with a large number of burgage tenants. The plan of the old part of Madeley shows the typical burgage tenements running off the High Street; the town plan of Much Wenlock itself suggests an element of plantation.

Some reference should be made here to Shifnal, which has the classic appearance of a planted town (see Fig. 16). There is, however, a good deal of confusion over the early history of the town. There appear to have been two manors here, one of which was abandoned in the fourteenth century and the other developed as a town. In 1591 there was a great fire at Shifnal, when some thirty-two houses were

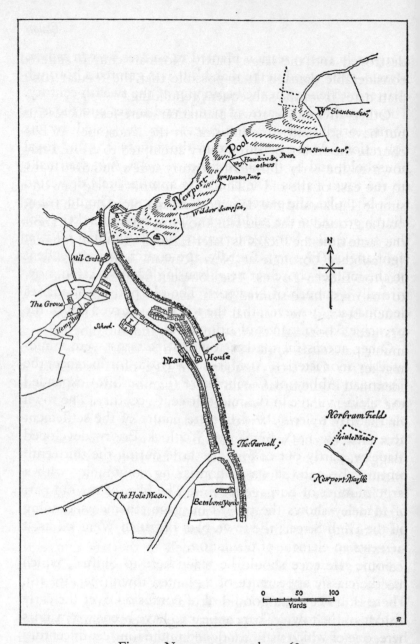

Fig. 17. Newport town plan, 1681

The planned town of Newport (S.R.O. 81/599). Around the church of
St Nicholas there is some colonisation; some of these houses to the
north of the church have since been demolished. Newport Pool,
probably the original fishpond on which the town was founded, was
later incorporated into the Shropshire Canal.

destroyed and the large, partly Norman church suffered considerable damage. It is possible that the regular town plan dates from the subsequent rebuilding.[1]

Other attempts at town plantation were less successful, but have still left some imprint on the landscape. At Baschurch, the Abbot of Shrewsbury attempted to create a new town in the early thirteenth century a few hundred yards to the east of the old village. The town was laid out on a simple T plan and the decayed burgage plots can be traced on the ground in the area still known as Newtown. At about the same time the Fitzalans (later Earls of Arundel) founded yet another borough at New Ruyton, better known as Ruyton-Eleven-Towns. The competition between the two towns must have stunted both, as neither settlement grew much beyond its original size; nevertheless Ruyton was granted a borough charter in 1308 and did not lose its municipal status until 1886, though it did lose its major market to Oswestry in 1407. Burgage plots can still be identified in the broad main street running westwards from the church and along a northern extension of the town on the road towards Wykey. Incidentally the road system in this area to the west of the Berth and to the south of Baggymoor has a regularity indicative of even earlier planning, possibly linked to a system of Saxon estates.

There appear to have been numerous other attempts to graft new towns or more frequently market extensions on to existing settlements. Robert Burnell, for instance, attempted to extend Acton Burnell in the late thirteenth century; by 1315 there were thirty-six burgesses here, but because of its comparative isolation the town had failed by the end of the Middle Ages. It was also too late, as by the middle of the thirteenth century there were enough market towns in the Welsh Borderland and attempts at plantation

[1] For discussion see P. A. Barker, 'Excavation of the moated site at Shifnal', *T.S.A.S.*, Vol. 57 (1966).

after this date were rarely successful. Apart from Shrewsbury, even those towns which did succeed never grew particularly large. Indeed, the first edition of the one-inch Ordnance Survey (1833) shows that they had barely expanded beyond their medieval boundaries. This changed with the coming of the railway, together with the need to provide municipal undertakings such as gasworks, and institutions like hospitals, workhouses and a prison (in the case of Shrewsbury), which meant that during the middle years of the nineteenth century the market towns of Shropshire finally broke their medieval girdles.

In order to understand more fully the stages of town growth, we may examine three towns in more detail— Ludlow, Bridgnorth and Shrewsbury.

Ludlow

Ludlow has long been recognised as a classic example of Norman town plantation[2] (Fig. 18). There is no direct evidence of any earlier Saxon occupation of the site, although place-name evidence suggests that there may have been an earlier hamlet here called Dinham. Two features dominate the town—the castle and the church of St Laurence.[3] Ludlow Castle was built about 1085, probably by Roger de Lacy. The castle, which dominates the town, was soon to become one of the most powerful in the Welsh Marches and in the late fifteenth century became the seat of the Lords President of Wales and their court of the Marches. It occupies a magnificent position—the cliff falls steeply to the Teme on

[2] W. H. St John Hope, 'The ancient topography of the town of Ludlow', *Archaeologia*, Vol. 61 (1909).

[3] Prior to the building of St Laurence's church in 1199 a great Bronze Age burial mound, the *Ludan Hlaw* ('Luda's Tumulus') was removed. Three stone cists—*tria maunsolea lapidae*, were found containing skeletons, these were revered as the bones of Irish saints, reflecting perhaps a folk legend that went back to the coming of Christianity to the region.

the west and the Corve on the north. This made it safe in the Middle Ages and makes its ruins picturesque now, especially when viewed from Whitcliffe on the Ludford side of the Teme. Within the inner bailey the remains of an unusual circular nave of a Norman chapel form an impressive monument.[4]

The original town was probably created by the de Lacys in the late eleventh century, immediately after the castle had been built. There seems little doubt that the plantation was in the manor of Stanton Lacy. The regular ancient parish boundaries to the north of Ludlow clearly show how the land was divided between St Peter's church, Stanton Lacy and St Laurence's, Ludlow, and later St Leonard's of Ludlow. Up until the late nineteenth century the keep of Ludlow Castle was still in the parish of Stanton Lacy.

Recent work on the morphology of Ludlow suggests that the town was built in several stages (Plate 24). The whole story is not yet fully understood and a new comprehensive history of Ludlow is needed. The last major study of the town to be published was Wright's *History of Ludlow* (1852). The infant borough of Ludlow appears to have been destroyed in the twelfth century when the High Street was laid down. This wide street which extends eastwards from the castle gates originally formed the old market place. Some of the temporary stalls were eventually replaced by more permanent buildings; thus the terraced shops at the eastern end of the High Street really represent 'fossilised' market stalls, with a narrow alley, Market Street, running behind them. It is probable that Old Street, which does not conform to Ludlow's regular grid plan, pre-dates the town, and was the original north–south routeway that crossed the River Teme some 200 yards to the east of Ludford Bridge,

---

[4] It has been suggested that the place-name Acton Round was derived from an early circular church there, possibly dating from the time the manor was under the control of the Knights Templars.

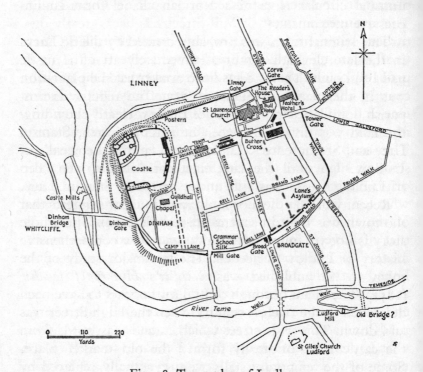

Fig. 18. Town plan of Ludlow

The town plan incorporates the various phases of medieval town plantation. The area of Dinham may mark a pre-Conquest settlement. The
dotted lines mark the line of an early street which was later blocked
with the extension of the outer bailey.

the present crossing point. This bridge dates from the fifteenth century when it probably replaced the old bridge.

Both Mill Street and Broad Street are slightly 'bow' shaped, a street-form commonly associated with town plantation and best expressed at Thame in Oxfordshire. The arrangement west of Mill Street has been greatly disturbed, but there is a narrow lane, formerly called Christ Croft, running parallel with it towards the river. This is probably original, since it has on its western side the twelfth-century chapel of St Thomas of Canterbury. Between this lane and Mill Street there is a strip of ground extending north and south, with gardens abutting on it east and west. This strip, which itself is now cut up into gardens, is strongly suggestive of having been laid down as one of the original streets of the town, and its breadth, though somewhat less than that of the main streets, is identical with that of the absorbed street east of Broad Street and probably that of Raven Lane before it was narrowed by encroachments. The abandonment of these streets is almost certainly linked with the addition of the outer bailey to the castle at the end of the twelfth century, cutting off the western end of the High Street and thus making redundant those roads immediately to the south of the castle.

St Laurence's church was given a chequer to itself on the north-east of the High Street; the earliest architecture appears to be late twelfth century, which probably dates an extension of the original town. This church, the largest parish church in the county, was built almost entirely by the burgesses of the town, made wealthy by the cloth trade. The imposing church and tower cannot be appreciated from within the town as later medieval infilling in the High Street has completely obscured the southern view. However, when Ludlow is approached from the north, the church along with the castle appears to dominate the town.

As the town grew more prosperous it apparently expanded in stages in the late thirteenth and again in the late fifteenth century, firstly around the Bull-Ring and Old Street, and later along Broad Street and Mill Street. King Street and Tower Street were both originally funnel-shaped. This, together with the extraordinary number of inns in both streets, suggests that originally they were intended as extensions to the market. Later still, planned extensions were added outside the town walls along Lower Broad Street, Oldgate Fee and Corve Street.

The town walls can still be identified on the modern map, but were not built until much of the town had already been planted. The enclosing of the town appears to have begun in 1233, following a visit of Henry III, but the many grants of murage between 1280 and 1317 suggest that the work was either postponed or a long time in hand. The sudden creation of such a town must have heavily taxed the population of the surrounding countryside. The adjacent village of Stanton Lacy appears to have experienced severe contraction as a result of the plantation at Ludlow. Not only was there a considerable movement of population to the new town, but Ludlow also took over the important north–south route previously controlled by Stanton Lacy.

There is no doubt that the plantation at Ludlow was successful, for by 1377 there were over one thousand taxable householders.[5] The town maintained a high level of prosperity throughout the Middle Ages, but many of the medieval timber houses were later encased in brick. As the majority of standing buildings are Georgian the overall impression that Ludlow gives today is that of a fashionable eighteenth-century town. It is certainly in many respects the most pleasant and best preserved of Shropshire towns.

[5] W. G. Hoskins, *Local History in England* (1959). Ludlow was the thirty-third largest provincial town in England at this date with a taxpaying population of 1172, compared with Shrewsbury's 2083 (seventeenth largest).

Bridgnorth

Bridgnorth lies on a ridge of old red sandstone overlooking the River Severn. It consists of two parts, High Town to the west of the river and Low Town to the east; these are linked by a cliff railway, the steepest and shortest inclined railway in the country, and by a bridge from which the town derived its name (*Bruge*). The present bridge was built in 1832, but earlier bridges may well have used the islands, or bylets, which lie in the River Severn here. Only one of these survives, to the south of the bridge, but a late sixteenth-century map marks two, the 'great billet' and the 'weures billet'. Until recently the town was less 'developed' than Shrewsbury, but it is rapidly becoming a commuter centre for the industrial West Midlands, with the result that the town now has a large northern suburban development. Even so, the castle park and walk remain amongst the best pieces of urban landscaping in the county (Plate 25).

The origins of the town are confusing. As early as 896 there was a bridge over the Severn at *Cwatbryg* (Quatbridge) and a *burh* was created on the river bank in 912 by Aethelflaed. The site of this fortification is not known. Possibly it is the earthwork known as Panpudding Hill, but Dr Mason convincingly argues that the *burh* stood on the site of the present castle. Florence of Worcester was quite precise about the site of the *burh*. It was, he says, on the western bank of the Severn, in the place called Bridge; later Florence states that Robert de Bellême refortified this *arcem* at Bridgnorth in the early twelfth century. Topographically too the present castle site seems the most attractive as a Saxon promontory *burh*. Bridgnorth is not recorded in the Domesday Book, but there was a *burgus* at Quatford, said to yield nothing. The entry appears under Eardington, a village on the opposite side of the river.[6] This *burgus* appears to have been an early but unsuccessful attempt at town plantation.

It is certain, however, that the present town of Bridgnorth was not founded until the beginning of the twelfth century. It is not known how long the bridge at Quatford continued to operate, but the use of the place-name 'Bridgnorth' to describe a second town to the north upstream suggests that it was not completely forgotten in the thirteenth century. This second town followed the transfer of the military site from Quatford in 1101, when Ordericus Vitalis records that the rebel Earl Robert de Bellême abandoned Quatford and transferred his castle, church (St Mary's) and borough to Bridgnorth. The new town lay originally within the parish of Morville and the initial parochial dependence on Morville reflects its artificial origin.

Bridgnorth Castle, the remains of which now form the centre-piece of the town-park, was originally built by Robert and later fortified by Henry II who granted the town its first charter in 1157 (incidentally the earliest surviving for Shropshire). Although Bridgnorth, along with Shrewsbury, was in the front line of defence against the Welsh in the eleventh and twelfth centuries, the defences were left to decay with the coming of more settled times in the late thirteenth century. By the early sixteenth century, the castle was said to be 'totally to ruine' and it was recorded that townspeople were building themselves houses in the bailey.

The early medieval town may have been contained within the outer bailey of the castle, as at Richards Castle and Caus. The new borough was probably laid out in the traditional

---

[6] The name Oldbury (old fort) is another complicating factor in the identification of the Saxon *burh*. For a full discussion of the late Saxon and early Norman history of the Bridgnorth region see J. F. A. Mason and P. A. Barker, 'The Norman Castle at Quatford', *T.S.A.S.*, Vol 52 (1961).

manner during the later twelfth century, with a broad high street and a series of streets running off at right-angles (Fig. 19). During this period a second church (St Leonard's) was built. Following the Welsh disturbances the new town was surrounded by a turf rampart and ditch between 1216 and 1223. Some forty years later the stockade was partially replaced by a stone wall, but by Leland's time the walls were all in ruin although remains are still to be seen at the west end of Lisley Street and the Half Moon Battery off Pound Street.[7] Of the five original town gates, only the North Gate, much remodelled in 1910, still stands. Whitburn Gate survived until 1761 and the Hungry Gate until 1821.

The area enclosed by the town walls was inadequate to accommodate the late medieval expansion and new suburbs grew up outside the North Gate, in New Town and Littlebrug, now known as Pound Street. A suburb also grew up at Low Town across the river. Although Leland dismissed it as "a pretty long street of mean buildings", on early maps it appears to be as large as High Town Bridgnorth.

By 1300 Bridgnorth was second only to Shrewsbury in importance in Shropshire, although it was closely rivalled by Ludlow. The key factors in the prosperity of the town were the river and bridge. Medieval Bridgnorth was an important route centre; the road from Chester to Bristol crossed the Severn here and the river itself was of major importance in the development of the town and, along with Bristol, Gloucester, Tewkesbury and Shrewsbury, Bridgnorth is one of five towns on the River Severn to be marked on Gough's 1360 map of Britain.

During the Middle Ages, the textile industry was

---

[7] It is interesting that the early Norman towns do not appear to have been walled. Several west Midland towns appear to have erected turf and timber defences in the late twelfth and early thirteenth centuries which were later replaced by stone walls.

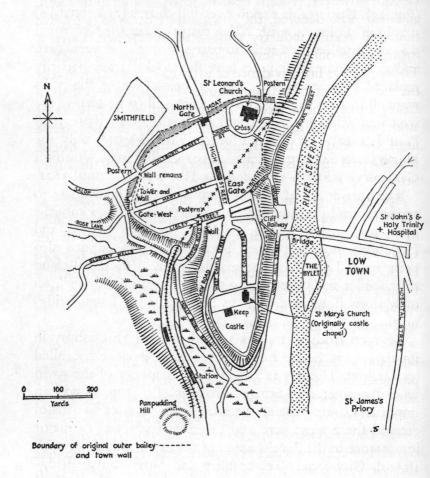

Fig. 19. Town plan of Bridgnorth

The town plan shows the area of the original castle and bailey which are probably co-extensive with the Saxon promontory *burh*. The later medieval planned town was added to the north.

important and so too were tanning and brewing. In 1540 Leland, however, records that the town "standeth by cloth, and that now decayed, the town sorely decayed"; by this time the textile industry was virtually extinct. Later it turned with only modest success to cap and hat making. Today there is little evidence of early cloth working, except the names Tainter Wall and Tainter Hill at the west end of Lisley Street; here freshly woven cloth was 'tented' or stretched out to dry. The carpet industry did not arrive until the end of the eighteenth century, when Joseph MacMichael established the first carpet factory in Lisley Street.

Because of destruction during the Civil War (much of High Town was burnt down), little remains of the buildings of medieval or Tudor Bridgnorth. At the bottom of the Cartway, which was the only way up from the river to High Town until the building of the New Road, stands Bishop Percy's house (1580), one of the few surviving half-timbered buildings in the town. An appeal to Parliament was made for aid, the fire having consumed "almost the whole subsistence of the Corporation, consisting of very faire and ancient buildings, to the value of ninety thousand pounds". The new Town Hall was completed in 1652 on a new site in the middle of the High Street, where it still stands today with the traffic flowing through it.

The real reconstruction, however, did not come until the eighteenth century when Bridgnorth emerged as a gracious and pleasant town with some fine Georgian terraces. In 1763 Bridgnorth was described as a "place of great trade, both by land and water". In Low Town new residences were built in Mill Street and St John's Street; the Post Office (*c.* 1700) is a very good example of this phase. In High Town, Anthony Weaver made a large-scale attempt to improve the inhabited area within the ancient limits of the castle. The ultimate sequel to these improvements came with the rebuilding of the fourteenth-century church of St Mary's (originally the chapel of Bridgnorth Castle), earlier described by Leland as a 'rude thing'. A new church in white freestone in the classical style was built by Telford at the end of East Castle Street late in the eighteenth century on a different alignment. The new church was designed to blend with the spacious street and buildings, and accordingly this part of the town still possesses considerable elegance. During the nineteenth century a number of large fashionable residences were built around the edge of the castle park. Ironically, in the sandstone cliff below there were squatter cave-dwellings occupied until at least the mid-nineteenth century.

As Bridgnorth lay only a few miles downstream from Coalbrookdale and the coalfield there were inevitably links with the iron industry in the town. From 1760 the Coalbrookdale Company leased the Town Mills as a forge and Thomas Cranage, the noted iron-worker, was employed here as 'master Hammerman' in 1766. On the east bank of the river behind Mill Street are remains of John Hazeldine's once famous foundry. Crude iron was stored at Bridgnorth before being shipped downstream to Stourbridge; this trade was mainly controlled by the Knight family who had furnaces at Charlcotte about eight miles from Bridgnorth and at distant Bringewood near Ludlow.

Until the coming of the railway in the 1850s Bridgnorth remained a major river port. During the eighteenth and nineteenth centuries coal from the pits at Broseley and agricultural produce from the surrounding countryside were the main cargoes. Although the New Road up to High Town was opened in 1786, coal and heavy merchandise continued to be taken in panniers by donkeys up the steps until the road was freed from tolls in 1852. The river warden's house built in the late eighteenth century can still be seen with an area of old wharves in front of it. Other surviving signs of the once-flourishing river trade include the flights of landing steps at the Old Quay, originally including Skinner's Load, Friars Load and Foster's Load opposite the entrance to Stoneway Steps, and the continuous iron lath (installed to protect the towing ropes) at the side of the riverside towpath. In 1674 the town had installed a 'capstay winde' on the bridge to unload vessels stranded at the Bylet. On a map of 1739 there were three dockyards on the Severn and about 1800 the river at Bridgnorth presented a "constant moving picture of boats and barges".

The coming of the railway did not bring any immediate advantages to the town. Indeed the first consequence was to kill the river trade; the last barge to use Bridgnorth came down the Severn in 1895. Ironically, this barge, which was carrying firebricks, sank after fouling one of the bridge piers. In 1892, however, the cliff railway provided Bridgnorth with the first (and now the only) inland inclined railway in England. The decision to build such a railway must have been influenced by the close proximity of a number of successful industrial inclined planes on the coalfield.

Bridgnorth has maintained its status as a market centre although now it is a rapidly growing commuter town. The construction of new housing estates began even before 1939, but after the war the pace accelerated. Today the town extends far beyond its medieval limits, but as with so much recent building in Shropshire these developments have little to commend them.

Shrewsbury

With some fifty-six thousand people, Shrewsbury was, until recently, by far the largest town in Shropshire and in many ways its history reflects that of the county as a whole. It owes its continuing historical importance to its unique siting on the edge of the Welsh uplands. The town lies at the very heart of the modern county of Shropshire within a loop of the River Severn which, as well as carrying its goods through the ages, protected the medieval town on all sides except the north. Even here marshy ground and an old river meander made defence relatively easy (Fig. 20). There were two fords, which were used by cattle-drovers up until the eighteenth century, roughly where the English and Welsh Bridges now stand. The present English Bridge was built in 1927 and the Welsh Bridge was rebuilt in 1795 by Mylne, the designer of the old Westminster Bridge. The earlier Welsh Bridge was described by Leland as "the greatest, fairest and highest upon the stream" (Plate 26).

Within the loop of the Severn, land rises abruptly on the east and south sides of the town with a more gradual rise on the west, where the ground was originally marshy in the area known as Mardol. Two small hills dominate the high ground; the High Cross with St Mary's church stood on one of these while on the other the old church of St Chad was sited.

There is evidence to suggest that Shrewsbury lay on a prehistoric trade route and that the Severn was used for transport before the Romans. Few Roman finds have been made in the town and the origins of the town lie almost certainly in the seventh or eighth century A.D. There is no evidence to show a direct movement from *Viroconium* to Shrewsbury, although this legend has appealed to antiquaries since the Middle Ages. Current archaeological thought suggests that the move was to the Berth, near Baschurch, rather than Shrewsbury (see Plate 4). Professor Finberg believes that the identification of Cynddylan's Pengwern with Shrewsbury "is nothing more than a bad guess on the part of Giraldus Cambrensis and his contemporaries". Subsequent to the collapse of Pengwern in the mid-seventh century, it seems probable that Shrewsbury

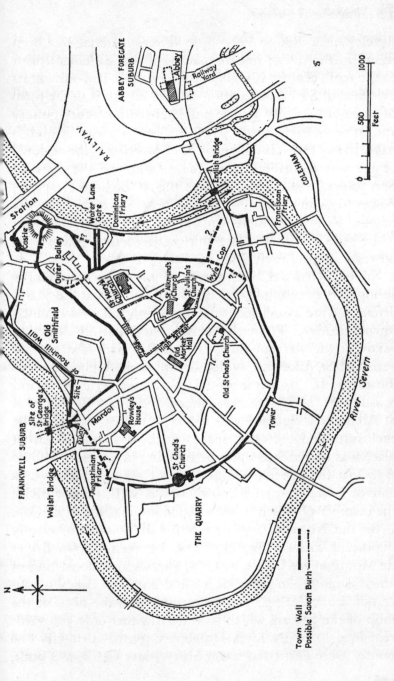

Fig. 20. Town plan of Shrewsbury

The basic town plan, showing the possible site of the Saxon *burh* and the town walls.

developed, although very little Saxon material has been found in the town; but the nature of the settlement prior to the tenth century is highly problematical. The only direct evidence of Saxon occupation at Shrewsbury is in the form of an eighth-century bronze pin, later-tenth-century pottery and some possible Saxon structures found under St Mary's nave. In any case it is unlikely that its position as the regional centre was formalised until the creation of the shire of Shropshire (*c*. A.D. 1000); after this it expanded rapidly, however. A mint was established near Shrewsbury in the reign of King Aethelstan (A.D. 925–40), and coins continued to be struck until the late thirteenth century (there was, however, a brief revival during the Civil War).

No trace has yet been found of pre-Norman defences although they certainly existed. It is possible that the Saxon defences were associated with the laying out of a planned town and Mr J. T. Smith has suggested that the defended Saxon town was roughly co-extensive with the ancient parish of St Alkmund, which occupied the highest part of the town. If this is the case High Street, Pride Hill and possibly St Mary's Street defined the limits of the *burh*. St Alkmund's church lay near the south-east corner of the enclosure, and the open space which served as a market place was encroached upon by building in the early Middle Ages. At the extreme southern tip of the *burh* there was a gate or movable barrier known as *Wil* (O.E. trap or trick), the memory of which is perpetuated in the name Wyle Cop.

By the Norman Conquest Shrewsbury was sufficiently important to have five churches. Between 1067–9 Roger de Montgomery built a castle at Shrewsbury, consisting of an oval motte, an inner bailey and an outer bailey of uncertain extent. It was thrown up between the neck of the loop of the Severn, which is so narrow that only 300 yards remained to be guarded. Domesday records that fifty-one houses were destroyed when Shrewsbury Castle was built, but these probably lay outside the Saxon town, between the outer bailey and the Saxon town defences and were cleared for strategic purposes. In 1069 "the Welsh, with the men of Cheshire, laid siege to the King's castle at Shrewsbury aided by the townsmen under Edric the Wild". It survived the ordeal successfully until relief was near, when the insurgents burnt the town and retired. The castle was rebuilt in stone in the time of Henry II, but in the thirteenth century it began to fall into disrepair. An enquiry of 1255 found that the motte had been undermined by river erosion and a wooden tower had fallen down, and the castle had been aggravated by the recent construction of a mill by the Abbot of Shrewsbury.[8] In addition to building the castle the Normans rebuilt the Saxon churches in stone and Roger de Montgomery introduced a Benedictine monastery on the eastern side of the river (1083–6). Shrewsbury Abbey, originally founded by Siward, was developed from a small Saxon wooden chapel, but by 1086 the Abbey was already endowed with thirty-four hides.

The town walls were not built until more than a century later than the castle;[9] in 1215, the Welsh leader Llewellyn captured Shrewsbury for a short time, revealing its weakness to siege, and in 1218–20 work was started on a stone wall. The construction of the new defences was interrupted by the Welsh wars of 1229, which led to the hasty construction of a temporary turf rampart, but the new defences were completed by 1242, when it was recorded that the Dominican friars were given 200 cartloads of stone "left over from the building of the walls of Shrewsbury". The new wall

[8] The monks were often in conflict with the town over the control of water; in 1298 there was a dispute over four islands which had arisen in the Severn between the Stone (English) Bridge and the Dominican Friary, probably as a result of the diversion of water to feed the Abbey Mills.

[9] However, Ordericus Vitalis describes the new Abbey of St Peter as being at the east gate, implying that by 1083 there must have been some sort of encircling defence, perhaps a simple rampart and ditch.

ran south-west from the castle to Roushill; from here it ran to Mardol to St Austin Friars, along Claremont Bank, St Chad's Terrace, Town Walls (which is the best preserved section and contains the one surviving wall tower), to the English Bridge and then north back to the castle. The town walls provided the security which was essential for the growing trade of the town.[10]

It is obvious that in Shrewsbury as elsewhere in the county during the Norman period there were deliberate attempts to foster urban life. Domesday records that already there were forty-three burgesses here in 1086. Later both Pride Hill and High Street were widened to accommodate markets; the Square and Mardol Head, too, appear to have been laid out afresh in the early thirteenth century on an area of reclaimed marsh. Rocque's map of Shrewsbury (1746) clearly shows a standardised frontage in this area.

Outside the town walls there was also substantial growth. Three friaries were established on the river in the thirteenth century; the Dominicans' (1232) immediately to the south of the castle, the Greyfriars' (1245–6) at the bottom of Wyle Cop and the Augustinians' (1298) near to the Welsh Bridge where the Priory Grammar School now stands. A small trading community grew up around the Abbey in the area of Abbey Foregate and at Frankwell, to the west of the Welsh Bridge, a community which had probably been planted in the eleventh century flourished and was able to live a virtually independent existence on the basis of the leather industry recorded here as early as the twelfth century.

By 1200 Shrewsbury was a substantial trading centre, to which Welsh Powys brought its produce, with trading links

[10] P. A. Barker, 'Excavations at the town wall, Roushill, Shrewsbury', *Medieval Archaeology*, Vol. 10 (1961). Llewellyn surrendered Shrewsbury to the English in 1221. Two years later, the Earl of Pembroke plundered the town, and in 1234, Llewellyn "again advanced with fire and sword and laid the country waste to the very gates of Shrewsbury".

as far removed as Ireland and the east coast ports. During the thirteenth century the wool industry became increasingly important, at least a quarter of the population being involved in the manufacture and sale of cloth. In 1209 the town obtained a charter by which it gained a virtual monopoly in the buying of raw hides and undressed wool in Shropshire. In 1266 a Royal Charter strengthened this monopoly and it was during this time that the great wool families that were to dominate Shrewsbury until the seventeenth century began to emerge. Typical of these was Nicholas of Ludlow, the builder of Stokesay castle, who in the late thirteenth century was exporting up to 240 sacks of wool a year, far in excess of the normal allowance. Other wool families included the Colles, the Prides (Pride Hill is named after John Pride) and the Vaughans. These merchants constructed large town houses, which also incorporated storage space for cloth. Little of these buildings can still be seen although Mr J. T. Smith has shown that there are substantial remains within standing buildings, e.g. Vaughan's Mansion, previously identified as the mint, next to Lloyds Bank on Pride Hill; the medieval street frontage here has now been successfully incorporated into a modern store, in a manner which must be applauded.

In 1326 Shrewsbury, along with Cardiff and Carmarthen, became a staple town for wool and leather for the whole of Wales, and thereafter had a virtual monopoly of trade in north and central Wales. Trade from central Wales came up the River Dovey to Welshpool and then down the Severn to Shrewsbury. The town also appears to have had control of trade in the Welsh Marches as far south as Hereford. There was evidence too of growing trade along the Severn to Bristol and even of continental export by this route. In addition to wool and leather industries, Shrewsbury had a wide range of conventional trades associated with medieval market towns, and in the fourteenth century there came the first streets named after specific trades, e.g. Butcher Row (1396) (Plate 27).

The prosperity of the fourteenth century (it was during this period that a great deal of church building went on) gave way to an apparent decline in the wool trade in the Marches. In the early fifteenth century it was recorded that "Divers and many houses messuages and tenements in the towns of Nottingham, Shrewsbury, Ludlow, Bridgnorth, Queensborough, Northampton and Gloucester now and for a long time have been in great ruin and decay and specially in the principal streets . . ." Trade, however, seems to have revived by the middle of the sixteenth century when the drapers' company claimed that they had "set at work about 600 persons of the art of shearmen or frizers" in Shrewsbury. Many of the Tudor and Jacobean houses, for which Shrewsbury is noted, were built as a result of this trade revival, when Shrewsbury enjoyed its most prosperous period. Ireland's Mansion, one of the best surviving examples of Elizabethan architecture in the town, was built by Robert Ireland about 1575, and characterises the prosperity and confidence of the Elizabethan wool merchants. Owen's Mansion (1592), a slightly less ostentatious merchant's house, stands nearby, facing the square. The Owens who lived at the fine Elizabethan hall at Condover also built the picturesque Council House Gatehouse in Castle Street. After this date merchants' houses tended to be of only two storeys and of more modest design. The earliest brick building in the town was Rowley's Mansion; Roger Rowley came to Shrewsbury shortly before 1600 and started business as a draper dealing in Welsh cloth and at the same time as a brewer and maltster, when he built or took over the half-timbered portion of the building known as Rowley's House which faces on to Barker Street. Rowley's son built the brick and stone portion known as Rowley's Mansion. This fine structure which now houses the town's museum

Plate 25 Air photograph of Bridgnorth. St Mary's church, built by Telford (begun 1792), stands prominently on the sandstone ridge in the foreground, near the castle and the park. Behind, the various phases of town plantation can be seen. In the background there is extensive suburban development belonging to the modern town.

Plate 26　The Welsh Bridge, Shrewsbury, in 1790, drawn by the Rev. E. Williams; the mast of a sailing vessel can be seen in the background. This is the medieval bridge, which has a large gate tower and houses on it; it was demolished only a few years after the drawing was made.

Plate 27　A photograph taken at the end of the nineteenth century of Butcher Row, Shrewsbury. The house in the foreground, which still stands, is known as the Abbot's House. It was wrongly claimed to have been the town house of the abbots of Lilleshall, nevertheless it is a town house of considerable interest, as it dates from before the Reformation. The ground floor is made up of original shop fronts; the timber decoration and jettying is typical of sixteenth-century town (and country) houses in Shropshire.

Plate 29

Plate 28   The general Market, Shrewsbury, in 1963 before it was replaced. This was the chief Victorian contribution to the public architecture of the town (1867–9). Although hardly functional, it compares favourably with its successor (*Plate 29*).

Plate 30 An abandoned lead-smelting chimney at Snailbeach. Behind the chimney, spoil-
heaps and scattered smallholdings can be seen.

has been cruelly treated. It now stands by itself, completely out of context, surrounded by car and bus parks.

By 1620 Shrewsbury drapers were paying over £2000 a week for Welsh cloth which was brought from Dolgelly and Mawddy by pack-horse. Soon afterwards the drapers moved the market from Oswestry to Shrewsbury, completing Shrewsbury's textile monopoly. The Merioneth clothiers had to travel the extra twenty miles and they were so late in arriving back home on Saturdays (the cloth was bought on Fridays) that in 1648 the rector of Dolgelly requested that the market be put back to Wednesdays. The Shrewsbury drapers compromised and agreed to buy the cloth on Thursdays. Such was the importance of the Welsh trade that Defoe on his visit to Shrewsbury noted "They speak all English in the town, but on market day you would think you were in Wales."[11]

As well as building themselves fine town houses the Shrewsbury merchants financed public buildings; typical of these is the Drapers' Hall (*c.* 1580) in St Mary's Place, the guildhall of the powerful drapers' guild whose religious meeting place was the south chancel of the chapel of St Mary's a few yards away. A little later the Old Market House was built (1596). Merchants were also responsible for municipal benefactions; foremost of these was the school founded in 1551. The old Shrewsbury School building, now the Library and Museum in Castle Gates, dates from the 1590s and 1630. The school, which was very stately for the period, makes an elegant partner for the castle nearby. Defoe described its buildings as "very spacious" and "the most considerable in this part of England".

During the seventeenth century the town changed from being a major regional market to a fashionable, though still busy, county town. In 1698 Celia Fiennes observed that the

[11] D. Defoe, *A Tour through the Whole Island of Great Britain* (1724–7), Vol. 2, p. 13.

lawns and gardens provided for the enjoyment of people of quality "more than in any town except Nottingham". And despite shortage of space several new elegant streets of residences were built within the town walls. One of the first of these was Belmont; houses built here overlooked lawns across the Town Walls to the river. Most of the houses on Claremont Bank and St John's Hill also date from the early eighteenth century. Swan Hill Court in Swan Hill was perhaps the most ambitious late eighteenth-century house in Shrewsbury; it was built for the Marquis of Bath by the Shrewsbury architect Thomas Farnolls Pritchard (1723–77). Pritchard was responsible for a number of other town buildings, including probably the Lion Hotel, and he also built country houses in the same style, including Hatton Grange at Shifnal and the Mansion House, Ford.[12]

There was still some space remaining for the large-scale development of Georgian squares and crescents within the loop of the river. The most concentrated development was along Town Walls overlooking the Quarry—anciently known as 'behind the walls'. This park of about twenty-five acres lies between the river and the old town walls to the west of the town. It was first laid with splendid lime avenues in 1719 and provided an admirable background for Georgian buildings. Despite the town's regrettable record in other spheres of preservation, the Quarry Park has survived virtually intact apart from the destruction of the lime avenues since the last war.

The circular church of St Chad (1790–2), the most ambitious Georgian structure in the town, was designed by George Steward, who was also responsible for Attingham Hall. It looks over the river to the present Shrewsbury School, originally built as a hospital in 1765. The school

---

[12] R. Chaplin, 'New Light on Thomas Farnolls Pritchard', *S.N.L.*, No. 34 (1970). It is also thought that Pritchard was one of the architects of the Iron Bridge, although he died four years before its completion.

moved from its cramped town site in 1882 (the old school buildings being now occupied by Shrewsbury Public Library). It is this area with its sweeping views and elegant buildings that has given Shrewsbury its not altogether deserved reputation for having used the river well. Finally, it is worth mentioning another of Telford's contributions to the county, though perhaps a less praiseworthy one. In 1790 he converted the castle ruins into a residence for Sir William Pulteney and among his additions was Laura's Tower, a red sandstone octagonal structure that overlooks the castle.

In 1801 Shrewsbury's population of rather under fifteen thousand was probably not much larger than at the end of the Middle Ages. By 1900 it had practically doubled, but this spectacular increase was modest compared with that of many industrial towns. Although the town had emerged relatively unspoiled from the traumatic Victorian years it had also changed into an ordinary county market town. It managed to become neither a fashionable resort such as Cheltenham nor a major industrial city such as Nottingham. The basic reason for this decline into relative obscurity comes from its isolated situation far from the coast and the arteries of trade. The fact that there was consequently comparatively little rebuilding in the town centre during the nineteenth century partly explains why so much medieval building survived, only to be destroyed by post-war 'redevelopment'.

However, the Victorians did make several major contributions to Shrewsbury's townscape. Among the most striking of these were the Eye, Ear and Throat Hospital built by C. O. Ellison (1879–81) on Town Walls and the railway station which was rebuilt (1903–4) to a design closely similar to the original earlier Victorian building. The station, built in the shadow of the castle, extends across the river, and now forms a convenient barrier between the ancient town centre and later industrial development. Two notable Victorian structures have recently been replaced; they were the Post Office (1877) on the site of the Old Butter Cross and the General Market (1867–9), a bizarre building in red, yellow and blue bricks in an Italianate style (Plate 28). The replacements can hardly be viewed as improvements (Plate 29). The Smithfield Market was built outside the town walls on the marshy section of the river loops in 1850. The present market was completed in 1958 and the old Smithfield has been developed as a shopping precinct and car park.

The textile industry still flourished sufficiently about 1800 to provide Shrewsbury with one of its most memorable monuments, Messrs Benyon, Bage and Marshall's flax spinning mill sited on the canal at Ditherington, the earliest of all factories with a complete iron frame. In 1831 there were six flannel manufacturers and two linen makers in the town. The coming of the railway brought heavy industry to Shrewsbury and with it new estates of workers' houses. Initially, tanneries and saw-mills grew up by the station and along Coton Hill. Later the Perseverance Ironworks and associated industry developed by the basin of the Shropshire Union Canal. Behind the railway station Castle Fields, a typical mid-Victorian housing estate of terraced houses with such characteristic street names as New Park, Victoria and Soho, was built. Similar, but smaller, developments took place outside the river loop at Coleham, where the remains of William Hazeldine's iron foundry can be found.

Later in the century, there was further eastward expansion along the railway, when Ditherington and Harlescott were developed for housing. In the twentieth century much industrial suburban development has taken place on this side of the town, and now reaches out almost to Battlefield, Pimly and Haughmond. Monkmoor, too, expanded rapidly during the late nineteenth and early twentieth centuries. The more spacious Victorian residential development, such as Cherryfields, can be clearly distinguished from later inter- and post-war housing schemes. Abbey Foregate itself was developed as a fashionable residential unit in the eighteenth century; the complex contains Lord Hill's Column (1814-16), a magnificent Greek Doric column (said to be the tallest in the world) and surmounted by a statue of Viscount Hill. To the west more prosperous residential Victorian and Edwardian development took place along the Mount, in the Kingsland area and Belle-vue.

The town has now spread well outside the river loop. The construction of a by-pass in the 1930s established a new limit of urban expansion, although some inter-war 'ribbon development' spread beyond. The traffic problem is now a considerable one and in the town centre the medieval street plan is quite incapable of dealing with an ever-increasing volume of vehicles. There has been little attempt to preserve the ancient and beautiful face of Shrewsbury. Although Shrewsbury claims to be a 'Medieval Town', only half-hearted efforts at preservation have been made. The story of the recent destruction of individual buildings is a sad and familiar one. Both the local authority and private developers must share the blame. Piecemeal destruction within areas of fine buildings is a common occurrence and more often than not there is little attempt to maintain the old scale or character with the new buildings. Within a generation Shrewsbury has changed from being a town of great charm and character to one virtually indistinguishable from dozens of others in England. Not only are ancient buildings being destroyed at an alarming rate, but the structures that replace them are stereotyped and not planned to blend in with the wealth and variety of architecture that the county town possesses. Shrewsbury's attraction lay in the atmosphere derived from whole streets of half-timbered and Georgian buildings. The gradual erosion of these streets by piecemeal redevelopment has been heart-breaking to those who have had to watch helplessly. It is true that at last there are schemes for the preservation of small areas within the town, for which we must be grateful. The planners have now grasped the nature of the problem, but their conversion is a little late and the hopes expressed in a recent planning publication ring hollow. ". . . We have a town centre of charm and character which has a great visual attraction, which unless it is to be lost to future generations of Salopians and to the nation must be conserved now."[13] The future of the town must surely lie in the exploitation of its remaining beauty, the ancient and delightful streets and mews with their entrancing diversity of building styles and materials.

SELECT BIBLIOGRAPHY

Beresford, M. W., *New Towns of the Middle Ages* (1968).

Conzen, M. R. G., 'The Use of Town Plans in the Study of Urban History', *The Study of Urban History*, Ed. H. J. Dyos (1968).

Eyton, Rev. E. W., *Antiquities of Shropshire*.

Mason, J. F. A., *The Borough of Bridgnorth* (Bridgnorth, 1957).

Owen and Blakeway, *History of Shrewsbury* (1825).

Pevsner, N., *The Buildings of England—Shropshire* (1958).

Smith, J. T., 'Shrewsbury: topography and domestic architecture to the middle of the 17th century' (unpublished Birmingham M.A. Thesis, 1953).

[13] N. Bennett and R. W. Gibb, *Shrewsbury Town Centre Study—Statement of Principle* (Shrewsbury, 1967).

11. Industrial Landscapes

Lead-mining. The Clee hill industries. The early iron industry. Coalbrookdale and the Shropshire coalfield. Settlement in the coalfield.

SHROPSHIRE IS STILL essentially a rural county and even the relics of early industry are preserved within a rural setting. It is difficult today to realise that during the eighteenth century it was the premier iron-producing county in the kingdom and that the Industrial Revolution, if not born, was certainly nurtured in a small valley in central Shropshire—Coalbrookdale. For it was here in 1709 that Abraham Darby first successfully succeeded in smelting iron ore, substituting coke for charcoal, and thereby heralding the introduction of the second Iron Age. Today Iron Bridge and the Coalbrookdale have largely reverted to rural tranquillity, although landmarks of the Industrial Revolution are still to be found in abundance.

The wealth of mineral deposits in Shropshire, usually lying in reasonably accessible places near to running water and timber, has meant a long history of extractive and manufacturing industry in the county. These extractive industries can be traced back to before the Roman Conquest, but the real impact on the landscape did not come until the sixteenth century and later. Even then most industry was ephemeral and much evidence of eighteenth- and nineteenth-century industrial activity has merged into the countryside. Only the occasional isolated row of cottages or a disturbed hillside tells of intense activity in the past. Today, apart from stone-quarrying, industry has survived only in the coalfield.

There are basically two types of industrial landscape within the county. Firstly, there are the open upland areas where lead, limestone or coal have been quarried for centuries. Such activities have left a scarred countryside of hollows and mounds, now overgrown and given over to rough grazing with scattered stone cottages straggling along the roads. Because of the comparatively small scale of activity in these areas miners tended to follow industry, often building squatter-cottages on common land. The miners were frequently part-time farmers and a tradition of smallholdings grew up in parts of the county. This type of landscape is confined largely to the foothill area of western Shropshire in such places as the Tanat Valley, the Stiperstones and the Clee Hills. Industry in these areas was largely unplanned, working on a piecemeal basis to the capacity of the primitive mining equipment, often resulting in the abandonment of a seam or deposit long before it was exhausted. Often these industries were not even served by railways and as the work was constantly moving there was little time for large settlements to develop.

The second landscape type, found mainly in eastern central Shropshire on the coalfield, was associated with the extraction of coal, iron and clay and also with the making of a wide variety of goods, principally ceramics and iron products. Industrial activity here has been contracting until recently, when the main area of ancient industry, the Coalbrookdale coalfield, was incorporated into Telford New Town.[1] Before tracing the imprint of the iron industry let us first examine two redundant industrial areas, where the scars of early industry have not yet completely healed.

[1] Prior to the building of the New Town, open-cast mining has been undertaken to clear up the coal seams, and during the course of this work many old shafts have been uncovered.

Lead-mining

Lead is found in the district between the Stiperstones and Corndon, in an area generally known as the Shelve country. This used to be one of the richest lead areas in Britain, but now the seams have been exhausted or so fragmented that mining is barely profitable. The activities of the lead-miners have left a stark and unique landscape which many consider beautiful in its poverty. The old sites are marked by great heaps of spar and rock, old workings in the form of deep trenches, shafts or open pits, ruined buildings and chimney stacks (Plate 30).

The most important mines were along the line from Snailbeach to the Bog and about Shelve Hill. There are deep shafts all over the district, and the volume of lead that has been raised here in the past is indicated by white tips of waste spar which can be seen up to a distance of twenty miles (Plate 31). The chief ore is galena, a sulphide of lead, which was smelted at Snailbeach and Pontesford, where tall chimney shafts, with hundreds of yards of flues, were erected to recover by-products such as arsenic. Tall abandoned brick chimneys are still to be seen in the area; at Pontesford, ruins of an engine house and of the old smelt are still standing.

The Romans began lead-working here and pigs of lead stamped with the name of Hadrian (A.D. 117–38) have been found near Linley. Other Roman remains found in the old workings include mining tools, notably wooden shovels and candles with wicks of hemp, as well as coins and pottery. During the early Middle Ages, Shelve became a major lead-producing area; in 1180 the mines here were leased for fifty-five pounds and lead was transported considerable distances to places as far away as Gloucester, Builth Wells and Wiltshire. Much of the lead must have been carried by

water from Shrewsbury, and the deeply entrenched tracks
running from the mines probably date from this period, as do
the slag heaps at Roman Gravels mine and East Grit mine
near Hope. Later, during the eighteenth and nineteenth
centuries, there were extensive workings here and the peak
of production came in the mid-nineteenth century when
nine mines were operating. At its height in 1883 the Roman
Gravels mine produced 3000 tons in one year compared with
3500 tons from all the Shelve mines in 1835, but by 1916 only
two mines were still working. Towards their latter days
many mines showed an increasing output of zinc ore, first
recorded in 1858, and of barytes, first recorded in 1860.
There was an overhead tramway here to deal with the
considerable quantity of lead ore.

Mining was always piecemeal, and even at its height
miners still built cottages with small attached pastures in
order to supplement their income by farming. During the
nineteenth century the Earls of Tankerville, who as lords
of the manor were responsible for much of the lead-mining,
encouraged miners to settle on the edge of the commons in
the northern portion of Stiperstones. By 1847 about 250 acres
of common had been taken up by ninety-three smallholdings
ranging from ten to four acres each, forming the communities of Pennerley and Perkins Beach. A few more had
appeared by 1881, but by 1902 some abandonment had
started in response to the decline of the mines; today only
thirty-five remain. The collapse of the lead industry at the
beginning of this century meant that the area was severely
overpopulated, and the subsequent economic story has
largely been one of painful adjustment to pastoral farming.
It is an unhappy if familiar story that wealth made in the
lead mines did not find its way back into the area. The
cottages, churches and chapels are all uniformly simple,
roads are only just adequate and the single-track railway
which used to serve the area has long since been taken up.

Today the landscape is one of rough grazing, small farms and decaying industrial remains. In recent years there has been more prosperity, new houses are appearing and some of the waste tips have been cleared. The Forestry Commission has been active on the higher slopes and has levelled and planted considerable areas of old workings. It may seem strange to regret the passing of this bleak landscape, but it has a strong character of its own. Perhaps we may be forgiven a little nostalgia for this area of Shropshire which had something of the pioneering spirit about it, even if the sepia photographs of the period do hide tales of horror and insufferable working conditions.

The Clee hill industries

One of the most striking landscapes in the county is to be found on the Clee hills in south Shropshire. The Brown, Titterstone and Catherton Clee hills contain a wealth of minerals—coal, iron, limestone, dhu-stone and copper are found here. The relics of past industrial activity on the Clees merge with a landscape of pastoral farming; for this is the region of the cottager and the southern slopes of Titterstone Clee, in particular, are covered with small stone cottages, scattered along the winding lanes or on the exposed hillside. The open heathland for common grazing and the work in the collieries and quarries on top of the hill have been constant attractions over the centuries. Even today, when there is no longer any work on Brown Clee and quarrying on Titterstone Clee is limited to the supply of road-stone, the Clee Hill Commoners Association still thrives.

The earliest recorded industrial activity on the Clee hills was coal-mining. In 1235 Wigmore Abbey received five shillings from the sale of coal at Caynham on Titterstone Clee and in 1260 Walter de Clifford granted land for assarting in Cleobury North with a licence "to dig coals within the Forest of Clee or to sell or to give it away". Piecemeal mining continued on the Clees for centuries; accordingly the summits of the hills where the coal is most readily accessible are dotted with bell-pit mines (see Plate 19). Some of these are medieval, but as the bell-pit technique continued until at least the seventeenth century it is difficult to distinguish the earlier workings.

The bell-pit coal mine takes its name from the profile of the working. The coal is mined in all directions from a central shaft, which reaches into the seam from the ground surface, eventually creating a small underground 'bell-shaped' chamber. The coal which was produced there was brought to the surface by the use of a simple windlass and bucket. When abandoned the mines collapsed or filled up, leaving a circular hollow around the old entrance. Areas which have been intensively worked over, such as that lying immediately to the east of Abdon Burf, thus appear to be pock-marked.

In the mid-sixteenth century Leland writes of "a blo shope on Titterstone Clee", possibly a reference to wind furnaces, which consisted of a pile of stones so placed as to allow the westerly winds which sweep across the Clees with great force at certain times of the year, to fire the wood and iron ore. He also noticed that the Brown Clee "is exceedyng good for lyme, whereof there they make much and serve the countrie about".

Although there was some ironstone quarrying for local furnaces, coal-mining remained far more important; by 1727 coal produced on Titterstone Clee was valued at £1500. Mining was still carried out in a haphazard manner; the nineteenth-century geologist Murchison records: "coal has been wrought from these hills from time immemorial, and innumerous old shafts attest the extent of the operations ... As the ground, however, has never been allotted, each speculator having begun his work where he pleased, and abandoned it when he saw a difficulty, it is impossible to say how much mineral has been wasted and what quantity may remain in unconnected and broke masses."[2] A map of 1769 shows the extent of coal-working on Catherton Clee and even gives the depth and quality of the coal (Fig. 21); it also shows the encroachments of the cottagers and miners. Plymley in his notes on the area in 1792 observes "some cottagers keep horses to carry lime and coal . . . some are colliers and lime men who earn 2s. and 3s. a day and maintain their families in decency."

One of the great problems of the mining and quarrying was to transport the material down the steep slopes of the Clees. There was not even a cart-track to the summit of Brown Clee and the coal and ironstone was carried by pack-horse or even on the backs of the cottagers' wives. Richard Jones of Ashford who attended Titterstone Wake in 1846 recalled the young women "fine handsome up-standing wenches they were, and well dressed too; but you wouldna know 'em the next day with a bag of coal strapped to their backs. For in them days coal from the Clee hill pits was carried down the hill on women's shoulders."[3] It was not until the middle of the nineteenth century that regular roads were built to the summits of the two Clees; before that the miners used the ancient tracks that had been engraved by the Clee commoners over the centuries.

During the nineteenth century mining on the Clees was rationalised, larger quarries and mines were opened up, and increasingly stone replaced coal as the most important product. Clee coal was still used locally until the end of the century, largely because there was no alternative source. Plymley observed that "the south-west parts of the county have not yet proved to contain coal; and the inhabitants

---

[2] J. I. Murchison, *The Silurian System* (1839), p. 123.
[3] C. S. Burne, *Shropshire Folk Lore* (1883), p. 368.

213

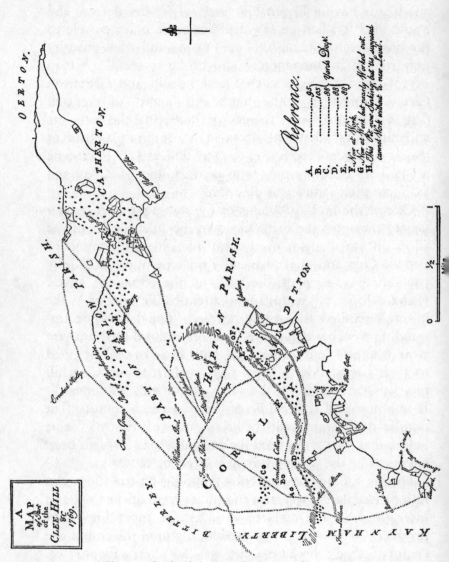

Fig. 21. Coal-mining on Catherton Clee, 1769
Copy of a plan (S.P.L. MS. 2481) showing the division of Catherton Clee between Coreley, Earl's Ditton, Hopton, Catherton and Farlow parishes. The dots mark bell-pit coal mines. Squatter encroachments can be seen around the edge of the common land.

purchase at great expense of land carriage coal from the Clee Hills." Plans drawn up by Telford to join this area to the Severn by canal—which might have resulted in extensive industry—were never implemented.

Both the Clees have a capping of basalt, which locally is known as dhu-stone ('black' in Welsh), and there is a small industrial settlement on Titterstone Clee with the same name. This stone is much prized for both building and road construction; Telford spoke highly of its quality and used it extensively. Some local villages including the churches are built almost exclusively in dhu-stone. When weathered, the stone turns a grey-brown colour, giving the villages and walled fields a rather sombre appearance, but like most local stone it blends harmoniously into the landscape.

In 1906 an inclined plane was built to move the stone from the summit of Brown Clee to the railway station at Ditton Priors. This enabled the Abdon Clee Stone Quarrying Company to extend their quarrying operations, and in doing so to destroy the hill fort that capped the hill known as Abdon Burf. Today the summit of Brown Clee is deserted. The quarrymen left in 1936 and the Burf cottages which housed the colliery overseers are in ruins. The mine workings stand gaunt and derelict, and some of the old industrial buildings rear like medieval castles out of a "vast rampart of rude and broken materials".[4] The turbulent years of industrial activity have left a dramatic fossilised landscape on the summit of the Brown Clee reminiscent of the Cornish white clay quarrying areas. There has been no reason for people to stay here, and slowly the heather and furze cover the pools and waste pits, leaving the summit abandoned and deserted for the first time in centuries.

The picture on Titterstone Clee is rather different, since the dhu-stone is still worked here and the top of the hill

[4] A. H. Cooke, *A Topographical and Statistical Account of the County of Salop* (1830).

is being systematically destroyed. Here secondary industries developed, iron at Knowbury and ceramics at Caynham, creating quite large industrial villages. Today, industry is largely confined to the summit of the hill, but legacies of earlier workings are everywhere to be seen.

The early iron industry

The beginning of Shropshire's involvement with the iron industry has now been traced back to the Middle Ages. The monasteries had for long been interested in the mining of minerals. In 1397, for instance, Crown permission was obtained by James 'Mynor' of Derbyshire to work a mine of copper and silver within the lordship (Wenlock Edge) of Wenlock Priory. In 1540 Wenlock was working two iron foundries as well as ironstone quarries in Shirlett Forest. One of the first references to iron working here was in 1559 when a man was killed digging in the Shirlett mines. Wenlock also had coal mines in Little Wenlock at this period.

At Wombridge Priory, situated in the middle of the coalfield, coal from two pits there brought in five pounds a year at the Dissolution and there was a small ironworks at Oakengates. The rather pitiful monastic remains are now engulfed by nineteenth-century coal and iron workings. Most significant of all, the Buildwas monks had a small iron forge on their demesne in the sixteenth century, possibly representing the beginnings of the Coalbrookdale iron industry. At the Dissolution these ironworks were taken over and developed by families such as the Reynolds, the Baldwins and later the Darbys, names closely linked with the Industrial Revolution.

During the sixteenth century there was a burst of industrial activity in south Shropshire, starting near the River Severn and spreading westwards. This industry was based

Plate 31 A derelict 'lunar' landscape of waste from the lead industry at Snailbeach.

Plate 32 A derelict mining area at Oakengates, disturbed by a frenzy of ironstone quarrying in the nineteenth century. In the foreground lies the Lilleshall Works, responsible for much of the spoliation. Note the scattered, unrelated terraces of workers' houses, built in a piece-meal way throughout the industrial period. Industrial activity in the region has very abrupt edges, corresponding to the outcrops of minerals.

Plate 33 The Iron Bridge (opened 1781). Probably the most outstanding industrial monument in the country. The small eighteenth-century town of Iron Bridge clings to the sides of the valley in the background.

Plate 34 The Roundhouse, Horsehay. Originally constructed as part of the Coalbrookedale Company's Potteries, probably in the 1790s, when it made chiefly refractory wares. The kiln closed well before the end of the nineteenth century, but was inhabited until recently when it was demolished.

Plate 35 Holy Trinity Church, Great Dawley. Built in 1845 by H. Egington in Perpendicular style. It is typical of the large, confident, stone-built churches found on the coalfield.

on charcoal blast furnaces, generally sponsored by local landowners. The blast furnace first appeared in England at the end of the fifteenth century, but it was almost a century before it completely replaced the ancient bloomery process in Shropshire, thus making way for the later developments in the iron industry. Like most early industry, iron-making was located on rivers and streams, generally close to the sources of raw material. Accordingly, we find the iron industry developing in comparatively remote places during the sixteenth and seventeenth centuries.

One of the earliest charcoal furnaces outside the Weald of Kent was built on the edge of the coalfield near Shifnal by George, Earl of Shrewsbury, in 1562, and one at Cleobury Mortimer was built by Robert, Earl of Dudley, at about the same time. Others were built at Lilleshall in 1591 and Bringewood (1601). The old blast furnace at Coalbrookdale, which may justly be considered the most famous in the world, was built by Sir Basil Brooke, Lord of Madeley Manor, in 1638. Later furnaces were built at Bouldon (1644) and Willey (1658).

The development of the iron industry rapidly led to the exhaustion of the remaining supplies of local timber. In 1561, for instance, licence was granted to Sir William Acton to fell trees necessary for making iron and to sell timber from Shirlett for his "lately buylded and set up iron mills in Morveld (Morville)." Because of the shortage of timber Crown authority was required to clear woodland within fourteen miles of the River Severn at this time. Supplies of accessible timber were badly needed for the emerging iron and glass industries and these were largely provided from newly planted coppices. With the widespread creation of iron furnaces between Willey Park to the east and Bringewood in the west, the first attempts at controlled coppicing were made. In 1550 Richard Minton and Richard Stokes coppiced an area of pasture in Shirlett valued at seven pounds. In 1583 a coppice in the Earl's wood, Shirlett, "was enclosed and fenced . . . and contained 1000 trees then standing and growing"; within ten years the coppice had doubled in size. In the early seventeenth century the inhabitants of Ludlow complained bitterly about the clearance of wood on Bringewood Chase for use in Bringewood furnace since they claimed it was common land. By 1650 there were regular coppices throughout south Shropshire, found mainly on valley slopes and escarpments such as Wenlock Edge. They were, however, planted wherever there was available land, for instance, in Aldenham Park near to the Willey furnaces (see Fig. 11). As late as 1728 Francis Canning undertook a major survey of his lands in Ditton Priors to determine how much coppice wood could be grown for the local iron furnaces, and between 1728 and 1760, 183 acres, some twelve per cent of the parish, was coppiced. Once established, the coppices became important not only for the iron furnaces but also for other industries and building. An enquiry into the state of Shropshire woodlands in 1791 clearly demonstrates the exhaustion of other forms of woodland, even hedgerow trees, which led to an ever-increasing dependence on coppice wood. Much of Shropshire's surviving woodland was originally planted for the iron industry, and it is interesting to observe that some of the most densely wooded parts of the county, such as the area to the south of Wellington, owe their tree cover to the needs of the charcoal blast furnace.

Many charcoal furnaces, however, had only short lives, leaving few visible traces of their activity. The site of a small seventeenth-century furnace at Abdon is represented by overgrown trackways and a wooded dingle with a slag floor but the furnace footings are still *in situ*. The furnace pond and weir can still be seen, and there is an abandoned road between the site and the deserted village lying half a mile to the east. Abdon furnace was operating in 1654 when

Sir Humphrye Briggs had "liberty of getting and carrying away all mines of ironstone off the Brown Clee hill", but by the end of the seventeenth century the furnace had ceased to function. Near Abdon there were three other furnaces at Bouldon, Charlcotte and Bringewood, the last lying on the River Teme a few miles west of Ludlow. During the eighteenth century these furnaces were all operated by the Knight family of Downton (now in Herefordshire). Some of the iron was treated in local forges such as those at Wrickton, Prescott and Cleobury Mortimer, but a considerable quantity was carried by cart to Bridgnorth and thence by barge to Stourbridge.

At its height the Charlcotte furnace produced over 400 tons of iron annually while Bringewood was making considerably more. Charlcotte is the best preserved of the three furnaces. The site, occupying a typical valley setting on the Clee Brook, consists of a stone-built furnace approximately twenty feet square and twenty-four feet high, with the foundations of an ore house to the north. Although the hearth has gone, the interior of the furnace is in good condition. Huge tree-covered mounds of charcoal furnace slag surround the site and give the farm its modern name of Cinder Hill. The site is within 200 yards of that of a paper-mill (now incorporated in the farm buildings) which was operating at the same time; the paper mill shared the same leat for water, provided that the furnace took precedence whenever it blew.[5] In the second half of the eighteenth century Charlcotte, however, drew upon coppice wood from increasingly distant parts and, being unable to compete with the coalfield furnaces, finally closed at the end of the eighteenth century. Bouldon furnace appears to have stopped iron production at about the same time, the mill and waterworks then being converted into another paper-mill. Today there is little legacy of the ironworks at Bouldon. Only the tree-covered

[5] N. Mutton, 'Charlcotte Furnace', *T.S.A.S.*, Vol. 58 (1967).

slag heap behind the mill bears testimony to the former ironworks here.

The same cannot be said of Bringewood, for although the
furnace and its buildings are now largely gone, there
remains a magnificent eighteenth-century bridge across the
Teme as a monument to the early iron-masters. At Burring-
ton, not far away, some fine seventeenth- and eighteenth-
century iron tomb-covers, cast at Bringewood, can be seen
in the churchyard. Below the bridge there is a small wharf
and a little further downstream there are the remains of a
tin-plating works; both are now completely overgrown and
forgotten. During the nineteenth century this area was part
of Downton Park which was created by the Knight
family from their iron wealth, and large numbers of exotic
flowers and shrubs grow on both sides of the Teme. This
part of the park has now run wild, and it is one of the
most delightful and completely rural spots in the whole of
the Welsh Marches.

Another area of early ironworking was the Tern Valley.
Recent work here has uncovered a number of late seven-
teenth- and early eighteenth-century iron forges at Upton
Magna, Tern, Withington, Wytheford, and Moreton Corbet.
It has been estimated that they were producing between 800
and 900 tons of wrought-iron a year.[6] Little obvious trace
of these sites remains, but intensive fieldwork around these
and other possible valley sites would be most profitable.

Coalbrookdale and the Shropshire coalfield

Charles Hulbert, in his *History of Salop* (1837), described
Coalbrookdale as "the most extraordinary district in the
world". And while we might find this language a little ex-
travagant it must be admitted that even today Coalbrookdale

[6] R. Chaplin, 'A Forgotten Industrial Valley', *S.N.L.*, No. 36 (1969).
See also p. 127 for a discussion on the history of Attingham forge.

has a charisma, deriving from both its beauty and its unique industrial history. The Dale runs northwards from the Iron Bridge gorge, where the River Severn cuts through a series of carboniferous rocks, exposing seams of coal, ironstone, clay and limestone. This has resulted in an extraordinary range and variety of industrial activity here in the past. In a description of Coalbrookdale of 1801, the writer explains:

> The works and the vicinity are frequently visited by numbers of people, of most ranks and stations in life, who seem much astonished at the extensiveness of the Manufactory, and the regularity with which it is conducted, oft expressing their surprise that a situation so passing excellent, should be fix'd upon for the seat of so large a Manufactory, but these ideas generally vanish, when they are inform'd that they are situated amidst ev'ry requisite for the purpose of carrying them on, viz. Coals, Ironstone, Limestone and water. Also the beautiful River Severn washing the bottom for the beneficial purpose of conveying the Goods to Market.[7]

The coal measures outcrop from Broseley in the extreme south across the Severn Gorge at Iron Bridge, to Donnington, Hadley and Wellington in the north. Originally the area appears to have been heavily wooded and Madeley, Dawley, Stirchley, Hadley, Broseley, Willey and Linley, the original settlements in the area, all have the characteristic -*ley* (woodland clearing) place-name ending. Today much of the area still appears wooded, providing a contrast with the adjacent industry. The steep-sided valleys carry coppices and many of the ancient spoil tips have been colonised by small trees and shrubs. However, little remains of the extensive medieval woods of Wrockwardine and

7 'A Description of Coalbrookdale in 1801 A.D.', ed. and annotated by B. S. Trinder, *T.S.A.S.*, Vol. 58, 1971.

Donnington; centuries of mining and quarrying have transformed them into a landscape of tips, shafts and railways. Much mining and quarrying waste to the south of the Severn has been reabsorbed into the rural landscape and it is only in the north of the coalfield around Oakengates that hundreds of acres of scarred land really illustrate the intensity of past industrial activity here (Plate 32). Most of the coalfield is characterised by the close juxtaposition of industry, houses, fields, and woodland. Throughout its history industrial exploitation in this area has been piecemeal, with the result that there are no extensive industrial slums and the small nineteenth-century towns possess a charm not generally found in other large industrial centres. Scattered throughout the area there is agricultural land, some of it reclaimed from waste heaps. In the north there is a very abrupt edge to industry, indicating the limit of the coal measures, and demarcated on the ground by the Newport–Wellington railway line.

There is some evidence of Roman mining in the Oakengates region, but the first surviving documentary reference concerned a coal mine at Benthall in 1250. In 1322 Walter de Caldebrook (Coalbrookdale) paid six shillings to Wenlock Priory to "dig for seacoal in Le Brocholes" (Brockholes survives as a place-name between Iron Bridge and Madeley Wood). But the first definite reference to ironworking here was in 1544 when there was a smithy at "Calbrookdale, where iron was made in blooms". By the sixteenth century coal-mining had extended northwards from the river; Leland (*c.* 1540) notes that "coles be digged hard by Ombridge where the Priory was", and at the Dissolution Wenlock Priory had coal mines in Little Wenlock and Broseley.

By this time the river traffic in Shropshire coal had reached quite significant dimensions as there was an attempt by Bridgnorth traders to control the price of coal being sold at Bewdley. The importance of the Shropshire mines is demonstrated by the attention paid to them during the Civil War, and by the end of the seventeenth century coal from Broseley and Madeley was by far the most important commodity on the Severn. In 1760 more than 100,000 tons of coal a year was shipped from these collieries, most of it downstream.

It is time now to look at the development of the iron industry in Coalbrookdale. The tale has been very ably told and retold, but its importance in terms of industrial history cannot be overemphasised; landscapes and cities far beyond this quiet Shropshire dale have been revolutionised by events here in the early eighteenth century.[8] It is at this point that Abraham Darby entered the already expanding Shropshire iron industry. During the following century the Darbys dominated the region and undoubtedly were the chief architects in converting the dispersed iron industry into one of concentration, with furnace, foundry, forge and engineering works close together connected by railway. They perfected the art of operating coke blast furnaces, making thin castings and utilising massive castings for steam engines, railways and bridges. They presided over an industrial enterprise which had a greater influence than any other, resulting in the expansion of the steel industry one thousandfold and laid the foundation of industrial development throughout the world.

The Darbys and the Coalbrookdale Works acted as a catalyst for other industrial innovations, and the discoveries and the developments of the eighteenth century within this small and remote area of eastern Shropshire must rate as an industrial renaissance, equivalent in its own way to the Florentine School of the fifteenth century. This was recognised in the early nineteenth century when visitors came here from throughout Europe to see at first hand the new

[8] A. Raistrick, *Dynasty of Ironfounders—The Darbys of Coalbrookdale* (1953).

wonders of the Industrial Revolution. It is only in recent years, however, when many of the unique industrial monuments have been threatened or even destroyed that Coalbrookdale and its hinterland have been rediscovered and have begun to receive the attention that they deserve.

Abraham Darby I moved from Bristol to Coalbrookdale in 1708. After he had repaired the Old Furnace damaged by an explosion caused by flood waters bursting the pool dam, he began to smelt iron ore using coke as a fuel. Darby blew the Old Furnace for the first time using coke early in January 1709. The initial output of iron was comparatively small and by 1717 had reached only five tons a week, but it gradually increased as techniques for smelting and casting were improved. By the middle of the eighteenth century, largely through the help of horse-drawn railways, the iron industry was able to expand away from the river. Iron furnaces were established at Horsehay, Ketley, Lightmoor (Little Dawley) and Madeley Wood in the late 1750s. Wooden rails appear to have been used as early as 1605 at Broseley when they were the object of "riotous behaviour". As early as 1711 the Rev. Francis Brokesby had written of a sophisticated railway system at Madeley where "small carriages with four wheels" were "thrust by men . . . along long underground passages to the boats on the Severn". About 1750 a plan for a waggonway between Little Wenlock and Coalbrookdale was proposed in order that "coals may be conveyed in the easiest and best manner, to make a waggonway and lay rails on sleepers in such a manner as is commonly used, and with coal waggons and horses and oxen to draw the same on or along the said railway to Coalbrookdale". Abraham Darby II considerably extended the railway system, radically cutting transport costs in the Dale. In 1768 Richard Reynolds began to replace the wooden rails with iron rails, and there is some controversy whether these or rails laid in Sheffield were the first in the world.

Between 1768 and 1771 Reynolds was responsible for the laying of some 800 tons of cast-iron rails. The new rails linked the iron-ore fields at Dawley with the coalfield and the furnaces and by 1785 Coalbrookdale had sixteen fire-engines, eight blast furnaces, nine forges and twenty miles of rails.[9]

About this time John Wilkinson developed his furnaces at Snedshill, Willey and Hadley; furnaces were later built at Broseley and Donnington Wood. Accordingly on the eve of the French Wars Shropshire had twice as many furnaces as any other county in Britain. Plymley estimated that the number of blast furnaces between Ketley and Willey would "exceed any within the Kingdom". Very soon Shropshire was overtaken by South Wales as the major iron-producing area, but it remained an important industrial region throughout the first half of the nineteenth century.

Apart from the introduction of iron rails there were other remarkable achievements at Coalbrookdale during the eighteenth century, some of them leaving tangible remains. The most notable of these, of course, was the casting and erection of the first cast-iron bridge. In 1777 Abraham Darby III re-designed the Old Furnace for casting the bridge, which was opened on January 1st, 1781. By a miracle the Iron Bridge across the Severn still stands today, the first metal structure of its kind in the world. It is a beautiful creation; the various parts are slotted together with carpentry techniques including dovetail joints and wedges (Plate 33).

Another equally remarkable, but lesser known, achievement of about the same time was the casting of an iron frame for Marshall, Benyon and Bage's flax-spinning mill at Shrewsbury, the earliest multi-storied iron-framed building ever erected. The building still stands set back from the

[9] R. Jenkins, 'Industrial History of the Coalbrookdale District', *Trans. Newcomen Soc.*, Vol. 5 (1923–4).

road between Shrewsbury and the engineering works at Harlescott. There is no absolute proof that the castings were made at Coalbrookdale, but a reference to 'arches for cotton work' contained in an inventory of Dale products in 1801 would strongly suggest their origin there. Other achievements such as Telford's iron aqueduct at Longdon-upon-Tern, which is discussed in the next chapter, are better authenticated.

In 1801 the great Cornish engineer, Trevithick, came to Coalbrookdale to ask for help with the construction of a locomotive to run on rails. His steam roadcarriage had worked successfully the year before, but he soon realised that smooth running on rails would greatly improve its efficiency. The textbooks give the name 'Penydarren' to this steam-engine, but recent research has given priority to Coalbrookdale as the first home of this important pioneer. It was to another Shropshire firm, Hazeldine of Bridgnorth, that Trevithick went for his first passenger train (1809), 'The catch-me-who-can', which ran as an entertainment in Regency London.

Other remarkable feats were performed on the coalfield to the south of the Severn, notably at Willey, where John Wilkinson successfully applied the Boulton and Watt steam-engine to ironworks at the New Willey furnace in 1776. Later he employed steam for forge hammers here (1786) and introduced the first steam-powered rolling and slitting mill (1786). Wilkinson also built the first iron boat called, fittingly enough, 'The Trial', at Willey Wharf in 1787; it was intended to carry the products of the Willey works down the Severn. However, these important developments have left few traces in the modern landscape. Willey today is remarkable for its tranquillity; here and there are pools and tree-covered slag heaps, but there is no longer any industrial activity. The visitor could well be excused questioning if these momentous events could have occurred in such a rural backwater, leaving so little permanent legacy to the landscape.

A mile or two south-east of Coalbrookdale at Coalport there are other reminders of former industrial glory. There is little industry here either since the world-famous pottery works which used to produce Coalport porcelain closed, although the south bank of the Severn is littered with pottery wasters and magnificent sombre brick-built kilns. At Caughley, the site of an immensely important porcelain factory, there is even less to see. The name Caughley Farm is the only reminder that this was the source of the world-famous Caughley Ceramics.[10] Industrial ceramics were made throughout the area and a vivid reminder of the Coalbrookdale Company's Horsehay Potteries survived until recently in the form of a conical pottery kiln known as the Roundhouse (Plate 34).

The Coalport incline, one of the wonders of the coalfield, is discussed in more detail later. At the very foot of this incline and driven under it is the famous Tar Tunnel, begun by William Reynolds, who (unconscious of the tar) hoped thereby to connect up with the lower workings of some pits at Blisters Hill and so obtain easy loading into river boats on the Severn. The walls of this tunnel discharged a tarry petroleum substance for a number of years which was "exported in large quantities to all parts of Europe". The Tar Tunnel was probably constructed about 1787 and when the tar spring was first struck the flow averaged about 1000 gallons a week, but by about 1793 this had considerably diminished. At the mouth of the tunnel there were extensive installations for the processing of the tar. By 1801, if not earlier, large quantities of coal were being conveyed through the tunnel to the barges on the River Severn. Its later history is much more obscure, although there is evidence to

---

[10] G. A. Godden, *Coalport and Coalbrookdale Porcelains* (1970).

show that the tar was still being exploited in the 1850s.[11] In the late nineteenth century the iron industry on the coalfield declined and today only the Lilleshall Company's steel-rolling mill at Oakengates survives as a direct legacy; the last blast furnace on the coalfield was blown out here in 1959. However, in recent years there has been considerable industrial diversification, and there are now a large number of light engineering and electrical works on the coalfield.

Settlement in the coalfield

The towns and villages on the coalfield are completely different from the settlement pattern elsewhere in Shropshire. Apart from the northern section the coalfield has remained, despite centuries of industrial disturbance, mainly rural. Everywhere small farms, fields, gardens, woods and orchards are interspersed between slag heaps and industrial buildings. However, in the Oakengates area during the nineteenth century the Lilleshall Company was responsible for raising thousands of tons of material in their search for ironstone, thus completely disfiguring the Donnington Wood area (Fig. 22).

The medieval villages on the coalfield, Dawley, Madeley and Broseley, all grew considerably during the eighteenth and nineteenth centuries and Iron Bridge developed as a

[11] B. S. Trinder, 'The Early Years of the Coalport Tar Tunnel', *S.N.L.*, No. 37 (Dec. 1969).

Fig. 22. Oakengates region, 1887

A plan based on the first edition of the six-inch Ordnance Survey showing the extent of industrial activity in the region. Note the very abrupt division between industrial working and the open countryside. The piecemeal spread of settlement along roads and railways is also typical of nineteenth-century Shropshire industry.

The Georgian Landscape

completely new town. In addition to this, however, rows of
workers' cottages seem to have been built wherever there
was an area of flat land available, along the river or canal
bank or along a road, or simply in the middle of a field.
The rows of terraced cottages, mostly in local brick and
stone, were never joined together as they were in other
industrial complexes. Accordingly it is common to see a
terraced block of artisans' cottages lying completely by
themselves amongst the fields. A block of this type has
recently been demolished at Dark Lane in Telford New
Town (Plate 40). Indeed, a row of true 'back-to-back'
houses, in a completely rural setting at New Dale, has
also only recently been pulled down. Thomas Telford made
some reference to such piecemeal building at Coalport in
the late eighteenth century.

> Formerly the place [Coalport] consisted of a very rugged
> uncultivated bank which scarcely provided even grass,
> but owing to the judicious regulations and encourage-
> ment of Mr Reynolds, joined to the benefit arriving from
> the canal and river, houses to the number of thirty have
> been built there and more are still wanted to accommodate
> the people employed at a large china manufactory, a
> considerable earthenware manufactory, another for
> making ropes, one for bag making and one for chains.

The chain works here were started by Gilberton Gilpin,
who at one time served with Wilkinson and had developed
chain-making at Stirchley before moving to Coalport.

There are small workshops and brick Nonconformist
chapels as well as the grander Gothic revival greystone
churches of the mid-nineteenth century such as Great
Dawley (Plate 35). The coalfield towns themselves grew
rapidly during the nineteenth century as can be seen from
the following census figures.

	1801	*1831*	*1871*
Dawley	3869	6877	9503
Madeley	4758	5822	9475
Wellington	7531	9671	13487

The towns mostly developed in a piecemeal way from existing villages, but some like Iron Bridge grew up on new sites. Iron Bridge was created on the northern bank of the Severn by the new bridge, largely to house Coalbrookdale workers as there was little room for settlement to expand in the Dale itself. The town clings to the valley bank, and some thought was obviously given to the planning of the town as immediately opposite the end of the bridge there is a large inn, known as the Tontine Hotel, as well as the former market house, built about 1800. To the east of this there is a small market place, and more than 100 steps above lies the church of St Luke, built in 1836, which from the southern bank of the Severn appears to tower over the bridge. To the east and west the town soon ceases, and after a mixture of miners' small yellow-brick cottages and bedraggled fields, the open countryside is quickly reached again (Fig. 23).

By good fortune the rural setting of Coalbrookdale and the Iron Bridge Gorge have survived much as they appeared in the eighteenth century, with hanging woods, Georgian houses, humbler dwellings and inns strung down the Dale and along Severn side. The Darby family, if they could return, would recognise the familiar surroundings of the works—more than could be said of Boulton and Watt, who would find that little was familiar in twentieth-century Birmingham. This most precious group of industrial monuments in the country—indeed the world—can still be seen in its original setting. It is to be hoped that the redevelopment in a new community of half a million people

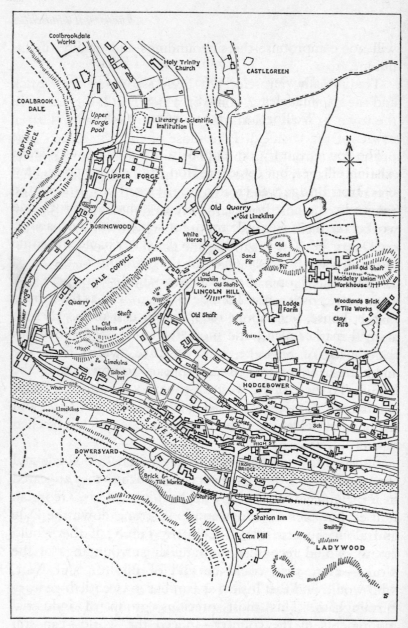

Fig. 23. Iron Bridge, 1884

The industrial town of Iron Bridge and Coalbrookdale; plan based on the first edition of the six-inch Ordnance Survey.

will not compromise the surroundings and quality of this unique area.

Traditionally, Broseley has been associated with brick and tile manufacturing, some of which is still carried on in the town. It is typical in many ways of the small industrial towns of the coalfield. Like most of them it reflects past prosperity through its buildings and general atmosphere. The church represents the heart of the old village, although it was rebuilt in 1845, and the industrial town has grown along the maze of roads northwards towards the Severn. As well as the terraced artisans' houses there are the large brick managers' houses, enhancing the air of decayed prosperity.

Of all the towns, Madeley is probably most evocative of the past. It is a town of yellow brick buildings, full of handsome Nonconformist chapels, halls and institutes. The parish church is octagonal and, appropriately enough, was designed by Telford. In the churchyard there are some unique local cast-iron tombs of the eighteenth and early nineteenth centuries, dedicated to members of iron-making families such as the Baldwins and Cranages. Madeley consists of three different segments: the open, elegant area around the church, which probably represents the site of the earliest settlement but was completely rebuilt in the eighteenth century; the High Street made up of regular but crowded shops, whose plan dates from the deliberate plantation by Wenlock Priory in the fourteenth century; and finally the irregular area of industrial growth to the north. Within half a mile of the church, Madeley Court, home of the Darbys, can be found. Originally Madeley Court was a grange of Wenlock Priory but was taken over by Abraham Darby from 1709 to his death. Until recently it was in a very dilapidated state, but it has now been restored.

SELECT BIBLIOGRAPHY

Court, W., *The Rise of the Midland Industries* (1938).
Dines, H. G., 'The West Shropshire Mining Region', *Bulletin of the Geological Survey of Great Britain*, No. 14 (H.M.S.O., 1958).
Life of Telford, Ed. J. Rickman (1838).
Mott, R. A., 'The Shropshire Iron Industries', *T.S.A.S.*, Vol. 56 (1961).
Mott, R. A., 'Coalbrookdale: the early years', *T.S.A.S.*, Vol. 56 (1961).
Mott, R. A., 'The Coalbrookdale Story: facts and fancies', *T.S.A.S.*, Vol. 58 (1968).
Murchison, J. I., *The Silurian System* (1839).
Plymley, J., *A General View of the Agriculture of Shropshire* (1803).
Raistrick, A., *Dynasty of Ironfounders—The Darbys of Coalbrookdale* (1953).
Randall, J., *History of Madeley* (1880).
Turner, E. A., 'Lead Mining in Shropshire', *T.C.S.V.S.*, Vol. 12 (1949).
Victoria County History, *Shropshire,* Vol. 1, pp. 415–81.

12. Communications

The River Severn.   Roads.   Canals.   Railways.

SHROPSHIRE IS A landlocked county situated at some distance from the main arteries of British trade. The main road link with the Midlands and the South-east is the A5 which, in Shropshire at least, still follows the Roman Watling Street. The county's rail links are now limited, with immediate outside contacts only with central and north Wales and the West Midland conurbation. This relative isolation is not new, but its sudden return in the past two decades has come as something of a shock. Some links with the rest of the country have been preserved in eastern Shropshire, and outside communications with the new Telford are to be improved. The rest of the county, however, is increasingly reliant on the motor car and the old road system.

The River Severn

The ancient link with the rest of the world was the River Severn (Roman *Sabrina*) which is navigable throughout the county. The river appears to have been used in prehistoric times as a trading link between the highland cultures of north Wales and the lowland cultures of Wessex, but there is little evidence of Roman or Saxon trading on the Severn, although it must have been used locally at least. In the Middle Ages the Severn linked the west Midlands with the port of Bristol and beyond, boats traded upstream as far as Pool Quay near Welshpool, just to the west of the Breidden Hills in Montgomeryshire. Toll lists taken at

235

Montford Bridge between 1285 and 1412 record a wide range of goods being traded, including cordwain (Spanish leather from Cordoba), tin, iron, wool, lead, wine, Cyprus silk and spice.[1] The Severn was also used for passenger traffic from an early date; in 1198 the sheriff of Shropshire paid 6s. 3d. for the hire of a barge to carry the wife of Griffin ap Rese from Bridgnorth to Gloucester. Buildwas Abbey's right to wash sheep in the Severn at Cressage and load barges there too suggests that wool was being shipped down river to Bristol in the thirteenth century. Attempts by riparian landowners to dam or obstruct the river for fisheries or mills were vigorously resisted by traders; in 1425 a commission was appointed to view the banks of the Severn in Shropshire, to repair defects and to see that the mills and weirs did not obstruct the river traffic. It is reported that the first barge-load of pit coal came down the Severn in 1520, and during the following centuries this was to be by far the most important commodity on the river.

During the Civil War, such was the value of the Severn coal trade that parliamentary forces seized Benthall to prevent coals going to Worcester.[2] Some idea of the extent of river traffic can be gained from the numbers of trading vessels attached to the Shropshire river ports in 1756:

	Welshpool	7
	Shrewsbury	19
Coalfield ports	Cound and Buildwas	7
	Madeley Wood	39
	Benthall	13
	Broseley	87
	Bridgnorth	75
	Between Bridgnorth and Bewdley	20

[1] G. Farr, 'Severn Navigation and the Trow', *Mariners' Mirror*, Vol. 32, No. 2 (1946).

[2] T. S. Willan, 'Severn Navigation and Trade, 1600–1750', *Economic History Review*, Vol. 8, No. 1 (1937).

The *Gentleman's Magazine* (1758) described the contemporary river trade in the following manner:

> The river, being justly esteemed the second in Britain, is of great importance on account of its trade, being navigated by vessels of large burdens, more than 160 miles from the sea, without the assistance of any lock; upwards of 100,000 tons of coal are annually shipped from the collieries about Broseley and Madeley, to the towns and cities situated on its banks, and from thence into the adjacent countries; also great quantities of grain, pig and bar iron manufactures, and earthen wares, as well as wool, hops, cyder and provisions are constantly exported to Bristol and other places, whence merchants' goods etc. are brought in return.

The Severn was not navigable all year round, however; up to five months in the summer the river was too low for loaded barges. Later in the eighteenth century attempts by Telford, amongst others, to improve all-year sailing between Shrewsbury and Worcester were thwarted by opposition to increased tolls. Consequently, a report of 1840 records that craft from Shropshire remained aground at Iron Bridge during droughts; when the river rose they came to Gloucester in fleets of twenty or thirty, taking between eleven and sixteen hours, unloading as quickly as possible, and then returning upstream before the water-level fell.

The coming of the canals seriously damaged the river ports, and their final demise came with the railways. The opening of the Severn Valley Railway (1862) saw the end of all but local trade; the last barge reached Pool Quay about 1890. Thereafter river vessels disappeared and the Severn ports decayed as if they had never existed. A few place-names such as Skinner's Loade in Bridgnorth survive;

elsewhere one or two small river settlements such as Hampton Loade to the south of Bridgnorth and old wharves at Iron Bridge serve as reminders of the former importance of the Severn trade.

As well as serving the county as a trading link, the Severn has also been a barrier. Even today there are only twelve road bridges (four of them in Shrewsbury) over the seventy miles of river in the county. There are towns at two of the bridging points, Shrewsbury and Bridgnorth, and the four bridges in the coalfield can be dated to the Industrial Revolution. The two other bridges at Atcham and Montford Bridge are worth examining in more detail.

There are two bridges at Atcham across the Severn, the modern one (1929) lying alongside a fine Georgian bridge (now for pedestrians only), built by John Gwynn (1769–71). Gwynn was a friend of Dr Johnson and a founder-member of the Royal Academy. He also built Magdalen Bridge at Oxford. The original Roman crossing point appears to have been at Brompton, where traces of a wooden bridge were found joining the island in the Severn just south of *Viroconium*; Brompton ford remained in use until the nineteenth century. It is possible that there was a crossing at Atcham itself in Saxon times, but the first reference to a ferry here was in the early Middle Ages. Up until 1222 the abbot of Lilleshall kept two ferry-boats here, then he had a bridge built and charged a toll on carts coming to and from Shrewsbury. In 1269 the abbot established a three-day fair at Atcham and in 1276 a second three-day fair was granted. The linear appearance of Atcham on an eighteenth-century plan, prior to the landscaping of Attingham Park, suggests that there had been some attempt to stimulate a town here during the thirteenth century.

The other ancient crossing was at Montford Bridge, a small settlement in the parish of Montford, on the road from Shrewsbury to Oswestry and north Wales. Montford

Bridge, like the Platt Bridge at Ruyton-Eleven-Towns, was traditionally a meeting place for negotiations between the English and Welsh in times of trouble. The first record of a bridge at Montford was in 1285, when reasonable compensation was demanded from "every float of firewood or timber descending with force against the piers of the said bridge to the injury of the same". This bridge was built of wood and stone. The list of items liable for toll at this date demonstrates the extent of river trade with north Wales,[3] and the receipts from tolls in 1292 were valued at almost twenty pounds.

The bridge now standing was built in local sandstone by Telford (1792) and was later incorporated into the Holyhead road scheme. Like Telford's other bridges in Shropshire it cuts the river at a right-angle, thus creating awkward bends on the approaches. These presumably were easily negotiable by carriage, but not by modern motor vehicles. Telford slightly realigned the bridge and built an embankment on the south side of the Severn. In doing so he by-passed the ancient settlement of Montford Bridge, which now lies down a cul-de-sac to the east of the small toll-house (1792) that overlooks the bridge. A small crossroad settlement grew up during the nineteenth century (Fig. 24).

Roads

Little detailed analysis has been carried out on the history of the county roads; much research work remains to be done. Parts of our modern road system can be traced to prehistoric times and reference has already been made to the Roman road system, which is still partially preserved. The distribution of major routeways was influenced by geographical considerations, particularly in the south. The run of

[3] Rev. C. H. Drinkwater, 'Montford Bridge: Tolls, Customs, 1285–1412', *T.S.A.S.,* Vol 31 (1907).

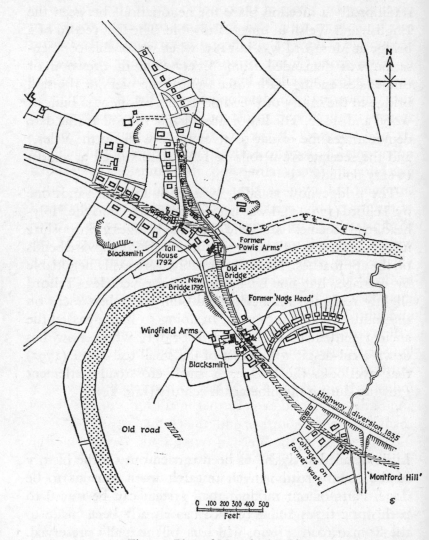

N

Blacksmith

Toll House 1792

Former 'Powis Arms'

Old Bridge

New Bridge 1792

Former 'Nags Head'

Wingfield Arms

Blacksmith

Highway diversion 1835

Old road

Cottages on Former waste

'Montford Hill'

S

0 100 200 300 400 500
Feet

Fig. 24. Plan of Montford Bridge
The plan shows the changes brought about in this ancient river settlement by Telford's improvements to the London–Holyhead road in the early nineteenth century.

the hard rocks, the ridges, and the longitudinal valleys, all give the upland part of the county a 'grain' trending north-east and south-west, and rarely do important roads run across this grain. For instance, it is extraordinarily difficult to travel from Church Stretton to Cleobury Mortimer in anything like a straight line. The siting of market centres also influenced the development of the medieval road system; eight major roads converge on Shrewsbury, and six on Oswestry. Of the five routes that centre on Bridgnorth only the road to Kidderminster does not include an exceptionally steep climb up the sandstone cliffs that surround the town—a clear demonstration that the siting of the town influenced the development of the subsequent road pattern. Apart from major roads the county is covered with a maze of minor roads. These simply served the villages and their fields and some were extinguished or gradually deteriorated after enclosure. Many minor roads in the south are deeply sunken with high hedges and are of undoubted antiquity.

For centuries Welsh cattle were driven into England by long-recognised routes, known as drove roads. By the mid-thirteenth century there was a well-established droving industry from all parts of Wales to markets at Gloucester and Shrewsbury and even further into England. The drove roads remained important until the coming of the railways; the importance of the Welsh droving trade was emphasised at the beginning of the Civil War when the north Welsh cattle farmers petitioned the king for unimpeded access to the English fairs and markets, particularly Shrewsbury cattle market. A number of drove roads, which had regular toll stops, crossed Shropshire. One of the best known was that which the Montgomery drovers took to Shrewsbury: it went by Bishop's Castle and then eastwards to Plowden, over the Long Mynd using the prehistoric Portway to Leebotwood, where the Pound Inn was a well-known drovers' hostelry. Other signs of cattle-droving are to be seen in place-names, such as Welshman's Meadow in Clun, Welshman's Ford at Ford and Cowlane in Worthen. A large stone-walled enclosure at Cowbatch Cross between Caradoc and Hope Bowdler has traditionally been regarded as a drovers' pound.[4]

Another type of cattle road that would well repay further investigation are the local driftways, or straker routes. Such routes were used by animals being driven to open common-land; particularly good examples of these can be seen around the Long Mynd, and those on Brown Clee have already been discussed (see Fig. 3). Often, they too are deeply sunken, although rarely used today. In south Shropshire such driftways appear to have been independent of other local roads. At the deserted hamlet of Cold Weston, for instance, a sunken driftway respects the earthworks and roads of the old village, and runs parallel but separately from those roads which obviously served the medieval community.

In the eighteenth century the general state of roads in the county appears to have been relatively poor—contemporary observers all remark on the difficulty of travelling by road. In 1762 John Wesley preached in Shrewsbury and a friend volunteered to send him and his companion on to Wem in a post-chaise, but the road was so bad that the chaise stuck fast and the horses broke their harnesses in endeavouring to extricate it. Archdeacon Plymley writes of Stoke St Milborough in 1793, "being within the Franchise of Wenlock the inhabitants must resort thither along a very bad road of fifteen miles for the purposes of justice." And in the neighbouring parish of Clee St Margaret "the roads are narrow

---

[4] P. G. Hughes, *Wales and the Drovers* (London, 1943), and H. C. Jones, 'The Cattle Trade between Wales and England in the Middle Ages', *T.C.S.V.S.*, Vol. 9 (1933). The Anchor, which lies in wild country just on the English side of the border in the Clun Forest, is another inn used by drovers since the Middle Ages.

and deep and during winter impossible to all except the natives who are well acquainted with their miry depths . . . most of the roads are impassable for horses even in summer through a part of this and neighbouring parishes."

Real improvement for many local roads did not come until widespread metalling earlier this century, though in some areas parliamentary enclosure roads replaced the old narrow winding lanes—in doing so such roads often by-passed the ancient settlements. A considerable number of Turnpike Trusts were established in the county and in 1854 some twenty-six Trusts were still operating in Shropshire. The Trusts built few new roads but were largely responsible for local improvements and maintenance. Their major visible contribution to the landscape were the small toll-houses, often built of local stone. Possibly the best known of these toll-houses is the grey stone 'umbrella' house to the west of Wellington, built as part of the Holyhead road. They are, however, found throughout the county, although in recent years a number have been destroyed. The end of the Turnpike era came really with the railways. It was observed that the opening of the Birmingham–Chester line (1849) in Shropshire "was the cause of removing all the traffic from the turnpike roads as if by magic".

The Holyhead road was probably the most ambitious piece of road-engineering in the county during the early nineteenth century, when there was increasing pressure for improved roads between London and Dublin. The condition of the existing roads was such that London mail coaches could not operate west of Shrewsbury. Between 1815 and 1817 Thomas Telford undertook a survey of the whole London–Holyhead road; and the work of rebuilding and improving was carried out at enormous expense over the next fifteen years. The most spectacular elements in the scheme are to be found in Wales, notably the Menai Bridge.

243

There were, however, important changes in Shropshire, although only a few stretches of completely new road were constructed.

The principal part of the route was constituted by Watling Street running from London to the port of Holyhead in Anglesey. Telford's new road, having come from Wolver-hampton via Shifnal, rejoined Watling Street just to the west of Oakengates. Sir Henry Parnell noted in his *Treatise on Roads* (1838) that the improvement at Shifnal was "partly over fields on the west of the town, and partly through some houses adjoining the market place". Telford's improvements were to be for the benefit of horse and carriage traffic, and accordingly some of the bends which he created on his Holyhead road, such as those at Shifnal, are hazardous for motor vehicles today. At Priors Lee, Parnell records that "there is much cutting and embanking". To the west of Wellington the road diverted slightly northward from Watling Street at Overley Hill, while at Shrewsbury the new road cut through the surviving monastic buildings of the Abbey, leaving only the refectory pulpit now by the side of a railway yard, and within the town there was further destruction. To the west of Shrewsbury several new stretches of road were created, notably between Gobowen and the Chirk Bridge. One of the immediate results of Telford's new road was to cut the time for the journey between Shrewsbury and London from three or four days to about sixteen hours.

Today the county's road system is essentially obsolete, as it developed mainly in the Middle Ages and has had to cope with the motor car for only just over half a century. Indeed the real revolution in motor transport did not come until after the last war, with the advent of popular motoring and rapid developments in road haulage. Although attempts are being made to by-pass some ancient settlements, many of Shropshire's towns and villages are in real danger of complete ruination by attempts to accommodate the new transport revolution.

Canals

In 1803 Thomas Telford wrote "although Shropshire was behind most of the other counties in adopting the plan of forthcoming artificial canals, it has of late made rapid progress . . . there has been more ingenuity displayed in the means taken for overcoming the various obstacles which lay in the way of the canals of this county, than has hitherto been shown in those of any other county in England."

Naturally, the first canal in the county was to serve the coalfield. Lord Gower, the Duke of Bridgewater's brother-in-law, who was no doubt familiar with the canal that ran into the Worsley collieries, built a canal for three-ton tub-boats from the coal mines on his estate at Donnington Wood to Pave Lane near Newport in 1786. The Donnington Wood canal can still be traced for a great deal of its length, but in places it has completely vanished. The coal wharf at the hamlet of Pave Lane can still be seen and the cut can be followed as far as the Duke's Drive from Lilleshall Hall, which was created in the mid-nineteenth century cutting through the canal. The cut can be picked up on the opposite side of the drive, and can be followed, with difficulty in some sections, as far as Lilleshall Abbey. From here it continues to Muxton Bridge, which is now an embankment cutting across the canal. Parts of the canal still contain water, but from Muxton Bridge to Donnington Wood the cut is largely filled in. The whole seven miles is upon the same dead level, and there was no lock of any sort. Its water was replenished by pumping from the coal pits.

Lord Gower had limestone quarries in Lilleshall and he used to burn the lime in kilns nearby. To obtain the necessary coal he cut another series of canals, which ran towards

245

the Donnington Wood Canal. This waterway also had no locks, and its course is still quite clear. It ran through the meadows, some seventy feet or more below the level of the main canal, and at first the coal brought from the pits was lowered in baskets from the upper canal into boats on the lower canal. Later, an inclined plane was built at Ketley along which boats could be hauled from the lower to the upper canal.[5] The success of the Ketley incline encouraged the builders of the Shropshire Canal to adopt this idea when making the very remarkable canal from Donnington Wood to Coalport. One end of this canal comes to the very edge of the Severn Gorge above Coalport,[6] some 207 feet above the level of the river, and the boats were lowered down an incline some 350 yards in length. The gradient is about one-in-three and on occasions the chains holding the carriages would break and allow a boat holding some five tons of iron pigs to rush violently down the incline and shoot its contents into the Severn. The canal never had any actual connection with the river, for at the foot of the incline and at right-angles to it was a short length of canal about three quarters of a mile long which followed the river bank as far as the Coalport Works. This portion has now been filled in.

The incline went out of use about 1884. A very good account survives of the incline when it was functioning.

Here is an Inclin'd plane 960 feet long falling 7in. and $\frac{3}{4}$ per yard, for the conveyance of boats up and down a high hill, the business being perform'd much quicker than by locks. The boats are convey'd upon carriages

[5] The Ketley incline was built by William Reynolds, son of Richard. It was based on a device that had been used with little success on Continental canals. The Ketley incline closed in 1817 after the price of pig iron had fallen from £18 to £7 10s. od. a ton.

[6] W. Howard Williams, 'Canal Inclined Planes of Shropshire', *Lock and Quay* (May, 1952).

constructed for the purpose, which are immersed in the Canals at top and bottom and the boats ['swim' crossed out] are conducted thereon. One person at top and another at bottom are sufficient to perform the business, with the assistance of a Steam Engine for raising the boats out of the upper canal to the summit of the Inclin'd Plane.

There is no trace of the original rails at Coalport, but the descent can be seen and appreciated! Recently the incline has been cleared of the undergrowth and parts of it have already been restored as part of an open-air industrial museum for Telford New Town.

While the Shropshire Canal (operational in 1793) was being built, another was proposed to bring coal to Shrewsbury, which town "and the country immediately around it", Plymley tells us, "are supplied with coal principally from the neighbourhood of the Oaken Gates, and which has hitherto been conveyed by land-carriage, about fourteen miles along the London road; and this part of the road, from the constant succession of heavy coal carriages, had become almost impassable, notwithstanding that large sums of money were annually laid out upon the repairs of it. The price of coals at Shrewsbury continued to rise year after year." The canal ran from Shrewsbury, where it had no connection with the Severn—the terminus basin lies near to the railway station, for seventeen miles by way of Wappenshall and Trench to join the Wombridge Canal. The canal had several features of great interest; the eleven locks, the aqueduct at Longdon-on-Tern, the inclined plane at Trench and the Berwick Tunnel.

The Longdon aqueduct was originally planned by Josiah Clowes who had begun work on a masonry structure, which had been partly destroyed by abnormal floods in 1795. Clowes died soon after and was replaced by Telford who consulted the Coalbrookdale Company about the possibility of constructing a canal aqueduct made of cast-iron. Until then aqueducts had been troughs of puddled clay carried on culvert-like arches. The new one at Longdon-upon-Tern consisted of a lightweight trough made of cast-iron plates bolted together, supported by three groups of cast-iron girders. Prophets of woe foretold that the first hard winter would crack it like a burst pipe, but it held water until the early 1960s, when it was drained. Telford used it as a prototype for his two enormous aqueducts on the Ellesmere Canal, built a few years later, at Chirk and Pontcysyllte, the most ambitious canal works of their kind in the world. The iron for the plates was cast at Ketley, and the aqueduct was sixty-two yards long and sixteen feet high, its masonry possibly being part of Clowes' original work (Plate 36). It was only the second aqueduct of its kind, the first was completed one month earlier than Telford's at the Holmes on the Derby Canal. The Trench inclined plane was 223 yards long, and had a fall of 75 feet downwards towards Shrewsbury. This plane remained in use until 1921, the last in Britain (Plate 37). The Berwick tunnel (970 yards) was remarkable for being the first of any length to have a towpath built through it. The tunnel was designed by Josiah Clowes, but the towpath, which was later removed, was added at William Reynolds' suggestion. An example of the exertions of a boatman's life on the Shrewsbury Canal is recorded in the *Shrewsbury Canal Minute Book* for December 1838. "When two trains of Boats shall have entered the Tunnel at the same time the party which shall have first passed the Centre of the Tunnel shall proceed and the other party shall return so as to allow the other to pass where both are laden, but when one train is unladen such train shall turn back."

The only canal still functioning in Shropshire is the Ellesmere Canal, originally intended to join the Mersey and Chester with Wales, Shrewsbury and eastern Shrop-

Plate 36 The iron aqueduct at Longdon-upon-Tern. It was designed by Telford and opened in 1796. The stone arches were probably built by Clowes.

Plate 37 The Trench Canal inclined plane, photograph taken when the incline was still in use earlier this century. It was closed in 1921.

Plate 38   Weston Wharf canal basin, which marks the end of an arm of the Ellesmere Canal, originally intended for Shrewsbury. Although the wharf was used well into this century, it is now overgrown and almost completely forgotten.

Plate 39   A typical abandoned Victorian railway station at Hopton Heath in south Shropshire. The station closed in the mid-sixties, although the line between Craven Arms and Knighton is still open.

Plate 40 Industrial housing at Dark Lane (Great Dawley parish) which has recently been demolished to make way for Telford New Town. This terrace, with houses consisting of living room, bedroom and kitchen only, was built by T. W. and B. Botfield as part of a coal-mining settlement.

Plate 41 A townscape of the late twentieth century: the Woodside estate, Telford New Town.

Plate 42   The massive cooling towers of the new power-station at Buildwas on the Severn; the earlier power-station is dwarfed. The remains of the Cistercian foundation, Buildwas Abbey, can be seen in the middle distance.

shire. The idea was to give the agricultural districts of Shropshire and Montgomeryshire direct access to Liverpool, but the canal never reached Shrewsbury, the arm from Frankton ended at Weston Lullingfields. The main canal was diverted via Ellesmere and Whitchurch to join the Shropshire Union Canal at Hurleston Junction. In July 1795 contractors were sought for the section of the Shrewsbury line from Hordley to Weston; this was opened in 1797 when "a wharf, four lime kilns, a public house, stables, a clerk's house and weighing machine" were built, and are still in existence. The canal got no nearer to Shrewsbury, because lime from Weston had to compete with that brought along the Shrewsbury Canal from Donnington, and the hoped-for coal did not materialise till Pontcysyllte had been finished. From time to time thereafter, an extension from Weston to Shrewsbury was reconsidered, but sufficient revenue could not be raised and no action was taken. Despite continued financial problems the Weston branch remained open until 1917 when the canal burst. Weston Wharf is today part of a quiet farm with an orchard growing in the barge basin (Plate 38).

Little commercial traffic uses the Ellesmere Canal but with the help of improvements by British Waterways it has become popular with holiday-makers. Canals, like many railways, had a comparatively short life, but their impact on the Shropshire landscape, quite apart from the embankments and earthworks, was significant; for instance, numerous characteristic humped red-brick bridges are to be found along the old canals. The creation of a canal often led to a shift in a village—Weston Wharf and Welsh Frankton are good examples of this—and a completely new hamlet grew up along the Ellesmere Canal at St Martin's Moor. Many of the new canal settlements were based on an inn; at Queens Head where the Holyhead road crosses the Shropshire Union Canal, just to the south of Oswestry, a small community developed, appropriately adopting the name of the inn. Fig. 25 shows the total extent of canals in Shropshire, and although most of these are no longer operating, traces of the waterways and their settlements are common throughout northern Shropshire.

Railways

The first railway to reach Shrewsbury was the line from Chester (1848); within two decades the county was served by a railway network which largely followed the river valleys and main roads. One of the most interesting branches was the Severn Valley Railway (1862–1962) which ran southwards from Shrewsbury to Bewdley and Worcester. Throughout Shropshire the railway kept to the right bank of the Severn. Its course through the Iron Bridge Gorge was very difficult as the rails were carried partly on a platform cut out from the rock and partly upon viaduct buttresses built up from the river bed and bank.

The history of the various Salopian railways has already been written, in part at least,[7] but an examination of the effect of the coming of the railway to the hamlet of Newton in the parish of Stokesay will serve as a detailed example of the physical impact of one line. Craven Arms, as Newton has been called for the past century, is Shropshire's only railway town, although Gobowen developed considerably after the coming of the railway. It occupies a textbook market-town site, where routes converge from all directions; the Welsh drovers crossed the River Onny here on their way to Bridgnorth. An inn called the Craven Arms, after the Earl, stood on the crossroads to the west of Newton

[7] E. S. Tonks, *The Shropshire and Montgomery Railway* (1949); M. Price, *The Cleobury Mortimer and Ditton Priors Light Railway* (1963); D. J. Smith, *The Severn Valley Railway* (1968). Sir G. Nabarro, *Severn Valley Steam* (1971). The latter contains an excellent photographic record of the early Salopian railways.

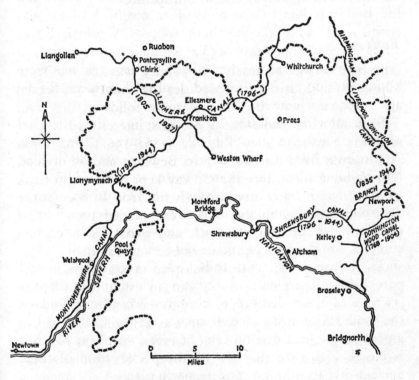

Fig. 25. Plan of Shropshire canals
The broken line represents the county boundary.

The following labels appear on the map:

Liangollen
Ruabon
Pontcysyllte
Chirk
Whitchurch
Ellesmere CANAL (1805-1937)
Ellesmere
Frankton
(1796-
Prees
BIRMINGHAM & LIVERPOOL JUNCTION CANAL
Weston Wharf
(1796-1944)
Llanymynech
BRANCH (1835-1944)
Newport
Montford Bridge
SHREWSBURY CANAL (1796-1944)
Shrewsbury
Ketley
DONNINGTON WOOD CANAL (1768-1904)
NAVIGATION
Atcham
Welshpool
Pool Quay
Broseley
MONTGOMERYSHIRE CANAL
RIVER SEVERN
Bridgnorth
Newtown

0   5   10
Miles

N

251

before the town was built. The present inn dates from 1841, but there was one here before that.

The first railway through Craven Arms was the Shrewsbury–Hereford line, late in the 1840s. It was followed by the Knighton line from Craven Arms to central Wales and the Buildwas line to the Shropshire coalfield which was constructed along the northern foot of Wenlock Edge. After Craven Arms was chosen as a junction, and terraces of houses were erected for the railway workers, sidings were built. Newington Terrace and Railway Terrace still lie apart from the later town.

Soon after the building of the Knighton line, the Earl of Craven saw the possibility of developing a town here. Accordingly he had a grid of streets laid down and divided into building plots, just as new towns in the Middle Ages were created. Market Street, Newton Street and Dale Street were built and a bridge was constructed to cross the Onny to the Corvedale. An auction mart was started and acted as a stimulus for the growing settlement. A market hall (1889), shops, houses and banks followed. Craven Arms is still parochially dependent on Stokesay church, but Baptist (1871) and Methodist (1880) churches were built. One of the roads, Albion Terrace, branches off the Clun Road at a peculiar angle, reflecting the open-field strips on which it is based. Fig. 26 clearly shows the preservation of these ancient divisions in the modern town plan.

In the early twentieth century Craven Arms looked like the growing nucleus of a large town, but subsequent growth was slower and it has fallen short of true town status. Some observers have condemned it out of hand as "the hideous

Fig. 26. Craven Arms: development of a railway town
Plan of Newton township in 1772 (S.P.L. MS. 2481), and the later plantation of the railway town of Craven Arms, from the second edition of the six-inch Ordnance Survey, 1904.

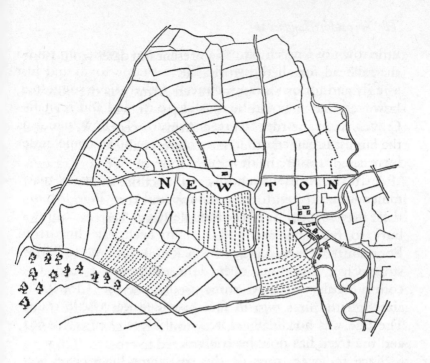

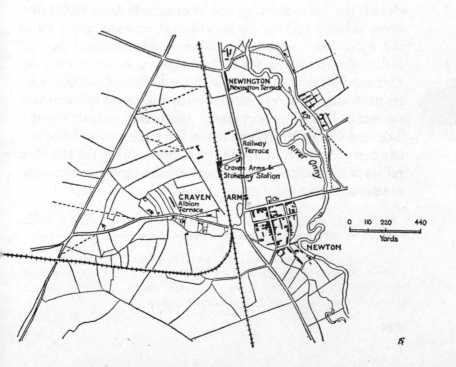

little town of Craven Arms . . . which has sprung up round the railhead for all the world like a prairie town and just as ugly and forlorn in appearance". Others have suggested, however, that it would be sensible to expand and revitalise Craven Arms in order to preserve nearby Ludlow, which as the largest urban centre in the area is bound to come under increasing pressure to develop.[8]

Apart from the main-line railways there were many mineral-lines through the coalfields and elsewhere. Among these may be mentioned the long derelict lines from Shrewsbury to the Breidden and Llanymynech, the line from Pontesbury to Snailbeach, and that from Ludlow to Titterstone Clee. This line, opened in 1864, was intended to convey coal, iron and stone found on the Clee Hills, although the first two in fact provided very little traffic. The line was not finally closed until December 31st, 1962, and the track has now been lifted.

Since the war most of the passenger lines have been closed, the rails taken up and the stations have fallen into decay (Plate 39). It is illuminating to read the accounts of the excursions of the Shropshire Archaeological Society earlier this century, when they were able to reach even remote villages like Longville in the Dale and Rushbury by train. Today only one north–south and one east–west line operates, linking Shrewsbury with the outside world. The mobility of the motor car in the mid-twentieth century has curtailed the railways in the same way that the speed of railways limited the effectiveness of the canals in the mid-nineteenth century.

[8] S.P.L., MS. Q.64, G. Evans, 'Craven Arms and District'; Q.66, F. Noble, 'A study of the history and development of Craven Arms'.

SELECT BIBLIOGRAPHY

Auden, Miss H. M., 'Old Roads', *T.C.S.V.S.,* Vol. 6 (1914).

Hadfield, C., *The Canals of the West Midlands* (1966).

Life of Telford, Ed. J. Rickman.

Robinson, D. A., 'The Vanishing Canals of Shropshire', *T.C.S.V.S.,* Vol. 11 (1939).

Rolt, L. T. C., *Thomas Telford* (1958).

Watkins-Pitchford, W., *The Port of Bridgnorth* (1934).

13. The Landscape Today

SHROPSHIRE REMAINS A comparatively empty county with a total population of no more than an average-sized industrial town.[1] Much of the county remains unscathed, with few traces of industry or suburban development. During the Second World War, Shropshire's comparative isolation was used to good advantage, with the building of a dozen or so airfields in the flatter northern and eastern parts of the county. When operating they covered a considerable area of ground. Today, however, less than one per cent of the county is under airfield and only Shawbury, Cosford and Tern Hill are still open, whilst most of the others are being reconverted to agricultural land. Remnants of airfields are still to be seen in such isolated places as Sleap and Childs Ercall, where runways and hangars lie incongruously amidst fields. Within a generation these too will have disappeared.

Over much of the county there is little evidence of mechanised farming, and the process of enlarging fields by removing hedges is found only in central and northern parts. The silence found in the rural areas of south and western Shropshire is, however, somewhat menacing. Rural depopulation is a real problem in the county and increasingly village communities are losing facilities such as schools, while many hamlets continue to shrink. Tugford, for instance, has now only two farms, three cottages and the church. The population of the whole of Tugford parish dropped from 168 in 1801 to 86 in 1961. It is more than a

[1] The population of Shropshire was just under 337,000 in 1971.

little sad to see the steady decay of settlements that have survived for over forty generations.

The decline of these villages is accompanied by the closing and subsequent decay of churches and historic houses. This silent process, which destroys medieval churches and fine Tudor buildings alike, must be seen as a danger to our landscape equal to suburban sprawl or industrialisation. At Upton Cressett, near Bridgnorth, the Norman church and brick Tudor gate-house were, until recently, gradually falling down through want of attention, and many buildings in the county are suffering the same fate. Country houses and parks, too, are disappearing at an increasing rate, Larden Hall on Wenlock Edge being one of the most recent to go. The scheme to break up Condover Park for a glorified housing estate has already been commented upon.

Nearer the towns, the problem is a different one. Here the villages are being developed as commuter settlements; places such as Bayston Hill and Pontesbury, all within ten miles of Shrewsbury, have been expanded to the size of small towns. Only a minority of villages are officially chosen for deliberate expansion, but most villages within easy access of Shrewsbury have changed radically within the past decade. The need for cheap homes has meant the insensitive intrusion of modern houses into many villages, often changing their essential character. Little if any attempt is made to blend the new buildings with the old. The fact must be faced that the villages and towns we are now creating are, on the whole, ugly. They are built with bricks foreign to the area and no longer have any ties with local soil and rocks. This could not even be said of much of the industrial building in the nineteenth century, when the bricks were made mostly from local clay, giving rise to a harsh, but integrated, landscape. One only has to look at the scattered cottages in Iron Bridge to appreciate this.

Do we really think enough before spoiling our ancient

villages? I fear the answer is no. Much more thought could be given to the scale and nature of new rural development. This is not a plea for indiscriminate conservation, or fossilisation, but simply a request in an age when we can change our landscape so rapidly, for consideration to be given about the environment we are creating. We cannot allow commercial considerations to be the sole criteria. There is a strong case to be made for the total conservation of parts of the county as a countryside 'park'. The growth of a massive city in eastern Shropshire will place increasing pressures on the countryside. Amenity and leisure needs for such a population would be best served by the preservation of sectors of the county as a properly financed country landscape. For many reasons there is a real need for areas of rural tranquillity to be preserved in parts of Shropshire which, as yet, are undisturbed.

The dual and somewhat contradictory problems of decay and insensitive development are to be found to an even greater degree in towns. The population of towns such as Bishop's Castle, Oswestry and Clun, if not declining, is static. These pretty towns have a slight air of decay about them and this is unhealthy, for it opens the door to shabby redevelopment. This is precisely what has happened in Shrewsbury.

Elsewhere the situation is not as bad, although there are unhappy signs that Bridgnorth is going the same way. There are hopes that parts of Much Wenlock, which lies in a particularly vulnerable situation close to Telford, can be conserved. Even here some damage has already been done; a sprawling estate on the southern approach to the town is a disgrace to the landscape. The desire for conservation both of ancient buildings and of countryside is not simply antiquarian. The importance of environment and the quality of life is increasingly being appreciated by planners and sociologists. The need for roots, visual as well as social, in new communities can be partly supplied by the proper preservation of old buildings and their integration into new developments.

The future of Shropshire, however, no longer lies in the traditional centres. Shrewsbury, no doubt, will continue to function as a market centre for the rural areas of Shropshire and mid-Wales, but to a very large degree Shropshire's destiny now depends upon Telford New Town. Telford is intended as an overspill city for Birmingham and the Black Country. Already the designated area contains the largest urban population in Shropshire, over 70,000 people, and by the end of the century it may house half a million subtopians. At the moment the older centres within Telford such as Wellington, Oakengates and Dawley, which gave its name to the original smaller new town project, maintain their own identity and authority. Eventually Telford will cover some thirty square miles, including much of the old industrial area of the Shropshire coalfield.

Already there are some good signs and some alarming ones. The concept of constructing a new town on areas despoiled by industrialisation is surely a good one. The use of sterile land, such as the old mining areas around Oaken-gates shown in Plate 32, instead of consuming farming land must be applauded. Similarly the proposed conservation of the industrial archaeology of the area in the form of a huge open-air museum is admirable. So too are the plans for the preservation of the Severn Gorge as an amenity area. All this shows a proper regard for the historical heritage of the area, particularly within a town that calls itself Telford.

There are, however, already some gloomy indications that the planners' aspirations are not to be realised on the ground. The first housing estates appear uniform and bleak, lacking even the character of the squalid nineteenth-century housing (Plates 40 and 41). There is little variation in colour, there are few trees and the skyline is monotonously even.

259

Nearby at Buildwas a massive new power-station has been constructed (Plate 42) dwarfing the old one and regrettably visible from most parts of central Shropshire.

It would be unrealistic to imagine that we are not going to see dramatic landscape changes in Shropshire in the next decades. Indeed, we have seen that the Shropshire countryside is a product of continuous change. Let me end, however, on a nostalgic and slightly inconsistent note with a plea for the preservation of at least some of the county's beauty and charm. We may then, in Housman's words, continue to walk:

> In valleys of springs of rivers,
> By Ony and Teme and Clun,
> The country for easy livers,
> The quietest under the sun.
>
> *A Shropshire Lad*

Index

Abdon, charcoal blast furnace at, 218–19; churchyard at, 81; deserted village of, 114, 116; enclosure of common land in, 160

Abdon Burf, 32; coal-mining on, 212, 215

Acton Burnell, castle at, 88–89; deserted hamlet of Allcot in, 108; Park, 131–2; shape of village, 131; town plantation at, 181–2

Acton Pigot, 131

Acton Reynald, chapel at, 80; park and deserted township, 133–4

Acton Round, enclosure of common land in, 156–8; mill at, 90–91; place-name, 183 fn.

Adderley Park, 133 fn.

Aethelflaed, Queen, 56, 187

Alberbury, priory at, 66; shape of, 59

Albright Hussey, 65 fn.

Albrighton, Domesday woodland at, 68; village green at, 74

Aldenham, chapel at, 80; park at, 125–7, 218

Aldon, Domesday manor of, 64

Alkington Hall, 164

Alnostreu Hundred, 79

Alveley, Hay House in, 68; village, shape of, 76

Amwithig, see Shrewsbury

Annales Cambriae, 84

Annscroft, growth of settlement at, 152

Ape Dale, settlement along, 70

architecture, domestic, 25, 97, 116 fn., 123, 186, 199, 200, 201–203

Arley, Worcestershire, place-name of, 102

Arundel, Earls of, *see* Fitzalen

assarts, 80, 96, 97, 102, 164, 175, 179

Asser, 54

Astley Abbots, chapel at, 80

Aston Eyre, 65 fn., church at, 78, 80

Aston Botterell, 65 fn.

Atcham, bridge, 238; movement of village, 116, 128; Norton, 39; St Eata's church at, 38, 48, 65 fn.

Attingham, Park, 127–9, 134, 202, 238; place-name, 45, *see also* Atcham

Baggy Moor, 165, 170, 181

Baker, Arnold, 35

Barrow, Saxon chapel at, 48, 77

Baschurch, agricultural improvements at, 170; the Berth, 43–44, 194; planted town at, 181; village shape, 76

Baucott, Tugford parish, abandonment of, 159

Bayston Hill, 257

Beckbury, 47 fn., 73

Bedstone, chapel at, 80

Beresford, M. W., 107, 178

263